CHAUCER STUDIES XXX

FEMINIZING CHAUCER

i

005
5

CHAUCER STUDIES

ISSN 0261–9822

Previously published volumes in this series
are listed at the back of this book

FEMINIZING CHAUCER

JILL MANN

D. S. BREWER

First published 1991 as *Geoffrey Chaucer*
Harvester Wheatsheaf, London

New edition 2002
D. S. Brewer, Cambridge

ISBN 0 85991 613 8
ISSN 0261–9822

D. S. Brewer is an imprint of Boydell & Brewer Ltd
PO Box 9, Woodbridge, Suffolk IP12 3DF, UK
and of Boydell & Brewer Inc.
PO Box 41026, Rochester, NY 14604–4126, USA
website: www.boydell.co.uk

A catalogue record for this title is available
from the British Library

Library of Congress Cataloging-in-Publication Data
applied for

This publication is printed on acid-free paper

Printed and bound in Great Britain by
Athenaeum Press Ltd, Gateshead, Tyne & Wear.

Contents

To St Anne's College, Oxford, and Girton College, Cambridge

Preface to the 2002 Edition

Feminizing Chaucer is a revised edition of the volume entitled *Geoffrey Chaucer* in the Harvester-Wheatsheaf Feminist Readings series, published in 1991. Since the nature of the book is no longer defined by the series in which it originally appeared, it has been re-christened with a title that reflects its contents and approach more directly. The new title has – as I suppose is readily apparent – a dual significance. In the first place, it signals that the book interprets Chaucer's work from a feminist standpoint, and in the light of modern feminist writings. Secondly, it aims to show that the ethos that pervades Chaucer's work is a 'feminized' one – that women are central to his imaginative vision and his explorations of ethical and religious problems. The central substance of this book remains unchanged since 1991, but it has been updated by means of additional references, footnotes, and bibliography, and a new Excursus on 'Wife-Swapping in Medieval Literature', which extends the discussion of the *Franklin's Tale*, has been added. In this Preface, I shall try to sketch some of the developments in Chaucerian gender studies over the last ten years, and to re-situate my own study in relation to them.

At the end of the 1980s, feminist criticism seemed rather thin on the ground. True, exploration of gender stereotypes played a significant role in the work of David Aers and Sheila Delany, but both these critics aligned themselves primarily with the tradition of Marxist criticism rather than with feminism *tout court*. Despite a number of pioneering articles by (among others) Mary Carruthers (1979), Louise Fradenburg (1986), Lee Patterson (1983), and Susan Schibanoff (1986, 1988), there was no book-length study of gender in Chaucer. All that changed in a short space of time, with the appearance of Carolyn Dinshaw's *Chaucer's Sexual Poetics* (1989), closely followed by Priscilla Martin's *Chaucer's Women* (1990), my own volume in the Feminist Readings series (1991), and Elaine Tuttle Hansen's *Chaucer and the Fiction of Gender* (1992). These volumes appeared so rapidly that in each of them there is barely a mention (if that) of any of the others. These first forays into the territory are also strikingly different in approach and attitude. If Priscilla Martin's book follows a relatively traditional line in focussing primarily on Chaucer's representations of women in various roles (as is indicated by the sub-title of her book, 'Nuns, Wives and Amazons'), Dinshaw's book traces a highly original trajectory, in pursuit of the 'figurative association of literary activities with human bodies' (1989, 4) that is her theme. This trajectory takes her from *Troilus and Criseyde* to the *Legend of Good Women*, and thence to the *Man of Law's Tale*, *Wife of Bath's Prologue* and *Tale*, and the *Clerk's Tale*, analyzing Chaucer's poetry 'in terms of its allegorical representation of the text as a woman read and interpreted by men' (12) – that is, the way in which the slipperiness of discourse, figuratively gendered as feminine, is subjected to attempts by 'distinctly masculine readers, narrators, interpreters, glossators, translators' (155) to limit and fix its meaning in the interests of patriarchal order (51). Dinshaw's concluding chapter, in an even more original move, links the sexual indeterminacy of the Pardoner with the fundamental instability and arbitrariness of language; he represents a 'eunuch hermeneutics' (159), rooted in lack, which undermines the certainties of patriarchal discourse, just as he himself undermines the binary opposition of male and female which constructs the male Same through contrast with the female Other (182).

Dinshaw's view of Chaucer's own relation to patriarchal discourse is, on the face of it, oddly double. In the *Wife of Bath's Prologue* and *Tale* and in the *Clerk's Tale*, she claims that he speaks for (and as) 'the excluded feminine' (129), albeit through a sense of what patriarchal discourse leaves aside. But this is in contrast to (though in response to) 'his representation of masculine narrators' misogynistic literary acts in *Troilus and Criseyde*, the *Legend of Good Women*, and the *Man of Law's Tale*' (ibid.). What might have motivated this change of stance is not made clear, and Dinshaw's habit of using the pilgrim-narrators to occupy the author-position in her analysis leads to an elision of the question (she speaks, for example, of the Man of Law as the 'voice of patriarchy' (103) on the one hand, and of 'the Clerk's identification or sympathy with the female' (154) on the other.[1] Reading these two (in many ways very similar) tales in terms of this supposed difference in their narrators leads Dinshaw to misread a striking instance in the *Man of Law's Tale* where Chaucer could be said to speak for the 'excluded feminine', in the last two lines of the stanza on Constance's 'unhappy plight as a token of exchange between men' (107):

> Allas, what wonder is it thogh she wepte,
> That shal be sent to strange nacioun
> Fro freendes that so tendrely hire kepte,
> And to be bounden under subjeccioun
> Of oon, she knoweth nat his condicioun?
> Housbondes been alle goode, and han ben yoore;
> That knowen wyves; I dar sey yow na moore. (267–73)

---

[1]   Dinshaw explains on p. 27 that she treats the pilgrims as having 'psychological dimensions', 'the capacity to make choices' (such as the Man of Law's choice not to talk about incest), and 'a certain interiority'; what is not entirely clear is how Chaucer's choices are related to the fictional choices of his pilgrims. Frequently they are spoken of as if they inhabited the same level of reality (see, for example, p. 158, where she speaks of 'the Clerk and Chaucer' as 'men who put themselves in the woman's place ... see things from the woman's point of view'). Does Chaucer also, then, put himself in the place of the misogynistic male narrator when writing the *Man of Law's Tale*? The habit of treating the pilgrims as quasi-independent authors of the tales they tell is surprisingly common in the other books referred to in this Preface; for just one example, see Laskaya's distinction between the Second Nun and the Man of Law as examples of female/male attitudes to virginity (1995, 168).

Dinshaw claims that the Man of Law is here speaking 'unironically' – that is, despite being able 'to sense that something is wrong in this gender asymmetry ... he has no way to think of it outside of patriarchal categories' (107). To me, not only is the irony obvious, but also the appeal to 'what wives know' is a clear invitation to the reader to take a cynical attitude to the patriarchal view of woman's 'subjeccioun'. It is the survival of such an attitude *within* a tale that makes female subjection a serious and powerful image of the human condition (cf. p. 118 below for a similar example in the *Clerk's Tale*) that constitutes the 'double perspective' that Dinshaw sees (as I do) as the mark of Chaucerian irony (154). The complexities of the Chaucerian voice are in my view evident throughout his work, and they make it impossible to identify some narrators as 'misogynistic' by virtue of an unquestioned masculine standpoint, and others as sympathetic to the female point of view.

For Elaine Tuttle Hansen, in contrast, it is precisely this complexity of voice that shows that Chaucer *never* speaks for the woman as the 'excluded feminine'. Dissociating herself from the view that 'the representation of women in Chaucerian fiction testifies to the poet's open-mindedness and even intentional subversion of traditional antifeminist positions' (1992, 11), she proposes that 'what is spoken in the name of women' actually voices 'an urgent problem for the gendered identity of male characters, male narrators, and (?male) readers' (12). While agreeing that Chaucer's poetic persona, and many of his male characters are 'feminized', she interprets this feminization 'in terms of the ambivalent, insecure, and inferior position that [the medieval poet] held in the fourteenth-century court' (37). Poet and woman are both 'marginalized and subordinated figures' (37), but this does not mean that the poet has any real sympathy with woman; instead, he displaces his own anxieties on to her, effacing and disguising his own voice 'in an attempt to remain as free of the constraints of fallen language, as powerfully apolitical, muted, unaccountable, unnamed, and unspoken as possible' (38). Hansen's rejection of 'the attempt to recuperate a feminist Chaucer who does not threaten the humanist Chaucer' (12) implicitly marks off her project both from my own book (see Introduction, p. 3, below) and from Dinshaw's (although she refers to neither).

In the period between Hansen's book and the present, this reluctance to credit Chaucer with a 'real sympathy' with women has persisted and intensified. It can be seen, for example, in the essays on Chaucer by Felicity Riddy and Lesley Johnson in the collection edited by Ruth Evans and Lesley Johnson (*Feminist Readings in Middle English Literature*) which appeared in 1994.[2] Sheila Delany's book on the *Legend of Good Women* (*The Naked Text*, 1994) argues that his attitude to women is 'ambivalent' (240) and ultimately conservative, 'entirely compatible with the orthodox Augustinian morality that suffuses both *Troilus and Criseyde* before it and the *Canterbury Tales* afterward' (12). Susan Crane's

---

2   See, for example, my account of the essay by Felicity Riddy, pp. 152–3 below.

book on *Gender and Romance in Chaucer's Canterbury Tales*, which appeared in the same year, is similarly sceptical. Crane provides some illuminating discussions of Chaucer's romances – for example, in her exploitation of Luce Irigaray's concept of mimicry, 'the deliberate acting out of prescribed femininity in an effort to thwart its limitations and reveal its hidden mechanisms' (59). Dinshaw had used this notion to interpret the Wife of Bath's appropriation of antifeminist stereotypes (1989, 115–16); Crane uses it to interpret Dorigen's invention of an 'impossible task' by means of which Aurelius might win her love as an exaggerated replication of the courtly lady's expected response to her would-be lovers. Since a lady's 'no' is conventionally read as 'yes' (see pp. 77–9, 91, 93 below), Dorigen's 'rash promise' reveals that 'her desire to refuse is at odds with courtly discourses that do not admit a language of refusal' (65). Equally insightful are Crane's notions of quoting 'against the grain' as exemplified in the speech of the female falcon in the *Squire's Tale*: Boethius's 'bird-in-the-cage' image and Jean de Meun's use of it are both refashioned so that both the bird and the instability it represents are masculine rather than feminine (66–72). She also makes good use of Joan Rivière's concept of masquerade in relation to the *Wife of Bath's Tale*: the Loathly Lady's switch from ugliness to beauty constitutes both these bodily forms as 'masquerades of womanliness, exaggerated facades reflecting back to the knight his own standards of repulsion and desire' (89). Crane is, however, reluctant to trace these instances back to any serious intention on Chaucer's part. Instead, she emphasizes the 'playful context' (72) in which these examples of mimicry and masquerade occur, a context which in her view leaves 'the masculine perspectives of dominant literary conventions' (73) untroubled – indeed, not only untroubled, but the necessary framework within which 'what is "feminine" about Dorigen, Canacee, and the falcon, works itself out' (ibid.). 'The latent masculine retort seems to be the necessary context for the feminine articulations that oppose it' (ibid.).

Chaucer's attitude to the relationship between 'pley' and its relationship to 'sooth' is, however, more complex than Crane's comments imply, as the exchange between the Host and the Cook makes clear (*Cook's Prologue* 4354–60). The whole of the *Canterbury Tales*, including its most apparently 'earnest' elements, comes under the heading of 'play', but it is in such play that new possibilities can be glimpsed and made available for lived experience. It seems apposite here to quote Judith Butler's well-known comments on performativity, in *Bodies That Matter* (1993, 241):

> Performativity describes this relation of being implicated in that which one opposes, this turning of power against itself to produce alternative modalities of power, to establish a kind of political contestation that is not a 'pure' opposition, a 'transcendence' of contemporary relations of power, but a difficult labor of forging a future from resources inevitably impure.

What one might claim for Chaucer's complex representations of the feminine is what Butler claims for performativity: 'though *implicated* in the very relations of power it seeks to rival, [it] is not, as a consequence, reducible to those dominant forms' (ibid.). This is why mimicry might be a fruitful way of reading not only Dorigen's 'playful' promise or the Wife of Bath's comic appropriation of antifeminist discourse for her own ends, but also the willed acceptance of female subjection expressed by Constance and Griselda – an acceptance so complete that it exposes and calls into question the nature of the power (not only masculine but also divine) to which they submit.

In the second half of the 1990s, studies of Chaucer's relation to gender issues have come thick and fast. 1995 saw the publication of Angela Jane Weisl's *Conquering the Reign of Femeny*, which, like Crane's book, focusses on the special relation between romance and the feminine,[3] and also of Anne Laskaya's book on *Chaucer's Approach to Gender in the Canterbury Tales*. Two years later there appeared Catherine S. Cox's *Gender and Language in Chaucer*, which extends Dinshaw's claim that 'woman may be understood to represent... the body of the text' by arguing that she may also be understood to represent 'its figurative capacity to generate and articulate meaning' (12). Florence Percival's book on the *Legend of Good Women* (*Chaucer's Legendary Good Women*, 1998) argued that the work is 'a debate between a presentation of idealized feminine virtue in the Prologue versus a somewhat compromised, certainly more naturalistic, view of women's goodness in the Legends' (327). Meanwhile, the growing sense of the need to problematize masculinity, evident in scholarship from the late 1980s (Laskaya, 1995, 12, n. 34), prompted a collection of essays, edited by Peter Beidler, on *Masculinities in Chaucer* (1998). And finally, Dinshaw's demonstration of the Pardoner's importance for queer theory was confirmed and developed in Robert Sturges's *Chaucer's Pardoner and Gender Theory* (2000), in which Butler's notion of performativity and Rivière's notion of masquerade again prove fruitful (78).[4]

---

[3]   The association between romance and woman had already been discussed by Fradenburg (1986).

[4]   However, Sturges rejects Dinshaw's 'concluding vision of the Pardoner's "poetics" as founded in the Incarnate Word or Body of Christ "in whom there is no lack, no division, no separation" [Dinshaw, 1989, 183]' as 'sentimental and over-optimistic' from a medieval perspective (Sturges, 2000, 202, n. 65). One point of possible contact between the present book and Sturges's work is his claim that the Pardoner 'resembles Baudrillard's Disneyland, which "is represented as imaginary in order to make us believe that the rest is real, whereas all of Los Angeles and the America that surrounds it are no longer real, but belong to the hyperreal order and to the order of simulation"' (2000, 76). That is, he might serve to draw a line between the 'feminized hero' described in my Chapter 5, who is nevertheless unmistakably heterosexual, and the homosexual; cf. Dinshaw's account (1994) of the way that homosexuality is deliberately suggested in *Sir Gawain and the Green Knight* in order to be shown as irrelevant. However, Sturges rejects Laskaya's suggestion that 'the Pardoner, by his very presence, becomes an "Other" Chaucer uses to reaffirm the male pilgrims' masculinity and his own culture's gender definitions' as 'too simple', since the Pardoner troubles masculine authority but nevertheless asumes it (Sturges, 2000, 105, quoting Laskaya, 1995, 192).

In most of these works, there is little sign of any notion that Chaucer seriously speaks for 'the excluded feminine'. The relentless critiques of Chaucer's representations of gender which have become their dominant theme have certainly produced some challenging readings of his work, but they also tend to flatten out its tonal, emotional, and intellectual complexities by assimilating it to the 'misogynistic literary culture' that it supposedly represents. Anne Laskaya states firmly that 'Chaucer's text is homosocial – written by a man, primarily about men, and primarily for men' (1995, 4); 'with regard to gender issues, the *Canterbury Tales* is best studied as a male-authored text containing representations which tell us much about late medieval constructions of masculinity/masculinities' (13). Although the *Tales* 'can be said to call gender ideals into question' (ibid.) by exposing their implicit tensions and contradictions, nevertheless 'in so far as Chaucer's text situates the issue of obedience and rebellion at the center of its depictions of women, the text can be said to reinscribe the culture's dominant codes of femininity' (141). Similarly, Catherine Cox's comments on Chaucer's ballades represent the approach that underlies her view of his poetry in general:

> ... we see conventional patriarchal codes at work, but their relentless foregrounding demands scrutiny. Chaucer, then, while no 'feminist' himself, exposes his texts' relationship to the cultural, ideological orthodoxy out of which they arise. His own position seems to resist the extremism of, say, Jerome or Walter Map, but his orthodoxy often operates covertly, leading readers to proclaim him a protofeminist even as he exhibits compliant participation in a misogynistic literary culture. (95–6)

The result of such an approach is that Chaucer's work is treated as a series of case studies in which the operations and inadequacies of the patriarchal codes that they embody are revealed.

What is particularly worrying – and surprising – in a number of these books is the way that they rely on traditional gender stereotyping, and indeed reinscribe this stereotyping within the terms of the critique itself. Thus, already in Elaine Tuttle Hansen, 'feminization' is an entirely negative term; if 'the courtly model of aristocratic behavior feminizes the male lover', it does so by 'rendering him subservient, weakened, infantilized, privatized, and emotional' (1992, 20). Likewise, an entirely traditional view of 'masculine' qualities underlies Cox's complaint that Troilus is 'wholly ineffectual and passive' (47). His actions in Book IV, she asserts, are 'hardly the behavior of a hero' (48), and his (alleged) unwillingness 'to risk himself for the woman he purports to love' (49) sets him in Cox's list of 'the men who fail' Criseyde – Pandarus, her husband (who very thoughtlessly 'dies and leaves her a widow'), and the narrator, who (allegedly) 'betrays Criseyde most of all by naming her as the betrayer' (48). The implicit demand for an active masculinity that will absolve Criseyde from the need to act is left unexamined. The essays on *Troilus and Criseyde* by Stephanie Dietrich and Maud Burnett McInerney in *Masculinities in Chaucer*

(Beidler, 1998) have a similarly conventional view of what constitutes 'manhood', claiming that Troilus is 'unmanned' by love. 'Troilus', says McInerney, 'regularly behaving like a heroine when he should be playing the hero, remains tragically unaware of the degree to which he is out of step with the world in which he has been placed' – and that is an Ovidian world 'in which the role of men ... consists largely of the pursuit of women' (234). 'The result is that, again and again, Troilus appears ridiculous when he should appear sympathetic and sensitive' (ibid.). The dispiriting aspect of such attitudes to Troilus is that they are essentially no different from those that were widely current in the 1960s and 1970s – in other words, the development of feminist criticism and gender studies was unnecessary for their deployment and indeed they are more easily derived from conventional presuppositions. The other side of this coin is Martin Blum's praise of Alison in the *Miller's Tale* for her 'virile womanhood' (Beidler, 1998, 51). It is instructive to contrast this latter phrase with Chaucer's careful deletion of Petrarch's admiring reference to Griselda's 'virile' ('virilis') mind; he speaks instead of her 'rype and sad corage' (*Clerk's Tale*, 220).[5] The substitution suggests not only that he is generally sensitive to the implicit condescension involved in praising women for exhibiting 'manly' qualities, but also that he is aware that in a story where masculinity is represented by Walter, it is a positive insult.

Fundamental to this book is the notion that gender is socially constructed, and that literature plays an important part in its construction. In saying 'socially constructed' rather than 'psychologically constructed', however, I differentiate my own project from the psychoanalytic approach that has provided the framework for much of the current work in gender studies, including writing on Chaucer (e.g., Hansen, Dinshaw, Fradenburg). The patriarchal bias of Freud and Lacan has often been recognized and criticized in these same writings (e.g., Dinshaw, 1989, 15–17, 165–7), although the usual response is to revise the theory so as to accommodate this objection. This enterprise seems both misguided and pointless to one who shares (as I do) the widespread and fundamental scepticism about the validity of Freud's work (see Webster, 1996, and Patterson, 2001). Robert Sturges has defended the use of psychoanalysis by arguing that 'even if one does not accept [its] validity ... for the understanding of psychic realities, it has shown itself a valuable tool in analyzing cultural productions such as literature – perhaps because it is derived from cultural productions rather than from life' (2000, xxii). Sturges's recognition that not everyone accepts the validity of psychoanalytical theory is welcome; as Patterson says, Freud is generally discredited everywhere except in literary studies. But I remain unconvinced that psychoanalysis can be valid for literature

---

5   See Bryan and Dempster, 1958, 302 (II.8). A few lines later (II.17), Petrarch describes her virtue as being 'beyond her sex and age' ('supra sexum supraque etatem'), whereas Chaucer speaks of 'hir wommanhede,/ And eek hir vertu, passynge any wight/ Of so yong age' (239–40), linking her virtue with her gender rather than seeing the two as contradictory.

when it is not valid for life (of which 'cultural productions' are certainly part). And the circularity of psychoanalytic criticism is evident in Sturges' formulation: if psychoanalysis derives its language and modes of thought from literature, it is not surprising that psychoanalytic critics often have very perceptive things to say about literary texts. Freud and Lacan mobilize a powerfully emotive set of metaphors which can serve as an imaginative prism through which to see life. But this metaphorical network does not have sufficient foundation in either scientific or philosophical analysis to merit the name of 'theory'; it exists at the level of rhetoric. I agree, therefore, with Patterson in preferring a historical approach – by which is meant not a naïve belief in the attempt to adopt a medieval point of view, but rather a dialectal engagement between the medieval text and the modern critic.

As I said in 1991, my belief is that this engagement will reveal that the medieval text is not just the inert object of a modern critique but has valuable things to say to us. This book was originally written out of a conviction that Chaucer criticism had not done full justice to the subtlety and complexity with which gender issues are treated in his work, especially in *Troilus and Criseyde*. I am not so much concerned, that is, to show how Chaucer's writings are (inevitably) embedded in the literary, cultural, and social matrices of his time, but rather to show that rather than simply reproducing these matrices in their own structures, they refashion them in ways that call to mind Butler's words about 'forging a future from resources inevitably impure'. My method is therefore – so far as is possible within the limits originally imposed on the length of this book – comparative. Setting Chaucer's work within its literary context, comparing and contrasting it with its sources and analogues as well as other medieval literature, makes it possible to identify its significant features and see them as the result of *choice* – not in order to vindicate Chaucer on intentionalist grounds, but in order to capture the full significance of the literary design. So, in the new Excursus on 'Wife-Swapping', I read the *Franklin's Tale* against a wide range of texts which similarly depict a husband who (wittingly or unwittingly) sends his wife to another man, in order to show that Chaucer's tale certainly *invokes* such stories of homosocial bonding as a context, but differs from them in ways that undermine homosociality. Or again, in Chapter 2, I show how Chaucer invokes the misogynist tradition of the *dissuasio de non ducenda uxore* but gives it a uniquely original twist that directs its laughter against men rather than women.

I also aim to compare Chaucer with *himself* – that is, to work back and forth between texts in such a way as to show how, in an important sense, they may be seen as variations on a theme. For that reason, each of these texts is provisional, representing the imaginative exploration of a particular situation, and representing the question 'what if ...?' rather than the declaration 'this is the way things are/should be'. Chaucer's tales are (to borrow the anthropologists' description of myths) 'good to think with', rather than mimetic representations of contemporary life. So one can see Chaucer meditating, for example, on betrayal and its roots in the human capacity for change (or rather its incapacity for *non*-change), shifting the gender of the betrayer from male to female and

back again, changing the context from a love-affair to a marriage to an envisaged death, showing it actualized or evaded (and, had he finished the *Squire's
Tale*, atoned for), asking if trust and love can survive a bodily betrayal. One
can also see him meditating on rape and its connection to gendered power-
relations, pondering the nature of the wrong and its sources in masculine
assumptions, asking why rape or the threat of it calls forth suicide or sacrificial
death, showing it averted by violent struggle (Constance) or submitted to,
albeit with horror (Dorigen), asking what would need to happen for it to be
eradicated. The extreme nature of the narrative situations though which such
questions are sometimes explored should not lead the reader to imagine that
they are proposed as everyday norms; it is evidently absurd to suppose, for
example, that a wife in Dorigen's situation would have done anything other
than protest 'but I didn't mean it'.[6] The quasi-magical power of the promise is
a way of constructing a situation in which actions can be seen as simultaneously willed and not-willed, and the limits of marital trust can be tested.
Despite their finely-attuned sensitivity to the way people behave, speak, and
feel, most of Chaucer's tales are anything but realistic in terms of their plots
and settings; they are permeated by the motifs of fairy-tale, religious miracle,
and fabliau farce, and are set for the most part in distant times and distant lands
rather than fourteenth-century England.

It is through such extreme motifs – Griselda's promise, Constance's rudderless boat, the Loathly Lady's transformation – that Chaucer explores the problem of power. One of the central claims made by this book is that Chaucer
complicates the binary opposition between active and passive, traditionally associated with the male/female binary. I suggested that Chaucer not only questioned
the superiority of active masculinity (as is evident, inter alia, in the general
absence of active male heroes in his work), but that he also questioned the nature
of active power itself, distributing agency through a multiplicity of causes which
embrace the apparently passive. I suggested that his notion of patience and pity
as *active* qualities might 'enrich the range of twentieth-century gender models,
limited as it is to shuffling the "active" and "passive" counters back and forth
between the male and female ends of the board' (see p. 144 below). Chaucer's
'careful integration of activity and passivity', I claimed, offers the vision of 'a
fully human ideal that erases male/female role-divisions' (ibid.). These claims
were met with sympathy but some scepticism by Susan Crane, who, while wel-
coming the 'departure from ... critical simplification and consequent impasse'
that they offer, nevertheless argued that

'the handling of gender-marked traits in romance suggests ... that the
"fully human ideal" is finally masculine. Traits marked feminine can indeed

---

6   It is true that Richard Firth Green (1999, 293) cites a real-life case where a woman
brought a legal action against a man who had made her a playful promise of marriage, in the
attempt to hold him to it; the point is, however, that the young man himself was not at all
disposed to take this playful episode seriously and the court took his side.

be integrated into masculine behavior, but the current does not run in reverse from masculine into feminine identity; and the complications of masculine behavior that femininity figures contribute to enlarging and universalizing rather than feminizing the masculine experience' (1994, 21).

While I can certainly understand this point of view, I do not, at the end of the day, find myself agreeing with it. In the first place, I do not think it is so clear that 'the current does not run in reverse from masculine into feminine identity'. Constance and Griselda, to take the most obvious examples, dominate the narratives in which they appear, reducing the men who are supposed to wield power over them to shadowy puppets. Their 'suffisaunce' involves a stoical courage and self-reliance that could well be said to represent a current running from the (conventionally) masculine to the (conventionally) feminine. It is the *same* Boethian 'suffisaunce' that is an ideal for men, who, however, need to be 'feminized' in order to achieve it, not because they thereby need to achieve a fuller humanity than women, but precisely because of the deficiencies of conventional masculinity. In the second place, since feminism assumes that the source of the problem lies with the masculine (patriarchy), which needs the feminine to function as the Other, it is reasonable to expect (particularly in the work of a male author) that the emphasis should be on the *re*definition of the masculine, in such a way that the feminine is not constructed as a necessary Other. So, for example, in the *Wife of Bath's Tale,* for example, we do not see the Loathly Lady transformed into a CEO, but into a beautiful and faithful wife, because the point of the story is the transformation of the *knight*, which is the condition and cause of the change in her; female ugliness is the accurate reflection of the deformity of male desires. What the ending shows is that men can have what they want only by renouncing their claim to it.[7]

Less sympathetic than Crane to the notion of an integration of activity and passivity is Anne Laskaya. Though she does not refer to this book in particular, it is worth quoting her on this point in order to clarify and re-articulate my own position.

It is possible to read articles claiming Griselde more powerful than Walter in the *Clerk's Tale* and Custance more powerful than the men residing in the *Man of Law's Tale.* Within an exclusively Christian framework, such arguments can stand, for these women exhibit superhuman, Christ-like obedience and humility in the face of oppression and suffering; however, they only have 'power' in the eyes of readers who fully believe

---

7   On this point I differ from Louise Fradenburg (1986, 54): 'through the transfiguration of the hag, the fantasy is reconstituted: the woman is represented as an other who can live in happy obedience to the same, provided that the same rescues her from fairyland and then worships her as the angel of the house'. This account of the ending of the tale ignores the essential condition of the transformation, which is the Same's surrender of 'maistrye' to the Other – a surrender which remains in place as the condition of the woman's voluntary 'obedience'.

that men should behave likewise and/or who fully believe in a hierarchical Christian afterlife with specific Christ-like prerequisites ... Attempts to ascribe 'power' to Chaucer's obedient female characters may well reveal how a modern reader who has spent years of her/his life studying literature would like to find Chaucer, would like to read the text as if it were advocating greater autonomy and power for women. Although such a reading is viable from an idealistically moral and Christian perspective, it runs the risk of praising women for using all their inner strength to achieve silence and a stillness of soul in the face of oppression; in other words, it runs the risk of appearing to endorse women as victims, as though passive-aggressive power were laudable, and as though martyrdom were a powerful and appropriate goal, particularly for women. (1995, 141–2)

Although I have certainly spent long years both studying and teaching Chaucer, I would never dream of reading his work as 'advocating greater autonomy and power for women'; the modern phraseology testifies unmistakably to the anachronism of such an idea. Nor does the phrase 'passive-aggressive power' accurately represent the integration of passivity and activity that I have tried to describe in this book. As for the 'idealistically moral and Christian perspective' which Laskaya assumes must underpin any sympathy for Chaucer's ' "ideal" women', I have made clear elsewhere that my own position is that of an unequivocal atheist (Mann, 1995). This does not mean, however, that my response to Chaucer's religious tales is limited to an exercise in social anthropology, the temporary suspension of disbelief. On the contrary, there is a very real point of contact, for the precise reason that what I most admire in Chaucer is his emotional and intellectual commitment to *questioning* the operations of divine power, whether explicitly (as in the constable's 'Boethian question' at *Man of Law's Tale* 813–16) or implicitly (as in the role of Walter in the *Clerk's Tale*). It is in the course of this questioning that Chaucer explores the nature of power, both human and divine, and shows active and passive as different sides of the same coin. As I say in Chapter 4, Chaucer does not so much attempt to redistribute power from active to passive as to *deconstruct* the idea of power, or at least ideas of simple 'possession' of it. His Boethian insistence on the determining role of chance limits human agency to the contingent, and leaves divine agency merely a matter of trust – a trust that can only be understood in terms of the *human* manifestations of love and faith.

It is also important that, if Chaucer's tales lead to the rediscovery of a Christian belief in the power of suffering, this rediscovery comes, not in the familiar forms of asserted doctrine or instructive *exemplum*, but as a surprise and an enigma. I was, I believe, among the first to claim that in Christian terms, Griselda offers a truer image of God than Walter.[8] Nowadays, this idea is casually mooted as simply one possible way of reading the tale. But the point

8   See Mann, 1983a, 180–82, and Mann, 1983b, 43–5. The article by Edward I. Condren (1984) which argues that Walter represents man tempting God was unfortunately unknown

is that this realization should come *as a surprise*, as a result of the experience of reading and allowing oneself to be troubled by the mysterious infinitude of Griselda's suffering love. It is only the experience of being troubled that gives value to the revelation that there is another way of reading the narrative. And the point is that this reading is not simply to be substituted for the alternative reading in which Walter plays the part of God, cruelly and gratuitously killing and torturing his victims. The two readings are inextricably intertwined; somewhat like the celebrated picture of the rabbit and the duck, it is not possible to settle for one or the other, and indeed they seem in some strange way to depend on each other. The tale structures the alternative readings not as objectively contemplated possibilities, but as an emotional experience, and one which takes full account of the suffering and loss involved.

Chaucer's exploration of gender roles, that is, is bound up with his exploration of cosmic power, and his engagement with the questions of chance, destiny, divine justice and human free will that Boethius had laid out so many centuries before. It is this cosmic perspective that I increasingly miss in the most recent studies of gender in Chaucer. One of my regrets about the limitation of length imposed on this book is that it inevitably led to the exclusion of important issues that are inextricably linked with gender in Chaucer's writings. The only one of these issues that has enjoyed much attention is language, which has been explored by Dinshaw and Cox. I have tried to indicate the importance of others (time, change, cosmic order, chance) in the course of my discussion, to indicate the larger network of ideas in which gender plays a part.

In 1991, I ended my Preface by stressing the 'dialogue between text and reader', which means that a writer's work is realized in different forms, not only by each century, but almost by each individual reader. It pleases me to think that this is the relation between text and audience that Chaucer represents in the *Canterbury Tales*, where the pilgrims react to each story in terms of their own personal experience and interests (Mann, 1991b) – the Reeve feels personally affronted by a story about a carpenter, the Host wishes his wife was like Griselda or Prudence, the Franklin wishes his son resembled the Squire. The Friar and the Summoner use their stories in the service of mutual aggression, the Pardoner thinks he can use his to make a fast buck. To call Chaucer a 'protofeminist' is pointlessly anachronistic, but his own shrewd observation of the uses to which literary texts are put licenses us to read him with feminist concerns uppermost in our minds. My continued conviction is that to do so is not just an exercise in unpicking masculinist assumptions, but is both a rewarding and enlightening experience.

The aim is not to rescue 'the humanist Chaucer', but to see in what ways his stories might enlarge our perceptions of human life and its possibilities, even though they were written out of and for a very different historical context.

to me when this book was first published. Condren, however, rejects the alternative reading in which Walter occupies the position of God, whereas my point is that the disturbing power of the tale depends on the co-existence of the two.

Sheila Delany puts it well when she says that we should not rewrite the past, but rather use it to rewrite the future (1994, 240).

My thanks are due to Derek Brewer and Richard Barber for offering to publish this revised edition, and to Caroline Palmer for help in the process of its publication. The Excursus on Wife-Swapping first appeared (in slightly different form) in *Viator* (Fall, 2001), and I am grateful to the editor, Blair Sullivan, for permission to reproduce it here.

In 1991 I thanked the Cambridge undergraduates with whom I had discussed Chaucer. In this revised edition, I should like to thank my wonderful students at the University of Notre Dame, both graduate and undergraduate, whose sharp insights and freshness of response have since January 1999 rejuvenated my pleasure in teaching Chaucer. I should also like to thank Maura Nolan and Chris Cannon for reading and commenting on this Preface in draft.

University of Notre Dame
January 25th, 2002

Preface

Chaucer is a major poet and women are a major subject of his poetry. In consequence, this book has turned out to be much longer than it should have been, and even so the reader will notice some obvious omissions. Among the more important casualties are the Prioress and her tale, St Cecilia, the Wife of Bath's fourth husband, the *Book of The Duchess* and the *Parliament of Fowls*. I can only plead in excuse that it seemed less important to give exactly equal coverage to all things female in Chaucer's work than to develop a coherent argument which would enable the reader to place individual works or passages in relation to a structure of poetic thought and practice.

The restrictions of space have had other consequences: I have had to omit any systematic survey of previous feminist writings on Chaucer, although I have dealt with numerous examples of them at appropriate points of my own discussion. I have also had to renounce any attempt to define the relationship between the fictional world of Chaucer's poetry and the social realities of fourteenth-century England. I hope that in doing so I shall not be thought to believe that when all is well in literature, all is well in life, but I do believe that literature is not only produced but also produces – that it is precisely in its imaginative engagement with the ideologies and myths of contemporary society that it can make a contribution to the formation of new social conditions. To concentrate on the text is therefore not an isolationist exercise, but a recognition that this imaginative engagement is itself a critique of prevailing ideologies and a visionary outline of the future, which must be grasped in its full subtlety if it is to be of any use.

As for the kind of 'feminist reading' that this book represents, I should make it clear that it is not tied to any particular school of feminist criticism, though I have formed many of my arguments in mental dialogue with their imagined representatives. Feminism as a historical movement belongs to the late nineteenth and twentieth centuries, and it is therefore legitimate to ask of the literary texts of this period how they stand in relation to the issues that were central to this movement (and which these literary texts themselves may well have helped to identify) – sexual freedom, the 'double standard', work, economic independence, domestic responsibility. There is nothing to stop us considering medieval texts in relation to these issues, as part of the constant re-interpretation and re-testing of past literature that brings it into meaningful relation with present-day culture. But adaptation to different historical circumstances will inevitably change them, sometimes out of recognition (the widespread existence of nunneries, for example, altered the pattern of choices for women – but whether towards greater freedom or greater repression is arguable). And we also have to be prepared for medieval texts themselves to throw up new questions, to point us to unfamiliar issues or unfamiliar areas of importance, if we are not only to avoid distorting the text, but also to see in what ways it can extend our own thinking. I have tried to describe Chaucer's 'feminism' in his own terms rather than ours, not with the narrow historicist aim of keeping him bounded in the past, but rather to avoid bounding him in the orthodoxies of the present. Rather than patronizingly awarding him praise to the extent that he managed to anticipate modern views or demands, I want to allow his text to speak in ways that can tell us something new as well as confirm what we already believe.

I should like to thank the three Harvester Wheatsheaf readers for their careful and appreciative comments, which I have used for last-minute improvements of the text. I should also like to thank Gillian Beer, Piero Boitani, Peter Dronke and Michael Lapidge, who likewise read the work and made helpful suggestions at an earlier stage, and the Cambridge students with whom I have discussed Chaucer and women over the last ten years.

Girton College
Cambridge
1991

Abbreviations

ChauR	*Chaucer Review*
CFMA	Classiques Français du Moyen Âge
CNRS	Centre National de la Recherche Scientifique
EETS, o.s., e.s., s.s.	Early English Text Society, original series, extra series, supplementary series
MED	*Middle English Dictionary*
OED	*Oxford English Dictionary*
PL	*Patrologia Latina*
PMLA	*Publications of the Modern Language Association of America*
SAC	*Studies in the Age of Chaucer*
SATF	Société des Anciens Textes Français

Introduction

'For al so siker as *In principio*,
Mulier est hominis confusio –
Madame, the sentence of this Latyn is,
"Womman is mannes joye and al his blis." '

(Nun's Priest's Tale 3163–6)

The polarized nature of medieval attitudes to women is notorious. Eve is set
against Mary, the sensual deceiver against maternal purity, rebelliousness
against meekness (Blamires, 1992). Yet this ambivalence is not a specifically
medieval phenomenon; its roots can be traced back at least to Roman antiquity,
where it is already visible in the two authors who contributed largely to the formation of these stereotyped images, and whose influence on Chaucer's works
is readily apparent: Ovid, whose amorous poetry represents women as cunning
strategists in the battle of the sexes, yet who is also ready in the *Heroides* to see
them as helpless victims of male cruelty; and Jerome, whose treatise *Against
Jovinian* is a major weapon in the arsenal of antifeminist texts deployed by
the Wife of Bath's fifth husband, yet is also cited by the God of Love in
the *Legend of Good Women* as a source for stories of women who were 'goode
and trewe' (G 270–304). In the Middle Ages, the oppositions that were the
by-product of Ovid's playfulness and Jerome's polemic hardened into opposing positions in a self-conscious debate about the nature of women of which
medieval writers seemed never to tire: were they good or bad, victims or pre-
dators, patient sufferers or aggressive shrews? Were their true representatives
Penelope, Lucretia and Griselda, or rather Eve, Delilah and Clytemnestra?
Often the same author could take up both positions in turn. The Latin writer
Marbod of Rennes (*c.*1035–1123) followed his poetic picture of 'the harlot',
an attack on women as the root of all evil, with an idealizing picture of 'the
matron', eulogizing female virtues. In the late twelfth (or perhaps early thirteenth) century, Andreas Capellanus, 'chaplain at the royal court' and author of
the well-known treatise *On Love*, imitated the volte-face between Ovid's *Ars
Amatoria* and his *Remedia Amoris*: the first two books of Andreas's work,
which instruct its addressee Walter in the art of wooing, present woman as the
quasi-divine goal and fulfilment of male desire, while the third urges him to
reject women's love altogether, bolstering its case with the antifeminist clichés
which represent the whole sex as predatory monsters. The virulently antifeminist *Lamentations* of one Matheolus, a cleric and native of Boulogne, written
in Latin in the late thirteenth century, were translated into French by Jehan
le Fèvre a hundred years later, and promptly answered by Jehan's own *Livre*

de Leesce, a vigorous defence of women against the accusations to which his own translation had given currency.[1] A fifteenth-century lyric (ed. Davies, no. 123) which appears to praise women for their fidelity, patience and discretion, is turned inside out by its own refrain: 'Of all creatures women be best/Cuius contrarium verum est [the contrary of which is true].' The refrain of Lydgate's poem 'Beware of Doubleness' undermines its praise of women's steadfastness in much the same way; 'beware of doubleness' is a pointer to the poem's own 'doubleness' – that it is to be read, as a manuscript gloss directs, 'per antifrasim' (*Minor Poems*, 2: 438–42).

If many literary productions of this sort testify to the medieval love of paradox, debate and disputation for its own sake, rather than to a principled misogyny, nevertheless their inevitable result was the creation and reinforcement of popular stereotypes of women whose consequences were serious enough. Christine de Pisan (*Querelle*, 1978, 136) tells of a married man who was accustomed to read aloud to his wife the antifeminist passages of the *Romance of the Rose*, beating her as he did so. Many a woman must have found herself in the position of Chaucer's Wife of Bath, tormented by the literary representations of 'wikked wyves', yet with no alternative model to turn to other than the role of suffering victim. When a woman, in the shape of Christine de Pisan, finally entered this debate, it was already centuries old, and its terms seemed unalterable. The weapons that Christine seized on had dropped from male hands; her *City of Ladies*, explicitly written as a reply to Matheolus's *Lamentations* (I.1–2), fights from the same corner as Jehan le Fèvre's *Livre de Leesce*, and manages no more than it does to shift the ground on which the battle is fought.

The problem confronting Chaucer when he began to write was thus not simply how woman was to be represented – as good or bad – but rather how she was to be represented in terms that broke free of these traditional polarities, and even more important, how she was to be represented *for herself*, rather than endlessly evaluated from the male standpoint that is equally evident whether she is portrayed as shrew or as patient helpmeet. The chapters that follow will attempt to show with what brilliant resourcefulness Chaucer solved both these problems, and also that he did so not by abandoning his literary inheritance, but by absorbing it into his work so fully that the biassed caricatures of polemical debate are invested with a completely new significance as they are subsumed into the ceaseless variations in the rhythm of lived experience. 'Woman' is not a sign that can be emptied of the meaning that has been poured into it for centuries, and Chaucer does not pretend that it can; instead, he crams in even more meaning, to the point where woman is at the centre instead of at the periphery, where she becomes the norm against which all human behaviour is to be measured.

[1]   In the Introduction to his edition of these three works, Van Hamel dates the Latin *Lamentations* around 1298, its French translation to 1371/2 and the *Livre de Leesce* to 1373 (2: CXIX–CXXVII, CLXXIX–CLXXXII). For further information on Matheolus (=French 'Mahieu') and Jehan, see 2: CVII–CXIX and CLXXXII–CLXXXIX.

This is a large claim, and it will not be fully substantiated until the final chapter of this book. The point I want to make at the outset is that a 'feminist reading' of Chaucer is not (as it might well be with other writers) essentially different from a reading *tout court*. If feminism has a contribution to make to Chaucer studies, it is not because it reveals what Chaucer did not consider or left to one side or was prevented by his historical position from perceiving; it is rather that it enables us to see the full significance of what is already there in his text. It makes it possible, for instance, to register so simple a fact as that the *Canterbury Tales*, for all its rich variety of mode and genre, contains not a single example of the story-type that embodies its ideals in the central figure of a male hero. Instead, the tales that mediate serious ideals are focussed on a series of women: Constance, Griselda, Prudence, Cecilia. The male hero enters only in the burlesque form of *Sir Thopas*, to be unceremoniously bundled out of the way in favour of the tale that celebrates the idealized wisdom of a woman, Chaucer's tale of *Melibee*. The twentieth-century interest in women as a serious subject makes it possible to acknowledge, without incurring the suspicion of distortion or special pleading, that they were an equally serious subject for Chaucer throughout his writing career. Twentieth-century critical theory has also taught us that literary meaning resides in the dialogic relation between text and reader; new types of reading do not subordinate or silence the text, but on the contrary allow it to speak to us in new ways. If feminism has created an audience ready to understand the significance and the importance of the role that Chaucer gives to women in the *Canterbury Tales*, then it will have made a major contribution to recovery of the full human meaning of his work.

1

Women and Betrayal

N'y sey nat this al oonly for thise men,
But moost for wommen that bitraised be
Thorugh false folk ...
(Troilus and Criseyde V 1779–81)

Woman betrayed, woman betraying – these were the alternative images of woman with which Chaucer engaged at the outset of his writing career. The image of woman betrayed was associated first and foremost with the series of examples that make up Ovid's *Heroides*, the collection of fictional letters supposedly addressed by the women of classical story and legend to communicate their anguish and despair to the men who had deceived, deserted or simply neglected them. The *Heroides*, like other works of Ovid, was read and commented on as a school-text throughout the Middle Ages,[1] and the names of these heroines – Dido, Phyllis, Ariadne, Penelope and the rest – became bywords for unhappy love in the writings of the period. But in uneasy contrast to this picture of woman as pathetic victim of male callousness and duplicity stands the picture of woman as temptress and destroyer of men. 'A young woman is fickle and desirous of many lovers' ('Giovane donna, e mobile e vogliosa/È negli amanti molti') is the warning that Boccaccio addresses to young men as the lesson to be learned from his story of Troiolo and Criseida; 'she is immune to virtue and conscience, as perennially inconstant as a leaf in the wind' (*Filostrato* VIII.30).

The contradictory images of woman betrayed and woman betraying do not always stand in simple opposition to each other. Ovid himself brings them into interesting relationship at the opening of the third and final book of his *Ars Amatoria*. The first two books have taught men how to seduce women, and how to hold their affections once won. In the third book, Ovid announces his intention to give parallel instruction to women, so that they may go into battle on equal terms with men. To those who might object 'Why do you add poison to serpents, and open up the sheepfold to the ravenous she-wolf?' (III 7–8),

---

[1]   See Hexter (1986); Bolgar (1954, 189) says of the eleventh and twelfth centuries that 'an analysis of the classical quotations of the literature of the time suggests that no works were more widely read and more lovingly remembered than the *Heroides*, the *Ars Amatoria* and the fourth book of the *Aeneid*'.

Ovid replies that not all women are bad, citing Penelope, Laodamia, Alcestis and Evadne as examples of selfless devotion to their husbands. What is more, he continues, men deceive women more often than women deceive men; he instances four of the women from his own *Heroides* – Medea, Ariadne, Phyllis and Dido – to make the point. So he urges women to make the most of their youth and beauty while they can: the day will come when no lovers will besiege their doors and they will lie cold and lonely through the night (15–76). He therefore sets about teaching them the arts by which they can manipulate men to their own ends. And ironically, one of his instructions is that they should allure men by reading aloud moving poetry such as his own *Amores* or *Heroides* (345). The pathetic pleadings of betrayed women are to become the instruments by which women ensnare men. Male betrayal and female deceit are set in a causal relationship.

This suggestion of a causal relationship between woman betrayed and woman betraying remains in Ovid merely implicit, an irony which the reader may privately relish. But it was an irony not lost on Jean de Meun, who repeated and reinforced it in his section of the *Romance of the Rose*. The lonely old woman conjured up as an imaginary figure in Ovid's warnings ('frigida deserta nocte iacebis anus': III 70) here takes on living form in the person of La Vieille, the crone set to guard Bel Acueil, personification of the Rose's good-will towards the Lover. La Vieille describes to Bel Acueil how the lovers who had battered down her door in the days when she was young and beautiful had all deserted her when she grew old (12731–826). Like Ovid, she concludes that a woman should play the field while her attractions last, squeezing as much money as possible out of her admirers before it is too late (12863–93). Women who do otherwise – who foolishly tie themselves in passionate fidelity to a single man – always come to a bad end (13008–9, 13120–42). She cites the familiar figures of the *Heroides* – Dido, Phyllis, Oenone, Medea – as examples, and concludes: 'In short, all men betray and deceive women; all are playboys, taking on all comers. And so women should deceive them in turn, and not fix their heart on one alone' (13143–239). She then proceeds to instruct Bel Acueil in the feminine arts of seduction with a thoroughness and a cynicism worthy of Ovid's *Ars*. As in Ovid, so in Jean de Meun, betrayal becomes the justification for deceit.[2] La Vieille preaches betrayal because she feels she has been betrayed. The causal relationship implied by Ovid is vividly realized in terms of an individual existence: experience is turned into motive.

This is one way in which the two stereotyped images of woman could be brought into meaningful relationship with each other – and even more important, could be imaginatively realized in an individual female life. In this respect as well as in more obvious ones, La Vieille provided an important model for the *Wife of Bath's Prologue*, as we shall see. But in dealing with betrayal Chaucer chose not to follow Jean de Meun's example directly. A superficial inspection

2   Cf. Richard Green's observation (1988, 11) that La Vieille's advice to deceive men is 'a witty reversal of Ovid's exhortation to male seducers, "Fallite fallentes" ("Deceive the deceivers!")'.

of his works might imply that he simply oscillated between the two alternatives. The *Legend of Good Women*, which follows the *Heroides* model in presenting women as betrayed victims, answers the picture of woman as betrayer in *Troilus and Criseyde*. The treacherous male falcon in the *Squire's Tale* is matched by the adulterous wife of Phoebus in the *Manciple's Tale*. *Anelida and Arcite*, which climaxes (at least in its present fragmentary form) in a *Heroides*-style letter from Anelida lamenting her betrayal by Arcite, is inverted in the *Complaint of Mars*, where narrative similarly leads into a lyric lament, uttered this time by a betrayed male lover. Yet this even-handedness between the sexes is only apparent, as a closer examination at once shows. I shall begin such an examination with the figure of Dido in the *House of Fame*, because it will demonstrate not only Chaucer's sympathy with the *Heroides* tradition, but also his acute sensitivity to his own responsibilities as a poet towards women.

In unsympathetic hands, even the female victims of the *Heroides* could become the targets of antifeminist sneers. Jehan le Fèvre's translation of the *Lamentations* of Matheolus lists Phyllis and Dido as examples of the excessive sexual passion characteristic of the female sex. Phyllis, mad with unsatisfied lust, was unable to wait patiently for Demophoon's return, and hanged herself from 'luxure desordenée' (II 1635–46). Dido's suicide is likewise treated as an act of 'trop grant outrage', committed out of 'fole amour' (II 1647–60).[3] It is, indeed, with the same brusque refusal of sympathy that the *Heroides* women make their first appearance in Chaucer's poetry, as the dreamer-narrator of the *Book of the Duchess* tries to persuade the Black Knight that his grief for his lost 'chess queen' is exaggerated:

> 'Ne say noght soo, for trewely,
> Thogh ye had lost the ferses twelve,
> And ye for sorwe mordred yourselve,
> Ye sholde be dampned in this cas
> By as good ryght as Medea was,
> That slough hir children for Jasoun;
> And Phyllis also for Demophoun
> Heng hirself – so weylaway! –
> For he had broke his terme-day
> To come to hir. Another rage
> Had Dydo, the quene eke of Cartage,
> That slough hirself for Eneas
> Was fals – which a fool she was!' (722–34)[4]

---

[3]   According to Leube (1969, 52–4), Jehan le Fèvre was here influenced by the *Ovide moralisé*, which likewise attributes Dido's death to 'sa folie et … sa rage/D'amours' (XIV 598–9).
[4]   The examples of Echo and Samson which follow (735–9) are possibly due to the influence of the *Romance of the Rose* (see n. to 710–58 in *The Riverside Chaucer*), which also includes references to Medea, Phyllis and Dido (see above, p. 6); the Ovidian character of the list remains however recognisable.

The forced heartiness of the tone in these lines suggests that the lack of sympathy here results from the dreamer's attempt at a therapeutic cheerfulness rather than settled disapproval, but it shows Chaucer's awareness that Ovidian pathos was not the only mode available for dealing with these heroines.

When Dido reappears in the *House of Fame*, however, this Ovidian mode uncompromisingly reasserts itself – and it does so all the more powerfully in that it grows with a quasi-spontaneous momentum out of a Vergilian narrative. Chaucer dreams he finds himself in a temple, on whose wall is 'a table of bras' inscribed with the following words:

> 'I wol now synge, yif I kan,
> The armes and also the man
> That first cam, thurgh his destinee,
> Fugityf of Troy contree,
> In Itayle, with ful moche pyne
> Unto the strondes of Lavyne.' (143–8)

To an educated fourteenth-century reader, this inscription would have been easily recognisable as an English rendering of the opening lines of Vergil's *Aeneid*, and it is duly followed by a lengthy résumé of the rest of the poem, which Chaucer claims he 'sawgh' on the wall – in what form, it is not entirely clear, since with dream-like vagueness, the words give way to pictures; the story is at one moment engraved (157, 193), at another 'peynted on the wal' (211), and shortly afterwards 'grave' again (256). Already, that is, the secondhand summary is assuming independent life; the words refashion themselves into mental pictures, on which attention may linger or focus in greater detail. And this is indeed what happens. Chaucer's résumé relates at an even pace the events described in the first three books of the *Aeneid*: the fall of Troy, Aeneas's flight with his father and son, the storm that scattered his ships, and his eventual arrival in Carthage. But as he relates the love-affair between Aeneas and Dido, 'quene of that contree', the narrative gradually dilates and lingers over this one episode, so that it becomes the focus and the climax of the whole. The pressure towards this dilation is Chaucer's discovery of a *general* significance in this episode; he is provoked to respond to and to comment on his own narrative summary by his recognition of its conformity with an eternally repeated pattern of human experience: the pattern of male treachery and female suffering.

> Allas! what harm doth apparence,
> Whan hit is fals in existence!
> For he to hir a traytour was;
> Wherfore she slow hirself, allas!
> Loo, how a woman doth amys
> To love hym that unknowen ys!
> For, be Cryste, lo, thus yt fareth:
> 'Hyt is not al gold that glareth.'

For also browke I wel myn hed,
Ther may be under godlyhed
Kevered many a shrewed vice.
Therfore be no wyght so nyce
To take a love oonly for chere,
Or speche, or for frendly manere,
For this shal every woman fynde,
That som man, of his pure kynde,
Wol shewen outward the fayreste,
Tyl he have caught that what him leste;
And thanne wol he causes fynde
And swere how that she ys unkynde,
Or fals, or privy, or double was.
Al this seye I be Eneas
And Dido, and hir nyce lest,
That loved al to sone a gest;
Therfore I wol seye a proverbe,
That 'he that fully knoweth th'erbe
May saufly leye hyt to his yë' –
Withoute drede, this ys no lye. (265–92)

I have quoted this passage at length because it is precisely its length that is surprising – even more so in the light of Chaucer's immediately preceding insistence that he cannot stop to recount the 'long proces' of the burgeoning love-affair because it would be 'over-long for yow to dwelle' (251–2). Although not itself based on the *Heroides*, this passage prepares us to interpret Dido's long lament over Aeneas's desertion of her, which follows immediately afterwards, in Ovidian rather than Vergilian terms. Chaucer's own comments, that is, encourage us to identify with Dido's perspective on the desertion, instead of seeing it, as we do in the *Aeneid*, framed and qualified within the dictates of Aeneas's historic destiny. When the long lament is over, Chaucer underlines this intrusion of an Ovidian perspective on the Vergilian narrative by directing his readers to 'Rede Virgile in Eneydos/Or the Epistle of Ovyde' if they want to know 'What that she wrot or that she dyde' (375–80).[5] And he reinforces the Ovidian terms of reference even further by interpolating a long passage rehearsing the similar fates of the other *Heroides* women – Phyllis, Briseida, Oenone, Hypsipyle, Medea, Deianira, Ariadne (388–426).

Dido's own lament harmonizes fully with Chaucer's conception of her as an exemplary victim of male deceitfulness. Leaving his literary models, Chaucer writes a quite new monologue, which consists almost entirely of generalisations

---

[5]   The early fourteenth-century *Ovide moralisé* similarly combines Vergil and Ovid (Leube, 1969, 43–4, 64–5), but the concluding moralisation takes Aeneas's side, allegorizing Dido as Heresy, which attempts to divert Holy Church from the true path of faith (XIV 302–596; cf. Leube, 1969, 45).

on male deceitfulness.[6] Gone are the specifics of the situation rehearsed by both Vergil's Dido and by Ovid's – her vulnerability to enemies and to other suitors, the opprobrium she has suffered for protecting and assisting Aeneas, the possibility of her pregnancy. Instead, Dido sees Aeneas's falsehood, as Chaucer has just done, as an instance of generalized male fickleness.[7]

> 'Allas, is every man thus trewe,
> That every yer wolde have a newe,
> Yf hit so longe tyme dure,
> Or elles three, peraventure?
> As thus: of oon he wolde have fame
> In magnyfyinge of hys name;
> Another for frendshippe, seyth he;
> And yet ther shal the thridde be
> That shal be take for delyt,
> Loo, or for synguler profit.' (301–10)

Her bewildered anguish is not directed to Aeneas alone, but to 'ye men' in general, just as she generalizes herself into 'we wrechched wymmen'.

> 'O, have ye men such godlyhede
> In speche, and never a del of trouthe?
> Allas, that ever hadde routhe
> Any woman on any man!
> Now see I wel, and telle kan,
> We wrechched wymmen konne noon art;
> For certeyn, for the more part,
> Thus we be served everychone.
> How sore that ye men konne groone,
> Anoon as we have yow receyved,
> Certaynly we ben deceyved!
> For, though your love laste a seson,
> Wayte upon the conclusyon,
> And eke how that ye determynen,
> And for the more part diffynen.' (330–44)

The prominence given here to the Dido episode is thus grounded in a general rather than an individual sympathy; Chaucer dramatizes his response to her

---

6   See Norton-Smith, 1974, 50. Fyler (1979, 36–40) comments on the way that the dreamer's 'progressively more subjective response to the *Aeneid*' leads to his 'increasing participation in his experience' in this section of the poem.

7   As Clemen points out (1963, 84, n. 3), 'this conception of Aeneas as a deceiver was supported by a tradition going back to Dares Phrygius and Dictys Cretensis, whereby the Greeks owed their capture of Troy to the treachery of Aeneas and Antenor'; for Chaucer, however, Aeneas's deceit is manifested only in the amatory sphere.

story as a response that arises out of a perception of its significance in illustrating and confirming the common lot of women.[8] It is at the point where her story makes contact with the everyday realities recorded and stored up in proverbial utterance (265–6, 269–72) that it moves away from its literary source and takes on its own independent life.[9] Once this moment of imaginative identification with woman's plight is over, Chaucer returns to his bald summary, disposing of the last eight books of the *Aeneid* in a mere thirty lines. No other event holds his interest or provokes him into spontaneous involvement. In Chaucer's retelling, Dido, and not Aeneas, is the centre of the *Aeneid*.

In creating Dido's lament, Chaucer is doing more than dramatize his sympathy for woman betrayed: he is also dramatizing his sense of the writer's responsibilities towards women as literary subjects. For his Dido not only contemplates her betrayal by Aeneas, she also contemplates her own humiliation as a figure of story and legend.

> 'O wel-awey that I was born!
> For thorgh yow is my name lorn,
> And alle myn actes red and songe
> Over al thys lond, on every tonge.
> O wikke Fame! – for ther nys
> Nothing so swift, lo, as she is!
> O soth ys, every thing ys wyst,
> Though hit be kevered with the myst.
> Eke, though I myghte duren ever,
> That I have don rekever I never,
> That I ne shal be seyd, allas,
> Yshamed be thourgh Eneas,
> And that I shal thus juged be:
> "Loo, ryght as she hath don, now she
> Wol doo eft-sones, hardely" –
> Thus seyth the peple prively.' (345–60)

It is in her role as victim of 'wikke Fame' that Dido claims entrance to Chaucer's *House of Fame*; she is the suffering human subject who must bear to be represented by the accounts of others – accounts that are circulated not only in oral form ('songe') but also in writing ('red'). At the head of this written tradition stands Book IV of the *Aeneid*. Vergil's account is not devoid of

---

[8]   Dronke ([1986] 1992, 451) comments on 'the wider, exemplary dimension' that Chaucer gives to Aeneas's treachery in Dido's lament; her story becomes meaningful 'insofar as the magnificent but remote queen of Carthage is seen to have an experience no different from that of any woman betrayed by any man' (452).

[9]   The possible source for one of these proverbs (269–70) in Dido's lament in the *Ovide moralisé* XIV 354–7 ('L'on selt dire un mot veritable:/Que feme a le cuer trop braidif/Qui d'ome d'estrange païs/Fait son acointe ne son dru') seems to have escaped notice so far.

sympathy for Dido; she is given a tragic stature that makes her suicide probably the emotional climax of the whole poem. Berlioz found this book of the
Aeneid so moving that it determined his whole conception of *Les Troyens*:
for him, Italy is founded on the bodies of dying women – Cassandra and the
Trojan women at the end of Act I, Dido at the end of the opera. But however
sympathetic Vergil's narrative is to Dido, it cannot allow her point of view to
predominate; the harsh necessities of masculine duty must have superior
claims. It is only from the firm security of this masculine point of view that
Vergil can allow himself (or fail to notice?) the glaring irony in Mercury's
exhortation to Aeneas to hasten his departure because 'woman is ever fickle
and changeable' (569–70). *Varium et mutabile semper/Femina*: the phrase that
became a proverbial expression of woman's fickleness has its origin at the
heart of the classic story of male betrayal.[10]

In reversing the balance of sympathies from Aeneas to Dido, Ovid brings
out a latent potential in Vergil's narrative, but he also prises the story loose
from Vergil's authoritative grasp. And in later centuries there were even stronger
challenges to the authority of the Vergilian account. Augustine, when recalling
with contempt his own boyhood tears over the death of Dido, points out that
the learned will admit that Aeneas never went to Carthage (*Confessions*
I.xiii.21–2). St Jerome, in his treatise *Against Jovinian*, lists Dido among the
chaste widows, attributing her suicide, not to despair at Aeneas's betrayal, but
to her desire to avoid marriage to her suitor Iarbas and to remain faithful to her
dead husband Sychaeus (I.43). This scepticism in the face of Vergil's account
passed on into the Middle Ages: John Ridevall, one of the fourteenth-century
'classicizing' friars studied by Beryl Smalley (1960, 130, 320–1), proclaimed
Vergil's story to be evidently false, since Aeneas lived three hundred years
earlier than Dido, whose dates are fixed by the foundation of Carthage. The
fourteenth-century chronicler Ranulph Higden took the same view, citing
Augustine as his authority. While Dante followed his master Vergil, Petrarch
and Boccaccio agreed with St Jerome in seeing Dido as a virtuous widow,
whose suicide was the final act of devotion to her husband's memory.[11]

What is at issue in these competing narrative versions is not only Dido
herself, but the nature of poetic truth. St Augustine's aim in mentioning Dido
in the *Confessions* is the scornful dismissal of poetic fictions ('poetica
figmenta'). Ironically, he himself is taken to task by Ridevall's commentary on
the *City of God* (I.2), for treating Aeneas's description of the fall of Troy as if
it were a reliable historical account ('veritatem historie') rather than a poetical
fiction ('fictionem poete') (Smalley, 1960, 360). It is likewise in the context of

---

10   Walther (1963–9) no. 32906.
11   Petrarch, *Familiares* IX. 15; *Seniles* I.4, IV.5; *Triumphus Pudicitiae* 10–12, 154–9;
Boccaccio, *De Mulieribus Claris* XLII; Higden, *Polychronicon* I.xxi; II.xxvi. Cf. also
Macrobius, *Saturnalia* V.xvii.5–6. This version of Dido's suicide goes back to Justinus's
Epitome of the *Historiae Philippicae* of Pompeius Trogus (XVIII.4–6), which Higden cites
as an authority alongside Augustine.

a discussion of the nature of poetic truth that Boccaccio refers to those who adduce Vergil's story of Dido as evidence that the poets lie (*De Genealogia Deorum* XIV.13). The 'truth' of Dido's story was traditionally bound up with the question of literary authority, with the kind of belief that is to be accorded to literature. Attitudes to women are determined by the endorsement or rejection of literary authority: when Jehan le Fèvre answered Matheolus's antifeminist accusations in his *Livre de Leesce*, it was on the grounds that his *literary* evidence was no evidence at all,

> Car de mençoingnes y a maintes
> En ces ystoires qui sont faintes. (754–5)

He points out that many of Matheolus's stories illustrate male treachery rather than female folly; but in any case, he says, writers such as Homer and Ovid are unworthy of belief because they are pagans.

> Leurs fables et leurs poësies
> En nostre loy sont heresies,
> Et pour ce ne font pas a croire,
> Ne ceulx qui suivent leur ystoire,
> Principaument quant il parlerent
> Des femmes et qu'il les blasmerent. (2697–702)

The question of literary authority is the central concern of the *House of Fame*, as critics have long agreed. In Book II, Chaucer comically protests a faith in bookish authority so extreme that it can entirely dispense with experiential proof: to the Eagle's offer to show him the stellar constellations so that he will be able to confirm what the books say from first-hand experience, Chaucer replies that he believes what he reads about them just as firmly as if he had seen it with his own eyes – and in any case, his eyesight wouldn't stand the glare (993–1017). The vision of the *House of Fame* in Book III shows the problems attendant on credulity of this sort: the medley of truths and falsehoods, of obliterating silences and unsubstantiated reputations, renders the recovery of historical truth effectively impossible. As in the *Livre de Leesce*, so here too Homer is accused of writing 'lyes,/Feynynge in hys poetries', which are to be dismissed as 'fable' (1477–80). Chaucer's vision of the true source of poetic authority is to be found not in Book III, but at the very outset of his dream, in the presentation of Dido. It is located, not in a rigorous historical accuracy, but in the liberating ability of the imagination to invest the two-dimensional outlines of a text with their own autonomous life and movement. If Chaucer's Dido visualizes herself shrinking to the two-dimensional figure of gossip and literary *exemplum*, then in imagining that moment of anguished anticipation Chaucer has reversed the process: he has in imagination gone behind the literary sources to recuperate the living individual from whom they take their origin. It is his own act of imaginative retrieval that Chaucer

emphasizes at the very heart of Dido's lament, intervening to make the point
that here he has left his literary sources behind:

> In suche wordes gan to pleyne
> Dydo of hir grete peyne,
> As me mette redely –
> Non other auctour alegge I. (311–14)

Ovid's importance to this passage is not that he creates a Dido more acceptable
to Chaucer; on the contrary, it is that his response to Vergil is the model for
Chaucer's similarly independent act of imaginative retrieval. Just as Ovid
could isolate a female perspective from Vergil's story of male destiny, so Chaucer
can reconstruct Dido afresh from the point where her story makes contact with
common human experience as he knows it.

The significance of this early work of Chaucer's, therefore, is not simply
that he takes the 'woman's side' in the Dido-and-Aeneas story; it is rather that
he dramatizes the adoption of this standpoint as *an act of retrieval*: the
woman's viewpoint is rediscovered in the story of male heroism. Chaucer's
Dido represents an affirmation of faith that such a retrieval is a permanent
possibility – that the writ of literary authority runs no further than the point at
which it meets the reader's own corrective or confirmatory experience.

To come to *Troilus and Criseyde* from the *House of Fame* is to see with full
clarity how surprising – indeed, how apparently inexplicable – is Chaucer's
choice of subject here. After his fervent identification with the victims of male
deceit, he chooses to tell the classic story of female betrayal. Like Dido,
Criseyde anticipates her own afterlife in story and song, but in her case there is
the added pain of knowing that her tale will fan the flames of antifeminism.

> 'Allas, of me, unto the worldes ende,
> Shal neyther ben ywriten nor ysonge
> No good word, for thise bokes wol me shende.
> O, rolled shal I ben on many a tonge!
> Thorughout the world my belle shal be ronge!
> And wommen moost wol haten me of alle.
> Allas, that swich a cas me sholde falle!
>
> Thei wol seyn, in as muche as in me is,
> I have hem don dishonour, weylaway!
> Al be I nat the first that dide amys,
> What helpeth that to don my blame awey?' (V 1058–68)

Criseyde's lament has a source in Benoît, whose Briseida similarly envisages
with dismay her own future disgrace in story and song ('De mei n'iert ja fait bon
escrit/Ne chantee bone chançon': *Roman de Troie* 20238–9), but his imagination
of her distress does not prevent him (as it does Chaucer) from drawing the

usual antifeminist moral (13438–56, 13471–91); for him, Briseida's prophetic vision of the meaning that will be given to her story simply repeats and endorses the meaning that he himself assigns to it – that women are inconstant and emotionally shallow (cf. Mieszkowski, 1971, 81–7, 103–4). The greater prominence that Chaucer gives to his own role as narrator of Criseyde's story invests the passage with a quite different significance: it becomes an accusation of his own role in adding to the 'bokes' that chronicle her shame. The responsibility is all the greater since Criseyde's very existence is a literary fiction; the poets invent the female inconstancy that they purportedly record. And whereas the *House of Fame* represents Dido's story as having painful consequences for herself alone, Criseyde's story is here represented as impinging on the real lives of other women, present and future. Chaucer here vividly realizes one of the special burdens that women have to bear: the knowledge that they cannot escape the burden of meaning. Whether good or bad, their actions will always be interpreted by reference to a model of 'woman', and will share willy-nilly in the responsibility for the nature of that model. The possible repercussions of this story on the lives of women are brought to the foreground again in the Prologue to the *Legend of Good Women*, where the God of Love upbraids Chaucer for having written *Troilus* precisely on the ground that women will be the sufferers from it.

> 'And of Creseyde thou hast seyd as the lyste,
> That maketh men to wommen lasse triste,
> That ben as trewe as ever was any steel.' (F 332–4)

Given this sensitivity to its antifeminist effects, why *did* Chaucer decide to tell this story? Are his expressions of sympathy for betrayed women to be seen as mere conventional gallantries, replaced at will by an equally conventional readiness to see women as fickle deceivers? That this is not the case is suggested by the fact that on two of the three occasions when Chaucer depicts female betrayal, he deliberately – even, it might seem, perversely – reverses the exemplary direction of his story when he comes to summarize its import. At the end of *Troilus and Criseyde*, he not only apologizes for his story to the female members of his audience[12] –

> Bysechyng every lady bright of hewe,
> And every gentil womman, what she be,
> That al be that Criseyde was untrewe,
> That for that gilt she be nat wroth with me.
> Ye may hire gilt in other bokes se;

---

[12] The audience addressed may be the implied rather than the actual audience, since Richard Green (1983–4) has shown that the number of women at court was probably small. Such apologies to women for anti-feminist material are frequent enough in medieval literature to be regarded as conventional (Mann, 1991); but Chaucer's use of the convention is differentiated from that of other writers by his immediate addition of remarks critical of men.

> And gladlier I wol write, yif yow leste,
> Penelopeës trouthe and good Alceste. (V 1772–8)

– he also, astonishingly, represents it as a warning to beware of falsehood in *men*:

> N'y sey nat this al oonly for thise men,
> But moost for wommen that bitraised be
> Thorugh false folk – God yeve hem sorwe, amen! –
> That with hire grete wit and subtilte
> Bytraise yow. And this commeveth me
> To speke, and in effect yow alle I preye,
> Beth war of men, and herkneth what I seye! (V 1779–85)

The same reversal of direction occurs in similar circumstances in the *Manciple's Tale*. Having reached the point where he has to relate the adultery of Phoebus's wife, Chaucer swerves aside into a long digression on the impossibility of eradicating natural characteristics, illustrating this point with the Boethian example of the bird who flies off to the wood the moment its cage door is left open. Similarly, he continues, a cat's appetite for mice will never disappear, no matter how well fed it is, and a she-wolf characteristically expresses her 'vileyns kynde' by choosing the 'lewedeste wolf that she may fynde' (160–86). This last example was a favourite with antifeminist writers,[13] and one awaits – given the nature of the story Chaucer is telling – the inevitable conclusion on female lustfulness. But the trait that Chaucer identifies as naturally implanted in human beings is not lust, but 'newfangelnesse', and it is not women whom he identifies as most tainted with it, but *men*.

> Alle thise ensamples speke I by thise men
> That been untrewe, and nothyng by wommen.
> For men han evere a likerous appetit
> On lower thyng to parfourne hire delit
> Than on hire wyves, be they never so faire,
> Ne never so trewe, ne so debonaire.
> Flessh is so newefangel, with meschaunce,
> That we ne konne in nothyng han plesaunce
> That sowneth into vertu any while. (187–95)

The 'we' is significant: not 'men', but 'we men'. With these at first baffling contradictions between story and moral, Chaucer delicately negotiates the problems of a male author telling a story of female betrayal. He acknowledges his own masculinity, rather than dissolving it in the impersonal authority of the invisible author, and deflects the moral of his story on to the sex of which he can speak

---

13   See Reid (1955); *Romance of the Rose* 7761–6; Matheolus, *Lamentations* I 904–6.

with personal authority. There are no such contradictory frameworks to complicate his stories of male betrayal; his exclamations against male deceit endorse and amplify the natural implications of the narrative rather than running against its grain. Setting the story at odds with the comment on it in the cases of female betrayal is thus not an instance of the 'ambivalence' so often invoked in Chaucer criticism as a convenient way of halting further analysis, but rather an overt recognition of the need for a male author to *situate himself* in relation to these tales, and thereby to redress the asymmetrical balance created by the alignment of the male author and the male victim in the story.

The *Manciple's Tale* has yet more light to shed on *Troilus and Criseyde*. For it shows us that the male author not only has a general responsibility for telling or not telling a story, he also has a specific responsibility for *how* he tells it. It is he who chooses the style that will determine whether we see sexual congress as romantic passion or as a bestial coupling. No sooner has Chaucer turned back to the story of Phoebus's wife than he digresses from it again, this time to comment on his own use of the word 'lemman' to denote her lover.

> Hir lemman? Certes, this is a knavyssh speche!
> Foryeveth it me, and that I yow biseche.
>   The wise Plato seith, as ye may rede,
> The word moot nede accorde with the dede.
> If men shal telle proprely a thyng,
> The word moot cosyn be to the werkyng.
> I am a boystous man, right thus seye I:
> Ther nys no difference, trewely,
> Bitwixe a wyf that is of heigh degree,
> If of hir body dishonest she bee,
> And a povre wenche, oother than this –
> If it so be they werke bothe amys –
> But that the gentile, in estaat above,
> She shal be cleped his lady, as in love;
> And for that oother is a povre womman,
> She shal be cleped his wenche or his lemman.
> And, God it woot, myn owene deere brother,
> Men leyn that oon as lowe as lith that oother. (205–22)

The story-teller determines attitudes to women by the style he chooses for his story; it is he who makes woman an Isolde or a whore. The power of rhetoric to re-create women in its own mould is depressingly illustrated in Phoebus's sentimental reconstruction of his wife after he has murdered her in jealous rage:

> 'O deere wyf! O gemme of lustiheed!
> That were to me so sad and eek so trewe,
> Now listow deed, with face pale of hewe,
> Ful giltelees, that dorste I swere, ywys!' (274–7)

Phoebus's wife is not only the victim of male violence, but also the victim of male rhetoric (Mann, 1991c, 222). We never penetrate behind this rhetoric to an intimate knowledge of her, her lover, or the nature of the relationship between them; we see only the various stereotyped models in terms of which she might be presented.

It is style that is crucial in Chaucer's telling of the story of Criseyde. It is his style, rather than his final protestations of good intentions, that prevents this story, against all probability, from being read as a classic example of feminine fickleness and deceit. So successfully did Chaucer fend off this apparently inevitable interpretation that scholars were long convinced that the hostile stereotyping of Criseyde came only *after* Chaucer, and was largely attributable to Henryson and Shakespeare. Gretchen Mieszkowski's exhaustive documentation of the Cressida story from its inception in Benoît de Sainte-Maure shows however that she was already a byword for female mutability (and worse) when Chaucer came to write. It is Chaucer who not only abandons Boccaccio's moral on the fickleness of women, but who also creates a Criseyde to whom this moral seems entirely inappropriate. Despite the fact that Chaucer makes clear from the outset that the story will tell how Criseyde 'forsook' Troilus 'er she deyde' (I 56), this inevitable ending fades from the reader's consciousness in the moment-by-moment excitements of the love-affair. When in Book III Criseyde exclaims, in response to Pandarus's trumped-up story of Troilus's jealousy, 'Horaste! Allas, and falsen Troilus?' (806), the idea of her being unfaithful to Troilus is as unthinkable to us as it is to her. The character of betrayer is one with which events invest her, not one we are persuaded is hers from the beginning, whether by virtue of her sex or by virtue of her individual character. The final moment when Criseyde visualizes her own entrapment within the bounds of this stereotyped character thus reveals to us the full extent of the living indeterminacy which Chaucer has recuperated from its unpromising outline. No less than Chaucer's Dido, Chaucer's Criseyde represents an act of imaginative retrieval. Yet the very success of this act of retrieval raises even more acutely the question of how the betrayal comes about. If it is *not* due to female fickleness, what is its cause?

In answering this question, we come near to the heart of Chaucer's continual concern with betrayal. For it is, in his eyes, the bitterest manifestation of the most fundamental characteristic of human nature: the capacity for change. On two occasions in the *Canterbury Tales*, Chaucer adapted the Boethian metre on the ineradicability of natural impulses, complete with its illustrative image of the bird in the cage (*Consolation of Philosophy*, III m.2). The passage from the *Manciple's Tale* which I have already discussed is one of these instances; the other is in the *Squire's Tale*, where it forms part of the lament of the female falcon, deserted by her lover, and thus accounting for his betrayal of her:

> 'I trowe he hadde thilke text in mynde,
> That "alle thyng, repeirynge to his kynde,

Gladeth hymself;" thus seyn men, as I gesse.
Men loven of propre kynde newefangelnesse,
As briddes doon that men in cages fede.
For though thou nyght and day take of hem hede,
And strawe hir cage faire and softe as silk,
And yeve hem sugre, hony, breed and milk,
Yet right anon as that his dore is uppe
He with his feet wol spurne adoun his cuppe,
And to the wode he wole and wormes ete;
So newefangel been they of hire mete,
And loven novelries of propre kynde,
No gentillesse of blood ne may hem bynde.' (607–20)

In both cases what Chaucer adds to his Boethian source is an identification of man's 'propre kynde' as 'newefangelnesse', the ineradicable movement towards change and 'novelries'. It is this same impulse towards 'a newe' that Dido had identified as the source of men's betrayal (*House of Fame* 302). Neither lust, nor greed, nor vanity, is necessary to account for betrayal: it is the simple and inevitable reflex of the changeability that is the very life of human beings.

Troilus and Criseyde is Chaucer's most extended and most profound exploration of human changeability, and it is worth investigating this in some detail in order to see how it can give rise to, and yet resist being reduced to, female betrayal. The long and complex narrative allows us to see change not only as the sudden reversal it appears to be in the condensed summaries of *exemplum* or lament, but also as a series of minute adjustments to the changing pressures of daily living. To this end, the first three books of the poem are even more important than the last two. For it is in the slow process of Criseyde's acceptance of Troilus that we learn to understand how, when the time comes, she will gradually abandon him for Diomede. Between the Criseyde who rejects Pandarus's first overtures with distress and indignation, and the Criseyde who in joyous ecstasy entwines her body round Troilus's as tightly as honeysuckle round a tree, there lies a linked sequence of shifts and adjustments so small that they pass almost unnoticed at the time; yet the change they effect is as major, when we stand back to take the long view of it, as the one effected in the betrayal. It is the comparability of the two processes that cleanses the betrayal of its antifeminist implications, and it is to the earlier process that we should look if we want to understand how Chaucer rescues the betrayal from an antifeminist meaning.

The pressure towards change in Criseyde comes from without – from Pandarus's revelation of Troilus's love in the first case, and from the exchange with Antenor and Diomede's wooing in the second – but these external stimuli would fail of their effect were it not for the internal mutability they find to work on – the capacity of the mind to adapt, to absorb the overturning of the status quo into its own processes until it becomes a new status quo, a point of new departure. Chaucer's first indication of this capacity for absorption comes in the carefully casual question Criseyde addresses to Pandarus when all the first agitations over his announcement of Troilus's love have died down, and the subject appears to have been dropped: 'Kan he wel speke of love?' (II 503). The threatening aspect of Pandarus's startling news is, we see, wearing off; fear is replaced by curiosity, rejection by a readiness to admit at least the hypothesis of a hypothesis. The knowledge of Troilus's love has become part of Criseyde's 'mental furniture'; tossed into the ceaseless play of her thoughts and emotions, it causes them to shift, to rearrange themselves around it, to regroup into new formations to take account of it (Mann, 1989, 223–6).

This process of rearrangement can be seen in all its subtlety of detail in Chaucer's account of Criseyde's private thoughts when Pandarus has left her and she sits down to reflect on the 'newe cas'. She has barely got beyond reassuring herself that no woman is obliged to love a man however passionately he is in love with her (II 603–9), when she is distracted by shouts outside hailing Troilus's return from the battlefield. Watching this young hero ride by, she sees him with new eyes in the light of Pandarus's revelation, and blushes with consciousness of the thought that this is the man whose life, according to Pandarus, depends on her mercy. The serene detachment of which she has just been assuring herself evaporates at its first test; the secret excitement that arises spontaneously with the thought that this brave and modest hero is dying with love for *her* creates an embarrassment that of itself constitutes an implicating relationship with Troilus, despite his obliviousness to her gaze or her blush. It is not – as Chaucer hastens to make plain – that 'she so sodeynly/Yaf hym hire love', but that the pressure of the moment creates a pull towards him: 'she gan enclyne/To like hym first' (II 673–5).

> And after that, his manhod and hys pyne
> Made love withinne hire [herte] for to myne,
> For which by proces and by good servyse
> He gat hire love, and in no sodeyn wyse. (II 676–9)

As Chaucer turns back to his account of Criseyde's thoughts, we can see this 'proces' getting itself under way, as her mind accommodates itself to the new fact of Troilus's love. In contrast to the deliberate calculations of Boccaccio's Criseida, who weighs pros against cons and allows Troiolo's handsome person to tip the balance (*Filostrato* II 69–78, 83), Criseyde's reflections proceed in a random, spontaneous, disorganized manner. Their zig-zagging movement is conveyed in the loose, additive nature of the phrases that introduce each new idea: 'Ek wel woot I ... Ek sith I woot ... And eke I knowe ... Now sette a caas ... I thenke ek ...' (II 708–36). The self-conscious organisation of thought at the opening, as Criseyde decorously addresses herself to questions of 'worthynesse' and 'honour', and attempts worldly wisdom ('better not to make an enemy of the king's son') dissolves into spontaneous wonder that this dazzling personage, who could claim the noblest lady in Troy as his love, has chosen *her*; equally spontaneous is the immediately succeeding thought that this is not, after all, so odd, since – as everyone says – she is the most beautiful woman in Troy. It would be a mistake to interpret this last reflection as revealing vanity in Criseyde; an outstandingly beautiful woman can hardly be unaware of her own beauty, although social decorum obliges her to conceal her knowledge, as Criseyde recognises ('Al wolde I that noon wiste of this thought': II 745). Criseyde's private awareness of her own beauty escapes being vanity precisely because the vigilant supervision of her more public self brings it under scrutiny and control. What is revealed by this most private of thoughts is the level of intimate reflection to which we have penetrated: we have moved from the level of thought that is prepared for public scrutiny – that would translate itself without difficulty into speech – to a level of instinctive reaction that could hardly be made public without changing its entire character. What it is not vanity to know, it is vanity to speak. This sense of *levels* of thought is the result of our perception of the constant movement between them; the self-conscious aspect of the mind (in our terms, the super-ego) constantly doubles back on what has been spontaneously thought, correcting and criticizing. As her awareness of her beauty is 'corrected' by the self-reminder that no one else must know of this awareness, the prudential consideration that Troilus is no boaster is immediately 'corrected' by the reflection that he will of course have nothing to boast of.

So it is that the possibility of loving Troilus, which first appears only as a hypothesis to be rejected ('although it is out of the question to grant him my love ...'; 'and he won't have anything to boast of ...') finally appears as a positive without any *logical* preparation for the change. Having begun to contemplate her own beauty – to look at herself, that is, with Troilus's eyes – she is led quite naturally into fashioning a new image of herself: the picture of sober widowhood which has been the model for her behaviour hitherto (II 113–19) gives way to a new conception of herself as her 'owene womman', in comfortable circumstances, 'Right yong', and free from obligations to a husband (II 750–6). For such a person love seems not only permissible but desirable.

> 'What shal I doon? To what fyn lyve I thus?
> Shal I nat love, in cas if that me leste?
> What, pardieux! I am naught religious.' (II 757–9)

So she admits the possibility of loving Troilus as one that is, indeed, open for her to choose.

What is important in this long sequence of thought is not so much its representation of *what* Criseyde thinks as its representation of *how* she thinks (Howard, 1970). Her mind moves of its own accord, flitting from one aspect of the situation to another, animated by the sudden emotional impulses that thwart the attempt at a logical progression by starting off in an unrelated direction. It is not surprising, then, to find that one of these impulses causes her thoughts suddenly to reverse themselves completely, the corrective agent here being not the super-ego but simple fear: *since* she is free, should she jeopardize this freedom by subjecting herself to the anxieties, quarrels, jealousies and betrayals so frequent in love? The spontaneous nature of this reversal in mood is emphasized by the natural image Chaucer chooses to express it:

> But right as when the sonne shyneth brighte
> In March, that chaungeth ofte tyme his face,
> And that a cloude is put with wynd to flighte,
> Which oversprat the sonne as for a space,
> A cloudy thought gan thorugh hire soule pace,
> That overspradde hire brighte thoughtes alle,
> So that for feere almost she gan to falle. (II 764–70)

Sun and shade alternate within the human mind as inevitably as in a March day; the mind too 'chaungeth ofte tyme his face'. So this reversal in turn eventually reverses itself.

> And after that, hire thought gan for to clere,
> And seide, 'He which that nothing undertaketh,
> Nothyng n'acheveth, be hym looth or deere.'
> And with an other thought hire herte quaketh;
> Than slepeth hope, and after drede awaketh;
> Now hoot, now cold; but thus, bitwixen tweye,
> She rist hire up, and wente hire for to pleye. (II 806–12)

'Now hoot, now cold': here is change working at its most fundamental and ineradicable level. The bold outlines of observable change are formed out of the *pointilliste* minutiae of this ceaseless movement of thought and emotion, absorbing and responding to external stimuli. In the sequence that follows we see how a new set of external stimuli gradually transforms the continual to-ing and fro-ing into a single directional flow: Antigone sings her song in praise of love which answers Criseyde's fears of 'thraldom'; the nightingale sings under Criseyde's window as she falls asleep; she dreams of the eagle who tears her heart out without pain. The current of events is pulling her towards love, but it could not do so without the existing presence in her mind of the thoughts and emotions which it can endorse and bring into the foreground. The seething possibilities in Criseyde's mind are the seed-bed for new developments; chance determines which of these possibilities – the attraction to nobility, openness to adventure – will realize themselves in the immediate sequence of events, but the other possibilities – cautious timidity, prudent self-interest – do not disappear; they remain, to be called into play by the new set of external pressures created by Criseyde's isolation in the Greek camp and Diomede's insistent wooing.

It is the slow process by which Criseyde's thoughts and feelings adapt themselves to the fact of Troilus's love until it becomes part of her own being that teaches us to understand how they can equally adapt to his loss and set

Diomede in his place. This time Chaucer does not show us her thoughts in detail, but his summary indicates with beautiful subtlety the way that this process mirrors that in Book II. After Diomede's first visit, Criseyde goes to bed in her father's tent,

> Retornyng in hire soule ay up and down
> The wordes of this sodeyn Diomede,
> His grete estat, and perel of the town,
> And that she was allone and hadde nede
> Of frendes help; and thus bygan to brede
> The cause whi, the sothe for to telle,
> That she took fully purpos for to dwelle. (V 1023–9)

The betrayal dissolves itself in the invisible flux of Criseyde's thoughts; the stanza concludes, not with a decision, but with the mere germination of the *cause* of a *purpose* – and a purpose that realizes itself not as action, but simply as the will's endorsement of a status quo, so that the moment of that endorsement is inaccessible to outward observation.

And yet, having shown us Criseyde's change of heart as a slow process of incremental adjustment, in the very next stanza Chaucer re-presents it with a brutal abruptness of style that becomes a characterisation of the deed itself:

> The morwen com, and gostly for to speke,
> This Diomede is come unto Criseyde;
> And shortly, lest that ye my tale breke,
> So wel he for hymselven spak and seyde
> That alle hire sikes soore adown he leyde;
> And finaly, the sothe for to seyne,
> He refte hire of the grete of al hire peyne. (V 1030–6)

The shift in narrative perspective effects a shift in emotional attitude. The first stanza takes a 'long view' of Criseyde's change of heart, seeing it as a gentle and quasi-inevitable process of reorientation; the second 'shortly' summarizes this process until its outlines appear in cruel clarity. Taken together, they answer the question of how betrayal comes about: the bewildering volte-faces castigated in the denunciations of 'newefangelnesse' spin themselves out into the subtle filaments of fluctuating mood and thought. We do not see Criseyde deciding to betray – we do not even see her betraying – we see her realizing, at the end of the almost invisible process, that she has betrayed (Mann, 1986, 82). Just as she never formally decides to yield to Troilus, but comes to realize that she has yielded ('Ne hadde I er now, my swete herte deere,/Ben yolde, ywis, I were now nought heere!': III 1210–11), so her betrayal too is a matter of retrospective acknowledgement ('I have falsed oon the gentileste/That evere was': V 1056–7) rather than present decision. In neither case is there a single moment of choice, but rather a gradual and spontaneous movement through a series of finely discriminated stages leading from common civility to declared love, each stage providing not only the basis for the next but also its *raison d'être*: 'since *that* has been granted, surely it obliges you to *this*'.

Criseyde's yielding to Diomede thus ironically repeats and mirrors her yielding to Troilus. The reorientation of the self which is applauded and welcomed when it leads to her ecstatic union with Troilus is bitterly parodied in her supine capitulation to Diomede. In the formal portraits of Criseyde and her two lovers which Chaucer interpolates into the narrative action of Book V, as if to freeze their outlines before they finally recede from us into history, the two manifestations of her capacity for change appear as two versions of her character:

> Ne nevere mo ne lakked hire pite,
> Tendre-herted, slydynge of corage. (V 824–5)

'Slydynge' is the adjective used to characterize Fortune in Chaucer's translation of Boethius's *Consolation* (I m.5.34); applied to Criseyde's mind, it underlines with brilliant economy Chaucer's profound perception that Fortune exists not only in external vicissitudes – the exchange of Antenor for Criseyde – but also as an ineradicable part of the human mind, as the constant variability which forms itself into the larger evolutions of an individual story. But if Criseyde's 'slydynge corage' is the ugly face of human changeability, its benign face is 'pite', the quality in the beloved on which the lover pins his hopes, as innumerable medieval love-poems – among them Chaucer's *Complaint unto Pity* – make clear. Criseyde's 'pite' leads to Troilus's happiness, her 'slydynge corage' to his betrayal.

It is at this point that we are ready to see how this story of betrayal both is and is not, in Chaucer's mind, appropriately told of a woman rather than a man. It is *not*, in the sense that changeability, as Chaucer shows it to us, is not specifically female but is simply a human condition. If Troilus remains faithful, that is not only because of his own stability, but also because his social context remains unaltered. For him, Criseyde's departure creates an absence, a vacuum into which his whole being strains; for her, it creates a new set of presences, obliterating the structure of relationships in which Troilus held the central place. The external change, not her own fickleness, precipitates her betrayal. Yet there is at the same time a special appropriateness in mediating the tragic experience of mutability through a woman, since it is in women that the capacity for change, for adaptation and graceful responsiveness, has been traditionally most admired. So in the *Knight's Tale* it is Emily's 'wommanly pitee' to which Theseus appeals in order to transform the grief at Arcite's death into rejoicing over her marriage to Palamon (3083). It is this womanly responsiveness which Chaucer surely has in mind in his generally misunderstood comment on Emily's 'freendlich' reciprocation of Arcite's happy gaze after he has won her in the tournament:

> (For wommen, as to speken in comune,
> Thei folwen alle the favour of Fortune). (2681–2)

The ready changeability which gives women a special affinity with Fortune can manifest itself as treacherous instability or as a blessed (from the male lover's point of view) susceptibility to external pressure; in Criseyde we see it in both its forms. Its role as part of an ideal of womanhood is manifest in Criseyde's graceful adaptations of her tone and manner to her companions and her situation: relaxed, poised and witty in her verbal fencing with Pandarus, she is dignified, open and passionate with Troilus. This is how men would have their women be, instinctively adapting to the contours of their personalities and moods. But if this is what they want, they must accept that women can be equally chameleon-like with *other* men, until they are changed beyond recognition.[14] The real tragedy of *Troilus and Criseyde* is not simply that Troilus is separated from Criseyde, it is that she ceases to exist as the Criseyde he has known and loved; she has become, in Shakespeare's words, 'Diomed's Cressid'. Troilus's fidelity is enslavement to a ghost.

To say that Chaucer roots Criseyde's betrayal in the fundamentally human capacity for change is to say that there is no reason why we should not take his final protestations against an antifeminist interpretation of his story at face value. But it is not to say that Criseyde's betrayal thereby becomes excusable or acceptable or a 'realistic compromise'. If Chaucer professes 'routhe' for Criseyde and an inclination to 'excuse' her in order to deflect *our* inclination to blame the tragedy on female weakness, this does not prevent him from narrating her betrayal in terms that make it far uglier than it is in Boccaccio's story. For one thing, Boccaccio's Diomede is a far nicer person, who has genuinely fallen in love with Criseida, and who has all the attractiveness and nobility of Troiolo. Chaucer's Diomede, in contrast, is a calculating seducer who seems simply to want another female scalp for his collection – and will even, it is suggested, boast about it afterwards ('som men seyn he was of tonge large': V 804). It is likewise Chaucer who displays in full the cheap dishonesty of Criseyde's letter to Troilus (V 1590–1631; cf. *Filostrato* VII 105; VIII 5), and who imports from Benoît (*Roman de Troie* 20275–8) the pathetic protestation of fidelity to her new lover with which she tries to cover over the implications of what she has done. Yet if we read the story aright, we understand how Chaucer can make these changes without incurring the charge of antifeminism. His aim is not to blacken women, but to show human change in its fully tragic dimensions, and for this Criseyde's loss is not enough: we need to see the deformation of her personality. But if antifeminism is not the aim of Chaucer's story, it may still be its unintended *effect*, as Chaucer himself acknowledges in the God of Love's accusations in the Prologue to the *Legend of Good Women*. It is to Chaucer's attempt to meet these accusations in the *Legend* that we must now turn.

*

---

[14] Cf. Saintonge (1954, 313): 'the same qualities that made [Criseyde] desirable brought about her fall from grace'.

In the *Legend of Good Women* there are no warnings against generalizing about a whole sex on the basis of an individual case; on the contrary, the false-hood and treachery of men is reiterated with a vigorous monotony that fully matches the unrelenting misogyny conventional in so much medieval litera-ture. What I shall argue here is that the *Legend* can only be understood *as* a riposte to misogyny – as adopting a single-mindedness and refusal of compro-mise which mirrors its own intransigence. In one sense, then, it is not fully 'serious'; it has the self-conscious extremism of polemic, an extremism which could be abandoned with a rapprochement from the opposite camp. But it is by no means frivolous or flippant in its indictment of men or its sympathy for women, and I shall try also to show the groundswell of seriousness beneath its mannered surface.

The tirades of medieval antifeminism are accepted without demur by modern scholars; the one-sidedness of the *Legend*, on the other hand, has provoked critics (especially in recent years) to question the seriousness of Chaucer's involvement with the work. Its (apparent) incompleteness has been ascribed to his boredom with what was probably a commission from the Queen or some other aristocratic patron.[15] Its strange variegations in tone have been read as signs of a deeply ironic detachment from its subject-matter.[16] Its 'real' concern has been identified as the search for 'a way of transforming courtly making into philosophical poetry' (Rowe, 1988, 51), or the affirmation 'that classical literature is important to Christians despite its lack of explicit Christian morality' (Kiser, 1983, 152). The poem's overt and obvious subject-matter – women – is usually disregarded, as if self-evidently too trivial to merit serious consider-ation. Lisa Kiser's comment is revealing:

> And if the poem was originally commissioned by Queen Anne (as many believe) merely to amuse or placate the ladies at court who wanted to read love stories that corrected the antifeminist clerical tradition, then Chaucer has certainly managed to convey more significant themes than one might ever think possible in a poem with such an undistinguished origin. (1983, 151–2)

I shall assume that the poem really is about what it says it is about, and more-over that correction of the antifeminist clerical tradition is an enterprise quite

---

[15] See R. W. Frank's excursus, 'The Legend of Chaucer's Boredom' (1972, 189–210), for the history of this view and the case against it. For a recent restatement (where, however, the boredom is attributed to the narrator, who 'makes his heroines and the fables boring because they would otherwise terrify'), see Dinshaw, 1989, 84–7.

[16] For sides taken in the question of whether the *Legend* is ironical or not, see the refer-ences given by Kiser (1983, 21, n. 6). See also the books by Delany (1994) and Percival (1998), whose position is briefly summarized in my Preface (2001), pp. ix, xi above. R. W. Frank (1972) gives due allowance to the local playfulness in the poem without taking it as the sign of a general scepticism towards women (see, e.g., 84).

as significant as any represented by the alternative themes that modern critics have 'discovered' in the work. On the issue of Chaucer's supposed 'boredom' with the *Legend*, it is worth noting that we do not know for certain that Chaucer *did* leave it unfinished, and indeed we have several indications to the contrary: the work as we have it contains only ten legends, but Chaucer's own *Retractions* refer to it as 'the book of the xxv. ladies', and the *Man of Law's Prologue*, in rehearsing its contents, lists legends of eight more Ovidian heroines (Deianira, Hermione, Hero, Helen, Briseida, Laodamia, Penelope, Alcestis herself) than we actually have.[17] As for the work's being commissioned, to see it as a *poème de circonstance* would go a long way to account for the self-conscious playfulness evident especially in the Prologue; the *Parliament of Fowls*, which is almost certainly an occasional poem, similarly transposes weighty subjects into graceful play. But that is no reason for supposing that the commission was not to Chaucer's taste, or that it did not harmonize with his own concerns. The playfulness of the *Legend* ripples over a serious subject – the subject that had occupied Chaucer in the *House of Fame* and that hovers in the background of *Troilus and Criseyde*: what is the poet's responsibility towards women (cf. Dinshaw, 1989, 68)? How can he control the *effects* of what he writes on individual human existences?

The playfulness and the seriousness are both evident in the accusations that the God of Love levels against Chaucer. Chaucer must have known perfectly well that *Troilus and Criseyde*, for the reasons I have already outlined, is not an antifeminist work. Yet he also knew (as his picture of Jankin's use of his 'book of wikked wyves' makes clear) that the subtleties of authorial intention are all too often submerged in the crude interpretations of the reading public. This being so, he both is and is not contributing to the antifeminist tradition in telling of Criseyde. He therefore avails himself of the conventional polarities of the 'woman debate' in order to make an equivalent contribution to the opposing stereotype of the suffering 'good woman'. It is in his consciousness of the intermediary role of literature in creating and nourishing these stereotyped interpretative patterns, rather than in the detailed exploration of female lives, that the real sophistication of the *Legend* lies.

Chaucer was not alone in this consciousness of literary responsibility. The relationship between *Troilus and Criseyde* and the *Legend of Good Women* has an illuminating analogue in the relationship between Jehan le Fèvre's translation of Matheolus's *Lamentations* and his own *Livre de Leesce*, written to answer and atone for the misogynist attacks of the earlier work. Already in the *Lamentations* itself, Jehan had intervened to express his unease with the material he was translating, and to assure his readers that he has no hatred for women

---

[17]   In addition, Stephen Hawes (writing in the early sixteenth century) referred to this work as 'the tragydyes so pytous/Of the nyntene ladyes' (*Pastime of Pleasure* 1326–7). He perhaps, however, takes the number from Lydgate, who ponderously jokes that Chaucer could not find so many examples of good women, and thus implies that the *Legend* as he knew it had a lesser number (*Fall of Princes* I 330–6).

('envers femme je n'ay haïne': II 1547); some women, he admits, may be cruel, but others are 'bonnes' and 'vertueuses' (1551). The violent exaggerations he is transmitting are not motivated by malice, but by the desire to 'colour' his discourse, to give it raciness and excitement (1548–9; cf. also II 2589–608). Jehan's rather naive attempt to marshal the principles of literary criticism in his own defence is somewhat undermined by the fact that – as far as we can tell – he freely expands and elaborates the material contained in his source. And the plea he makes for himself as 'only a translator' (*Leesce* 1–11), paralleling Alceste's excuses for Chaucer (*Legend of Good Women* F 369–72), will take him only so far: if he were really as embarrassed by his material as he claims, he could of course translate something else.

Nevertheless, there are no indications that the defence of women in the *Livre de Leesce* is to be read ironically; and the fact that so much of its material has to be freshly thought up, in contrast with the tired old antifeminist commonplaces, gives it an extra ring of sincerity. Jehan does not content himself with citing the usual counter-examples of good women, he appeals to daily experience for evidence that women are more pious than men (3740ff.), and that they are better at growing plants and caring for children (3694ff.). His picture of women slaving away at their weaving and cheese-pressing while their husbands drink in the tavern or waste their time in blood-sports (3763–75) would fit comfortably into the pages of today's *Guardian*. What is most interesting for the *Legend of Good Women*, however, is that Jehan does not simply counter claim with claim: he bases his argument on literary-critical grounds, rejecting Matheolus's case as supported by purely literary authorities. Fabliau-tales of women's lust and trickery are nothing but 'truffes' and 'frivoles' (787, 797–8); Ovid's story of Scylla is nothing but 'mençonge' and 'fable' (1517–21). Matheolus's selectivity distorts the evidence: he cites Vashti but omits to mention Esther – and so on.

Chaucer similarly opens his own poem in defence of women by raising the question of literary authority:

> A thousand tymes have I herd men telle
> That ther ys joy in hevene and peyne in helle,
> And I acorde wel that it ys so;
> But, natheles, yet wot I wel also
> That ther nis noon dwellyng in this contree
> That eyther hath in hevene or helle ybe,
> Ne may of hit noon other weyes witen
> But as he hath herd seyd or founde it writen;
> For by assay ther may no man it preve.
> But God forbede but men shulde leve
> Wel more thing then men han seen with ye!
> Men shal nat wenen every thing a lye
> But yif himself yt seeth or elles dooth;
> For, God wot, thing is never the lasse sooth,

Thogh every wight ne may it nat ysee.
Bernard the monk ne saugh nat all, pardee! (F 1–16)

The comfortable blandness of Chaucer's assurances here is reminiscent of the contented credulity with which he refuses the Eagle's offer to show him the stars in the *House of Fame*; the good-humoured irony becomes even more apparent as he goes on to claim for the writer the poetic equivalent of a licence to print money.

Than mote we to bokes that we fynde,
Thurgh whiche that olde thinges ben in mynde,
And to the doctrine of these olde wyse
Yeve credence, in every skylful wise,
That tellen of these olde appreved stories
Of holynesse, of regnes, of victories,
Of love, of hate, of other sondry thynges,
Of whiche I may not maken rehersynges.
And yf that olde bokes were aweye,
Yloren were of remembraunce the keye.
Wel ought us thanne honouren and beleve
These bokes, there we han noon other preve. (F 17–28)

What cannot be proved is precisely what we must believe, on the authority of 'olde bokes', when 'other preve' is lacking. But among the 'sondry thynges' which books treat of are women, and here we not only have 'other preve', but we find the books themselves at variance; in opposition to the antifeminist tradition which is represented in the *Legend*'s Prologue by the *Troilus*, there are the 'sixty bokes olde and newe' in Chaucer's possession which the God of Love cites as containing innumerable stories of women who chose to die rather than be unfaithful (G 273–310). How can the notion of literary authority survive such contradictions?

The question has a contemporary relevance, as the blindness of contemporary critics to the radical nature of this question and its implications for the legends that follow amply demonstrates. Where Jehan le Fèvre insists with clear-sighted accuracy that the classical legends are nothing more than poetic fictions, modern Chaucer critics speak unthinkingly of these stories in terms of 'objective truth' (Rowe, 1988, 58). Chaucer is said to have falsified the legends in his collection by omitting, for example, Medea's murder of her children or Philomel and Procne's grisly revenge on Tereus, or by presenting Cleopatra as a willing martyr for love or (once again) taking the Ovidian rather than the Vergilian view of Dido and Aeneas. Fyler (1979, 98–115) argues that 'what Chaucer deletes from his source is often as much a part of the poem's meaning as what he includes'; the informed reader, recognizing 'a consistent pattern of censorship', will be prompted to read Chaucer's versions in an ironic light. Recognisable distortion is likewise assumed by Donald Rowe when he scornfully dismisses the narrative stance of the Dido legend as due to the sentimentality of the narrator-persona he distinguishes from Chaucer himself:

> he pities Dido as victim and scorns Aeneas as victimizer. But of course he is the author of Dido as victim, Aeneas as victimizer. The pathos in which he revels is enabled by his misperception and misrepresentation.
>
> (1988, 138)

What this comment ignores is precisely what the Prologue's questioning of literary authority has encouraged us to perceive: that Vergil is *equally* the author of his Dido and his Aeneas. There is no truth to be 'misrepresented', only a series of poetic fictions, each with its own claims to authority. Chaucer has the same liberty to represent Aeneas as victimizer that Vergil had to represent him as a dutiful hero.

Nothing is more characteristic of the Middle Ages than the constant refashioning of old stories, and this refashioning depends precisely on the reader's willingness to suppress the details of the older versions and accept the new one on its own terms as a valid account. Matheolus's *Lamentations* provide one example of this refashioning which is particularly instructive when compared with the *Legend*. Among the stream of *exempla* which Matheolus uses to 'prove' women's failings, there appears the story of Orpheus and Eurydice, offered as illustration of women's disobedience; they are incapable of obeying any command. So Eurydice, Matheolus says, was released from hell on condition that she did not look back as she left; her husband enjoined her not to do so, but 'la fole' disobeyed him and was promptly reclaimed by hell (II 1315–36). Now, in all the classical versions of this story it is of course Orpheus and not Eurydice who disobeys the command not to look back, and so loses his wife. Although this version of the story was often moralized in ways unflattering to Orpheus (Friedman, 1970, Chapter IV), no writer in either classical or medieval times, so far as I know, interpreted it as illustrative of the innate unruliness of *men* – although this would be an entirely plausible conclusion to draw from it – because there was no pre-existing stereotype to prompt such a reading. Matheolus however fundamentally alters the story in order to read it across the grain as 'evidence' of female refractoriness. The learned (male) editor of the *Lamentations*, who usually comments in detail on Matheolus's sources and their transformations in his handling, does not appear to have noticed this startling alteration to the story and has no comment to make on the passage; nor has anyone in this instance proposed that Matheolus's readers would read the story as heavy irony, correcting it in the light of their knowledge of the 'true' version. Indeed, when Jehan le Fèvre gives his critique of Matheolus's *exempla* in the *Livre de Leesce*, his objections to this one are founded not on its falsification of the original version, but rather on the grounds that it is 'against nature' for a dead person to be brought back to life, and the story should therefore be rejected root and branch as a self-evident 'fable' (2089–102).

Chaucer has the same licence to refashion the story of Medea or Cleopatra as Matheolus has to refashion the story of Orpheus and Eurydice, without eliciting suspicions of irony (cf. Ames, 1986, 69). Elaborate efforts to 'prove' irony by appealing to the traditionally hostile presentations of these heroines (e.g., Taylor, 1977) are thus beside the point. It is against exactly this sort of literary background that the one-sidedness of the legends finds its justification: it represents the weight of insistence necessary to redress the balance of male-oriented literature. Jehan le Fèvre answers the possible objection against his *Livre de Leesce* that it cites only good women and ignores the bad, by saying that this is only fair, since men are equally silent about such male villains as Nero or Herod (3794–819). He then gives a long list of good women which sets 'Cleopatre, qui fu bonne' (3821) – the only one to be dignified with this epithet – alongside such figures as Ruth, Rachel, Sarah, Octavia and Lucretia, without any hint of incongruity or irony.[18]

If the Prologue to the *Legend* raises the question of how much 'feyth and credence' (F 31) should be given to books, it is not because Chaucer wishes to undermine the credibility of his own legends, but rather the authority of the 'olde bokes' which slander women. The legends do not need 'correcting'; they are themselves corrective of the antifeminist thrust of earlier writings, as the Prologue makes plain.[19] This corrective role is evident, for example, when Chaucer changes his source and transfers from Medea to Jason the comparison between sexual desire and the appetite of matter to form so that it refers to male rather than female promiscuity (Frank, 1972, 84). It is equally evident in his alteration of Aeneas's reaction to the depiction of the fall of Troy on the wall of the temple at Carthage: whereas in the *Aeneid* Aeneas takes comfort from this evidence that the sorrows of the Trojans arouse general sympathy, in Chaucer he reacts with distress at the publicisation of their disgrace – a distress that is clearly meant to mirror the distress of Chaucer's Dido as she visualizes the publicisation of her own shame.

> 'Allas, that I was born!' quod Eneas;
> Thourghout the world oure shame is kid so wyde,
> Now it is peynted upon every syde.
> We, that weren in prosperite,
> Been now desclandred, and in swich degre,
> No lenger for to lyven I ne kepe.' (1027–32)

The fate that Phyllis wishes on Demophoon is similarly that he should be 'peynted' so that 'folk may rede forby as they go' and deride him for his

---

[18] Lowes (1909, 547–65) provides other examples of the women of the *Legend* being presented in a positive light by medieval poets.

[19] Delany ([1986] 1990, 84–5) argues a similar case with respect to Christine de Pisan's *City of Ladies*, and cites the *Livre de Leesce* as a precedent, but since she interprets the *Legend* as ironic, she does not connect it with these examples. Ames (1986) argues on lines similar to my own here.

treachery (2538–42). The legends are to bring shame on men in the same way that the antifeminist *exempla* bring shame on women.[20]

But Chaucer does not simply slant the old stories so that they favour women; he also makes them into expressions of a peculiarly female ethos, based on the 'pite' to which Criseyde had given such a bad name. The word 'pite', together with its cognates and synonyms, is a leitmotiv in the *Legend*; 'pite' is the quality that dominates in the women, and the quality that is totally lacking from the men. The 'pite' which prohibits Hypermnestra from murdering her husband is presented as characteristic of her sex:

> Pyëtous, sad, wis, and trewe as stel,
> As to these wemen it acordeth wel. (2582–3)

Wherever the story makes it possible, Chaucer emphasizes that it is pity, rather than sexual attraction, which draws these women to love.[21] Ariadne and Phaedra have 'compassioun' for the imprisoned Theseus and think his fate 'gret pite' (1974–6); when he is brought before them he begs for 'mercy' and looks so pitiable that anyone seeing him would have wept for 'routhe' (2073, 2076–7). Dido's relationship with Aeneas is paradigmatic in this respect. At their first meeting Aeneas's misfortunes elicit her 'routhe and wo', and by an inevitable progression, her love.

> Anon hire herte hath pite of his wo,
> And with that pite love com in also;
> And thus, for pite and for gentillesse,
> Refreshed moste he been of his distresse. (1078–81)

Alone with Dido in the cave, Aeneas pleads on his knees for her love until she takes pity on him ('rewede on his peyne': 1237). Her pity is generalized to her sex in Chaucer's wondering lament:

> O sely wemen, ful of innocence,
> Ful of pite, of trouthe and conscience,
> What maketh yow to men to truste so?
> Have ye swych routhe upon hyre feyned wo,
> And han swich olde ensaumples yow beforn?
> Se ye nat alle how they ben forsworn? (1254–9)

As in the *House of Fame*, Dido's story is the wand that conjures up a larger vision of women's trusting generosity and its abuse by men. The men call forth

---

20   Green (1988, 15) sees Chaucer's willingness to call these male lovers 'traitors' as an 'indication of the underlying seriousness' with which Chaucer treats the heroines of the *Legend of Good Women*.
21   Frank (1972, 68) comments on Dido's pity for Aeneas that it 'is not the pity of the lady for the beseeching lover but a more general, humane quality of heart'.

the women's pity, but they do not reciprocate it: the abandoned Dido's plea to Aeneas – 'Mercy, lord! Have pite in youre thought!' (1324) – falls on deaf ears. Ariadne futilely begs Theseus to 'turn ageyn, for routhe and synne' (2200). The men cynically milk women's pity for their own ends, without being touched by it: Jason 'loketh pitously' to win Hypsipyle's love (1549); Tereus weeps 'pitously' while relating his false tale of Philomel's death (2344). The power of weakness – the power on which women are taught to rely – is in the *Legend* something to be exploited not by them, but by men.

The masculine imperviousness to pity may be seen not only in the *Legend* itself, but also in its modern critics. Donald Rowe's summary of his reading of the poem is a classic example of the way its emotional claims may be resisted:

> Our pity for the heroines is now a response to their frailty, not a participation in their feelings of innocent victimization. At extreme moments the narrator's pity is virtually transformed into its opposite – as when we respond with contempt and scorn to the narrator's pity for Ariadne. Similarly, our participation in the narrator's anger at the legends' villains is often tempered by our perception that they are victimized as well as victimizing. Thus the narrator's pity and scorn are transformed into the poet's sympathy and satire, which are directed not least of all at his own persona. (1988, 139)

Such comments are reminiscent of ·the medieval commentators on the *Heroides* who turn Dido's epistle to Aeneas into a moral warning against *stultus amor* (Hexter, 1986, 183), and are as little sympathetic to Chaucer's tone and style as these commentators are to Ovid's. This rejection of pity is the more serious in that it is through pity, and not through historical veracity, that the legends achieve authenticity. It is in the chord they strike in the reader, the point at which the individual story makes contact with knowledge of a general human experience, as Dido's story spreads itself into the innumerable lives of 'sely wemen', that they establish themselves as 'truth'. Pity, that is, is not only a quality exhibited within the narrative, it is also the emotion it elicits from the reader.[22] The pity the men withhold, the reader is to supply, with Chaucer leading the way. 'Allas, for thee myn herte hath now pite!' (2184) is his response to Ariadne; his 'routhe' is too great for him to bring himself to transcribe Dido's lament to her sister Anna (1345). The womanly ethos of pity extends to envelop the reader: the reader is feminized, as it were, by the process of reading. The 'olde ensaumples' are not in themselves the goal of the reading process; its aim is to permeate the reader with the female responses that are crushed and set aside in the male-centred narratives of heroic legend.

Chaucer marks his intentions in the Prologue to the *Legend* by embodying the ethos of pity in the figure of Alceste, who defends Chaucer against the

---

[22] Cf. Frank's comment that Dido's passionate plea for pity 'is aimed as much at the audience as at Aeneas' (1972, 72).

God of Love's anger, and urges him to practise 'compassyoun' in place of 'tyrannye' (F 390, 375). Alceste's 'pitee' is the very mark of her identity:

> The god of Love gan smyle, and than he sayde:
> 'Wostow,' quod he, 'wher this be wyf or mayde,
> Or queene, or countesse, or of what degre,
> That hath so lytel penance yiven thee,
> That hast deserved sorer for to smerte?
> But pite renneth soone in gentil herte;
> That maistow seen; she kytheth what she ys.' (F 498–504)

The 'wommanly pitee' that in Criseyde's case had become tainted by its kinship with her 'slydynge corage' is here renewed as a positive force. Changeability manifests itself only in the benign form of an open responsiveness, symbolized in the heliotropism of the daisy, Alceste's flower, opening and closing in harmony with the changing rhythms of day and night (F 60–5).[23] Change, that is, becomes the essence of constancy. So in the legends 'pite' is intimately linked with 'trouthe'; Hypermnestra is feminine not only in being 'Pyetous' but also in being 'trewe as stel'. The commitment prompted by pity endures through all subsequent vicissitudes because it meets them with the same open responsiveness that brought it into being. Cleopatra's 'routhe' for Antony's death leads her to replicate it in her suicide, as the daisy replicates the motions of the sun; it is the inevitable culmination of her passionate identification with his being.

> 'And in myself this covenaunt made I tho,
> That ryght swich as ye felten, wel or wo,
> As fer forth as it in my power lay,
> Unreprovable unto my wyfhod ay,
> The same wolde I fele, lyf or deth –
> And thilke covenant whil me lasteth breth
> I wol fulfille; and that shal ben wel sene,
> Was nevere unto hire love a trewer quene.'
> And with that word, naked, with ful good herte,
> Among the serpents in the pit she sterte,
> And there she ches to have hire buryinge. (688–98)

In this passionate identification with their lovers, the women demonstrate the courage they share with men: imbued with 'strengthe and hardynesse' by her love, Thisbe repeats Piramus's suicide, smiting herself with the same sword, 'That warm was of hire loves blod, and hot' (914) to show that a woman can be 'as trewe in lovynge as a man' (911). As two souls entwine themselves into a single sentient entity, male courage and female courage become indistinguishable.

---

23 This feature of the daisy is frequently mentioned in French Marguerite poetry; see Wimsatt, 1970, 30–1.

The corollary of this *ought* to be that 'wommanly pitee' manifests itself in men, and indeed it does so in the idyllic world of the *Legend*'s Prologue: the pity Alceste shows to Chaucer is replicated in the God of Love. The Prologue also has importance as the place where Chaucer begins to develop a vision of male subjection to 'wommanly pitee' in contexts quite outside the erotic. Pity here is independent of love, and as a result its own power appears more clearly. What is important is that this power originates not in the stronger but in the weaker: it is not the God of Love who magnanimously decides to take pity on Chaucer, but Alceste who pleads with him on Chaucer's behalf. His pity manifests itself as a subjection to her pleas. And this subjection does not lie in his arbitrary will but is the spontaneous result of his nature: his 'gentil kynde' makes him *inevitably* responsive to pity's claims (F 384–96); like Alceste, he 'kytheth what he is' in his capacity for pity. In the God of Love we can see an outline sketch for the ideal of feminized masculinity more fully represented in the Theseus of the *Knight's Tale*.

If the God of Love represents the ideal, the men of the legends represent its antithesis. Even Piramus is made to contrast the 'mercy' he asks from Thisbe with his own mercilessness in sending her into danger (835–9). Tarquin, 'a kynges eyr', ought 'by lynage and by ryght' to show his nobility as the God of Love does in his responsiveness to pity (1819–24); instead he exemplifies the male 'tirannye' that the God renounces (1883) in its most extreme form, the crime of rape.

It is with the two stories of rape that I want to end discussion of the *Legend*, because they constitute in my view the clearest indications of the seriousness underlying Chaucer's defence of women, whatever its occasional digressions into playful gallantry. The stories of Lucretia and Philomel are two of the four in the *Legend* (as we have it) that have no parallel in the *Heroides*.[24] The other two – the stories of Cleopatra and Thisbe – are, like the Lucretia legend, stories of female suicides. No critic seems to have addressed the question of what dictated Chaucer's choice of these legends, but for me the fact that they contain three suicides and two rapes between them is in itself indicative of Chaucer's wish to give emotional seriousness to his work by representing female suffering in its most extreme forms. The violence that women are unable to turn against men (as the legend of Hypermnestra shows), they turn against themselves. The deaths of Cleopatra and Thisbe repeat the suicides of Dido and Phyllis but in a more positive form: suicide appears less as the response of emotional frustration and more as an impassioned expression of emotional union. Lucretia's death is in quite another category. Suicide here takes on an entirely different significance by virtue of its link with rape. It is neither the climax and consecration of romantic passion nor the catharsis of a romantic agony; that is to say, it expresses no previous surrender of the self to

---

[24] The story of Lucretia is based on Ovid's *Fasti* (II 685–852), that of Philomel on Ovid's *Metamorphoses* (VI 424–674), as is the Thisbe-legend (IV 55–166). The Cleopatra-legend has no single obvious source; for discussion of possible secondary influences, see Frank (1972).

a lover which can find satisfaction in the mimetic surrender of the self to death. There is nothing of willed surrender here, as Lucretia's swoon during the rape symbolically underlines; what her death mimetically repeats is the simple obliteration of the female by male 'tirannye'. Her suicide realizes in public and demonstrable form the brutal extinction of personality that constitutes the invisible horror of rape:

> And openly the tale he tolde hem alle,
> And openly let cary her on a bere
> Thurgh al the toun, that men may see and here
> The horryble dede of hir oppressyoun. (1865–8)

The emphasis on male 'tirannye' protects Chaucer's Lucretia legend from the dangers inherent in a story that represents female heroism in the form of suicide – dangers that are intensified when the suicide is a response to the fact or threat of rape. For suicide seems merely to confirm and lend approval to the notion that female virtue should express itself only in passivity; moreover, when it follows rape, it doubles the crime by visiting its penalties on the victim rather than the perpetrator. 'If she was an adulteress, why is she praised? and if she was chaste, why was she put to death?', as St Augustine puts it in the *City of God* (I.19). Chaucer stresses the 'gret compassioun' that 'the grete Austyn' expresses for Lucretia (1690); he omits Augustine's suggestion that her suicide is a boastful demonstration of her purity: 'she intended to show this punishment to the eyes of men as a witness to her state of mind for those to whom she could not show her conscience' (ibid.). For Chaucer, what Lucretia's suicide makes manifest is not her mind but Tarquin's deed, 'the horryble dede of hir oppressyoun'. Female martyrdom manifests male aggression, and it is this that justifies the telling of the story. The stories of rape move the *Legend*'s indictment of male cruelty on to a level of seriousness that the recriminations of slighted love can never reach. Charges of falsehood and betrayal can be bandied back and forth between the sexes interminably, but rape is a crime that only men can commit. 'I see no woman who wounds her lover nor who takes him by force' says Jehan le Fèvre (*Leesce* 3927–8), though he makes nothing more of this point. For Chaucer, on the contrary, rape remains a constant touchstone for determining justice between the sexes; in the *Canterbury Tales* as in the *Legend* it appears as the definitive form of male tyranny, representing a fundamental imbalance between the sexes which human relationships must seek to redress.

In the Philomel legend the indictment of men threatens to become an indictment of God. The opening launches without warning into metaphysical questioning:

> Thow yevere of the formes, that hast wrought
> This fayre world and bar it in thy thought
> Eternaly er thow thy werk began,
> Why madest thow, unto the slaunder of man,

> Or, al be that it was nat thy doing,
> As for that fyn, to make swich a thyng,
> Whi sufferest thow that Tereus was bore,
> That is in love so fals and so forswore,
> That fro this world up to the firste hevene
> Corrumpeth whan that folk his name nevene?
> And, as to me, so grisely was his dede
> That, whan that I his foule storye rede,
> Myne eyen wexe foule and sore also.
> Yit last the venym of so longe ago,
> That it enfecteth hym that wol beholde
> The storye of Tereus, of which I tolde. (2228–43)

The passage echoes Boethius's interrogation of God's justice in the *Consolation* ('Why suffrestow that slydynge Fortune turneth so grete enterchaungynges of thynges? So that anoyous peyne, that scholde duweliche punysche felons, punysscheth innocentz...'), and Tereus may be counted among the 'schrewes' who are guilty of 'fraude covered and kembd with a false colour' (I m. 5.34–7, 44–6). The God whom Chaucer addresses is also recognisably the Platonic Father of Forms hymned by Boethius:[25]

> Thow, that art althir-fayrest, berynge the faire world in thy thought, formedest this world to the lyknesse semblable of that faire world in thy thought. Thou drawest alle thyng of thy sovereyn ensaumpler and comaundest that this world, parfytely ymakid, have frely and absolut hise parfyte parties. (III m.9.11–17)

The invocation of the Father of Forms seems on the face of it irrelevant, but taken together with the suggestion that the very telling of Tereus's story corrupts ('Corrumpeth') the world, and infects those who behold it, it seems to imply that the divine thought itself is polluted by the presence of this story within it. At any rate, he suggests, the reader of the story is so polluted. Chaucer here throws into question his own relationship – as reader, as writer – to the story of rape; if to read it is to be infected by its 'venym', what is the responsibility of the writer who tells it? It is perhaps for this reason that he emblematizes it so that its horror is muted into pathos. It both describes and enacts a process of silencing; her tongue torn out, Philomel can tell her story only by writing it (not picturing it) in the dumb 'letters' of her tapestry (2358, 2364). Her writing speaks only her mutilation. Procne's response to the tapestry is a replication of her sister's muteness: 'No word she spak,

---

[25] Young (1944) discusses other ways in which this Platonic notion could have been mediated to Chaucer, including a passage in the *Romance of the Rose*; its connection with the Boethian question on the origin of evil shows however that the *Consolation* was the primary impetus behind this passage.

for sorwe and ek for rage' (2374). Participating in their grief, the tale itself
falls silent:

> The remenaunt is no charge for to telle,
> For this is al and som: thus was she served,
> That never harm agilte ne deserved
> Unto this crewel man, that she of wiste. (2383–6)

When woman is thus silenced, to speak on her behalf seems like another kind
of violation.

Chaucer's pondering of his own role as reader and as writer here takes up in
deeply serious form the Prologue's dramatisation of his sense of his responsibilities to his subject-matter. And it is to the Prologue that we return for the last
time to consider some aspects of these responsibilities still not mentioned. For
his relationship to the *Legend* offers almost as many problems as his relationship to *Troilus and Criseyde*. The first difficulty is how he can exculpate
himself from his relentless accusations of male duplicity – a difficulty he
acknowledges with his little joke at the end of the Phyllis legend:

> Be war, ye wemen, of youre subtyl fo,
> Syn yit this day men may ensaumple se;
> And trusteth, as in love, no man but me. (2559–61)

More important, there is the difficulty of how to write of the pitiable sufferings
of women without appearing to patronize them, to arrogate the right to 'rescue'
them with a gallantry that assumes their inability to defend themselves. This is
where Alceste's role becomes doubly important. If the legends represent
Chaucer 'rescuing' women, the Prologue shows us Alceste 'rescuing' Chaucer;
his pity for suffering woman is mirrored in her 'pite' for the accused poet.
However playful the Prologue's mood, there is a serious point behind
Chaucer's representation of his story-collection as written in obedience to a
woman's command. Whether fact or fiction, the commissioning of the *Legend*
by a woman is freighted with an essential significance: the male author signals
his abnegation of his independent authority, and his subjection to women and
the story they have to tell.

2

Antifeminism

'Who peyntede the leon, tel me who?'
(*Wife of Bath's Prologue* 692)

And yet, and yet. The *Legend of Good Women* can be no more than a provisional response to antifeminism, contradicting but not obliterating it. Created as antifeminism's mirror-image, it derives the very substance of its being from its antagonist's power, and relies on that power to justify its own extremism. There thus arises the danger acutely described by Elaine Showalter:

> The [feminist] critique ... has a tendency to naturalise women's victimisation, by making it the inevitable and obsessive topic of discussion ... This comes dangerously close to a celebration of the opportunities of victimisation, the seduction *of* betrayal. (1979, 28)

The focus on victimisation in the *Legend* carries not only this risk, but also the risk of stasis: the polarisation of male treachery and female suffering immobilizes not only the women in the legends, but also the poetic discourse itself, perennially arrested by pity. In the *Canterbury Tales*, Chaucer solves this problem by setting both antifeminism and 'wommanly pitee' within dynamic structures that enable him to go beyond the old stereotyped polarities even while acknowledging their powerful grip on human lives. And the first step is to turn away from the mirror-image to engage directly with antifeminism itself. This direct engagement is apparent above all in the *Merchant's Tale* and the *Wife of Bath's Prologue*, which will form the focus of attention in this chapter.

For Chaucer, the *éminence grise* behind the medieval tradition of antifeminist literature was St Jerome, whose treatise *Against Jovinian* offered a rich stock of materials on which misogynist writings throughout the Middle Ages drew. Jerome's work is a polemic directed against 'a certain Jovinian', who had (among various other heretical arguments) denied that virginity was a state superior to marriage. Women are thus not the primary target of the polemic, but are as it were civilian casualties sacrificed to Jerome's saturation bombing.[1] Thus,

---

[1]   Wiesen (1964, Chapter IV) shows how 'Jerome's attachment to the cause of extreme asceticism' led him into antifeminist polemic, despite the warm relationships he enjoyed with his own female followers.

since Jovinian had instanced the much-married Solomon in support of his case, Jerome replies by quoting antifeminist proverbs from the Solomonic books of the Bible as 'evidence' of what Solomon's experience of women had taught him: (for example) 'It is better to dwell in a corner of the housetop, than with a brawling woman in a wide house [Prov. 21:9]' (*Adv. Jov.* I.28). Jerome calls on contradictory images of women as the needs of his polemic dictate. When he wants to show that even the pagans have always held chastity in high regard, he cites the well-worn examples of feminine purity and marital fidelity – Alcestis, Penelope, Laodamia, Lucretia, Portia (I.43–6). But immediately afterwards, he launches into an extended portrayal of woman as shrew, gossip and adulterer. This time he is quoting an otherwise unknown 'Golden Book on Marriage' (*Liber Aureolus de Nuptiis*) by a pagan named Theophrastus, which argues that no wise man should ever take a wife (I.47). Theophrastus's trenchant summary of female vices is followed up with literary anecdotes to the same effect, among them the stories of Socrates' shrewish wife Xantippe, of Pasiphae, Clytemnestra and Eriphyle, which reappear centuries later in the *Wife of Bath's Prologue*.

This relatively brief section of Jerome's treatise exercised a quasi-hypnotic influence on medieval antifeminism (Delhaye, 1951). The Solomonic proverbs, the anecdotes illustrating women's vices, the gibes of Theophrastus against marriage, form a recognisable cluster of antifeminist motifs in a whole series of texts from the twelfth century to Chaucer's time and beyond: passages in John of Salisbury's *Policraticus* (VIII.xi) and Pope Innocent III's *De Miseria Condicionis Humanae* (I.16), the speech of the Jealous Husband (Le Jaloux) in the *Romance of the Rose* (8436–9330), Jehan le Fèvre's translation of Matheolus's *Lamentations*, Deschamps's *Miroir de Mariage* (to name only some of the most important). All the texts I have instanced, as well as Jerome's text itself, were either certainly or very probably known to Chaucer,[2] so that it is often difficult to isolate one in particular as the source of a Chaucerian line or motif; in this vast echo-chamber of antifeminist commonplace, the voices blur into each other, endlessly repeating the same message.

The literary form into which Theophrastus cast his antifeminist material, the dissuasion against marriage (*dissuasio de non ducenda uxore*), was a traditional one.[3] The virulently antifeminist Sixth Satire of Juvenal, for example,

---

2   Chaucer translated both the *Romance of the Rose* (*Legend of Good Women* G 255) and Innocent III's treatise (ibid., G 414–15). His knowledge and use of Jerome is abundantly evident in the *Wife of Bath's Prologue* and the *Franklin's Tale*. He probably knew John of Salisbury's *Policraticus*, which was widely read in the fourteenth century, and also the French translation of Matheolus's *Lamentations*, though many of the detailed parallels suggested by Thundy (1979) are unconvincing. His knowledge of Deschamps's *Miroir de Mariage* is disputed (Lowes, 1910–11; Thundy, 1979). For further bibliography, see the relevant entries in Morris (1985).

3   For a survey of the *dissuasio* tradition, see Wilson and Makowski (1990). They discuss the *Wife of Bath's Prologue* in Chapter 4, but fail to recognize the opening of the *Merchant's Tale* as a disguised *dissuasio* (see p. 47 below).

purports to be written to dissuade the poet's friend Postumus from his insane intention to get married (21–32); why resort to such desperate measures, pleads Juvenal, when there are so many easier forms of suicide? The popularity of the *dissuasio* was assured by its use as a set theme for rhetorical exercises, in both antiquity and the Middle Ages;[4] it is quite probable that one of the best-known medieval examples of the type, the *Epistola Valerii ad Rufinum*, began its life as a school-exercise of this sort. This is the 'Valerie' included in the 'book of wikked wyves' owned by the Wife of Bath's fifth husband (*Wife of Bath's Prologue* 671).[5] The *dissuasio* here takes the form of a letter written by the fictional Valerius to his friend Rufinus, a 'man of philosophic life', who plans to get married – a step which will, in Valerius's opinion, put an end to his scholarly pursuits. Another twelfth-century example of the type is Peter of Blois's letter to 'the deacon R.', which includes the familiar Theophrastan material. Yet another is the Goliardic poem *De Coniuge Non Ducenda*, a piece even more popular than the *Epistola Valerii*,[6] in which the poet relates how he was warned against a projected marriage by three angels, Lawrence, John and Peter. In the late Middle Ages, the miniature genre of the *dissuasio* was swollen to gigantic proportions with Deschamps's *Miroir de Mariage*, which casts the debate in the form of personification-allegory. The central figure, whose name is Franc Vouloirs (Free Will), is urged to marry by Desir, Folie, Servitute and Faintise. On applying to his friend Repertoire de Science for advice, Franc Vouloirs receives from him a letter more than 7,000 lines long, exhaustively rehearsing the arguments against marriage. The climax of this rich medieval tradition, as of so many others, is to be found two centuries later in Rabelais; the whole of the Tiers Livre of *Gargantua and Pantagruel* is devoted to Panurge's plan to get married and his efforts to get advice from Pantagruel and others on the subject.

In all these instances, the *dissuasio* is a purely male affair: it is addressed to a man by another man (or men). This makes it all the more surprising that it is a woman – the remarkable Heloise – who is responsible for one of the earliest medieval examples of the form.[7] Peter Abelard relates in his autobiography,

---

[4] Quintilian, *Institutio Oratoria* II.4.25, instances 'ducendane uxor' ('to take a wife or not') as a suitable theme for practice in suasory rhetoric.

[5] Walter Map claimed authorship of the *Epistola Valerii* when he incorporated it into his *De Nugis Curialium* (Dist. IV, cap. iii–iv), which was written between 1180 and 1193. The *Epistola* was already in independent circulation at this time, and continued to be so; it is mentioned in library catalogues, and is the subject of numerous commentaries (Dean, 1950) which indicate its role as a school-text. For Chaucer's use of it, see the section on the *Wife of Bath's Prologue* in Bryan and Dempster (1941), with further references.

[6] There are fifty-five manuscripts extant (ed. Rigg, 1). Rigg dates the poem between 1222 and *c.*1250, and locates its origin in England or Northern France (11). Lydgate translated it into English (*Minor Poems*, ed. MacCracken, 2: 456–60; Utley no. 75).

[7] There are earlier or roughly contemporary examples of the type of *dissuasio* which is addressed by a male cleric to a female religious and which contrasts the miseries of earthly marriage with the bliss of spiritual union with Christ: the poem *Ad Muriel* by Serlo of Bayeux (*c.*1050–*c.*1120), which is preserved in BL, MS Cotton Vitellius A.XII, and two

the *Historia Calamitatum*, how, after the discovery of their love-affair and the birth of their child, he offered to make reparation by marrying Heloise, but she resolutely refused, on the grounds that it would involve him in disgrace, and the loss of his clerical and philosophical career (trans. Radice, 70–4). Heloise's dissuasion against marriage, as reported by Abelard, follows the familiar pattern established by Jerome's treatise. Like Jerome, she cites St Paul and Theophrastus; she re-tells Jerome's anecdotes about Cicero's refusal to remarry and Socrates' shrewish wife, in order to prove the incompatibility of marriage and the life of a philosopher. The importance of Heloise's *dissuasio* to the *Wife of Bath's Prologue* is not only that it earns her a place in Jankin's antifeminist book, but even more important, that it is to my knowledge the only other case in medieval literature where antifeminist satire is uttered by a woman. Speaker and speech are thus set at odds with each other in an ironic relation which Chaucer reproduces – albeit in a different way – in the *Wife of Bath's Prologue*. Heloise's dissuasion is no rhetorical exercise or literary game; it is delivered in passionate earnest. Yet not only does it issue from a woman, but from the very woman who stands to gain most from the man's decision to marry. Thus, the more passionately Heloise argues against her own interests, the more apparent is the contrast between the picture of woman painted by Jerome and Theophrastus on which she founds her case, and the self-sacrificing loyalty that drives her to argue it.

It may be thought that in reporting the *dissuasio* Abelard is putting words into Heloise's mouth, since it was he who had first given general currency to Jerome's vituperations against marriage, including his quotation of Theophrastus, by incorporating them into his *Theologia Christiana* (II.94–106), written a decade earlier.[8] But Heloise's first letter to Abelard confirms that he has reported her arguments accurately, even if incompletely (trans. Radice, 114), and it is entirely plausible that her knowledge of Jerome's treatise was acquired from Abelard. In any case, the question of which of them bore final responsibility for the form of the dissuasion as reported by Abelard does not affect either way the ironic contrast between speaker and speech, or the unique meaning that the *dissuasio* takes on in this instance. It is an ironic contrast to which the medieval readers of the *Historia Calamitatum* (who took it for granted that the *dissuasio* represented Heloise's own words) were quite alive; for them, antifeminist content is dissolved in admiration for the woman speaker (Dronke, [1976] 1992). The same contrast appears in the correspondence with Abelard which is appended to the *Historia Calamitatum*, as Heloise's

letters (22, 40) by Osbert of Clare (died after 1153). The Middle English *Hali Meiðhad* includes a *dissuasio* of this type. Bugge (1975, 88) assumes a relationship between this line of the *dissuasio* tradition and the classic type addressed by a man to a male philosopher or scholar, but they remain distinct types, and it is from the latter that Heloise's *dissuasio* derives.
[8]   The *Theologia Christiana* was written *c.*1124; thus it was composed after the real-life *dissuasio* would have been delivered (1117–18), but before the composition of the *Historia Calamitatum c.*1132 (Dronke [1970] 1986, 147). On Abelard's rare uses of anti-feminist material, see Dronke, ibid., 147–9.

reflections on the disastrous consequences of their marriage – Abelard's castration, their final separation and their entry into religious orders – provoke her to self-recriminations.[9] Nothing would have been more natural for Heloise at this point, it should be noted, than to identify herself with the deserted women of the *Heroides* – separated from her lover, persuaded by him to enter monastic life, for which she felt she had no vocation, still suffering the terrible pangs of a love that Abelard could not reciprocate physically, and would not reciprocate verbally. Alexander Pope's *Heloisa to Abelard* shows how natural and indeed inevitable was this assimilation of Heloise's experience to the Ovidian model. But instead, Heloise sees herself as the temptress of antifeminist tradition, as one of those women who are the ruin of men. She applies to herself the Solomonic warnings against women: 'I find woman more bitter than death; she is a snare, her heart a net, her arms are chains.' [Eccles. 7:26]. She cites Adam and Eve, Samson and Delilah, Solomon and his wives, Job and his wife, as traditional examples of the general banefulness of women. The paradoxical relationship between speaker and speech here was evident to Jean de Meun: 'Now Heloise is arguing against herself' ('Or argue Heloys contre li mesmes') is his comment on her bitter exclamation 'Alas, that women are the general and the greatest ruin of great men!' (Dronke, [1976] 1992, 276).

It is easy – too easy – to see this passage as no more than the demonstration of a woman's internalisation of male values; this, although true, is not the whole truth. What we see most of all here is the role of this internalisation in an individual woman's life: the last bitter torture offered her is the knowledge that her proud uniqueness – her pre-eminence in learning, the distinction of Abelard's love – is dissolved into the banality of crude antifeminist commonplace. Like Chaucer's Criseyde, she is forced to acknowledge that the woman she knows from the caricatures of proverb and anecdote now wears her own face. It is when we see the stereotypes in this punitive role that we can measure their cruelty in terms of the individual lives of medieval woman. But there is another reason why to talk of Heloise as a mere mouthpiece for male values is not the whole truth, and that is precisely the fact, mentioned earlier, that her male contemporaries never concur in this antifeminist view of her role in Abelard's life (such hostile responses as there were, were directed against Abelard, not Heloise; Dronke, [1976] 1992). Indeed, the most striking feature of the medieval responses to the Abelard–Heloise story is the absence of any inclination to interpret it in antifeminist terms, despite the fact that Heloise herself had pointed the way to this interpretation. For Peter the Venerable, she is raised above women and men alike by her 'wealth of religion and learning' (trans. Radice, 281). 'You act in all things, Heloise, with the greatest sweetness

---

[9] The letters accompany the *Historia Calamitatum* in the manuscripts; see Monfrin's introduction to his edition of the *Historia*, 9–31. The controversy over the authenticity of the Abelard-Heloise correspondence does not affect my argument, since it was certainly taken to be genuine in the Middle Ages, and it is its contribution to the medieval tradition which matters here.

and gentleness' is one of Petrarch's marginal comments on his copy of the correspondence (Dronke, [1976] 1992, 290). Abelard himself never takes the course, as obvious for him as the Ovidian role was for Heloise, of blaming her for his own downfall. Her seduction he presents as calculatingly initiated by himself, spurred on by the challenge of conquering a girl of some beauty and unparalleled learning. Although he excuses himself to her uncle, when revealing the affair, by saying that 'since the beginning of the human race, women [have] brought the noblest men to ruin' (trans. Radice, 70), he never makes this male weakness a matter of reproach to Heloise herself. For him, she is not the biblical temptress, but a figure of 'piety and wisdom, unequalled gentleness and patience' (trans. Radice, 97). To Heloise's lament that whereas they had both sinned, God had unjustly visited the punishment of castration on him alone, he replies that God rightly spared her, for she, although weaker in sex, had been stronger in continence (trans. Radice, 154). Whereas Heloise rehearses the jibes of antifeminism, Abelard insists on the dignity of women, combing the Bible and the works of the Fathers for evidence of their special favour with God.[10] Speaker is again implicitly contrasted with speech. But it is not only a sense of the speaker that complicates the interpretation of the *Letters*: it is also a sense of the listener, the implied presence of an addressee. The listening presence of Abelard, as addressee of Heloise's *dissuasio* or as reader of her letters, guides our own imaginative response; the antifeminist elements in Heloise's utterances are thus deflected and contradicted not only by our sense of the nature of their feminine speaker, but also by our sense of the scepticism of the male listener. The dialogic framework of the dissuasion and the letters weaves the antifeminist commonplaces into a complicated network of human feelings and transforms their meaning.

That Chaucer had direct knowledge of both the *Historia Calamitatum* and the letters is suggested by his listing of 'Helowys,/That was abbesse nat fer fro Parys' among the antifeminist authorities in Jankin's book (*Wife of Bath's Prologue* 677–8).[11] But whereas Jankin sees only the flat outlines of antifeminist stereotype in the work, Chaucer seems to have been vividly alive to the way it realizes the dialogic quality implicit in the form of epistle, *dissuasio* or polemic – to the way it shows us speech as speech act. Whether or not this was his source of inspiration, the examples I am about to discuss show how Chaucer plays constantly with the complex relations between speaker,

10   See Radice's translation of the *Letters*, 122–3, and Letter 6. Abelard's views on women incorporated traditional assumptions about their secondary status and greater weakness (*Letters*, trans. Radice, 188–9, 206, 210–12; cf. d'Alverny, 1977, 116–18), but he is in general notably free of the misogynist attitudes characteristic of other medieval clerics (Dronke, 1970, 136–7; McLaughlin, 1975).

11   The report of Heloise's *dissuasio* in the speech of Le Jaloux in the *Romance of the Rose* (8729–801; see pp. 61–2 below) does not include the traditional anti-feminist material which would qualify her for inclusion in Jankin's collection; and Jean de Meun's translation of the letters survives in only one manuscript. I therefore assume that Chaucer most probably knew the Latin original.

listener and speech, with the dialogic qualities of monologue, and the mono-logic tendencies of dialogue. It is thus only by paying attention to speaker and listener that we can fully understand what is being said, and perceive the complexity of the new meaning Chaucer forges from the old antifeminist commonplaces.

In the *Merchant's Tale*, Chaucer gives us a dramatized version of the *dissuasio de non ducenda uxore*. The old knight January assembles his friends and announces his intention to put an end to his life of lechery by getting married. Placebo, the type of the flatterer, happily endorses his plan, but Justinus advises against it. Echoing the *Epistola Valerii*, he bids him take care to whom he gives possession of his person (1523–9). Taking a wife requires a good deal of deliberation: one needs to enquire into all her possible vices, and make sure they are outweighed by her good qualities. Marriage, as he knows from experi-ence, is no picnic, even though his female neighbours assure him that he has the best of wives – 'But I woot best where wryngeth me my sho', he says, again echoing the *Epistola Valerii*, which is itself echoing Jerome (*Adv. Jov.* I.48). He counsels January to be especially wary of taking a young wife, whose sexual fidelity even a young man would find it difficult to ensure (1530–65). January's response to this vigorously argued *dissuasio* is to dismiss it out of hand:

> 'Wel,' quod this Januarie, 'and hastow ysayd?
> Straw for thy Senek, and for thy proverbes!
> I counte nat a panyer ful of herbes
> Of scole-termes. Wyser men than thow,
> As thou hast herd, assenteden right now
> To my purpos. Placebo, what sey ye?' (1566–71)

Placebo reaffirms his support, and the marriage is duly decided on.

Such is, Chaucer implies, the usual, nigh-inevitable, fate of the dissuasion. Of the examples of the genre mentioned so far, the *De Coniuge non Ducenda* concludes with the would-be bridegroom's capitulation to the dissuasion and his abandonment of the projected marriage, while the *Epistola Valerii* leaves Rufinus's response open. The *Miroir de Mariage* breaks off incomplete, but the most likely ending is abandonment of the marriage. Heloise's dissuasion is the only one that evidently fails of its effect, but the deadly earnest of Heloise and Abelard's situation is far removed from the comedy of January's consult-ation. Chaucer transforms the meaning of the dissuasion by showing us the disbelieving listener who renders it ineffectual. Dialogue collapses into mono-logue; if January asks for his friends' opinions, it is because he wants them to echo his own wishes. Rabelais's version of the *dissuasio* shares Chaucer's comic perception and gives it an extra twist: when Panurge asks Pantagruel for counsel on his decision to marry (which, like January, he announces in advance), he is completely disconcerted to find that his friend nonchalantly

changes his advice one way or the other, according as Panurge himself brings
forth reasons for or against.

> 'Well,' replied Pantagruel, 'since you have cast the dice once and for all,
> and have decreed and taken a firm resolution in the matter, there's no need
> for further talk. All that remains is to put your resolution into effect.'
> 'Yes,' said Panurge, 'but I shouldn't want to put it into effect without your
> counsel and good advice.'
> 'I advise you to do it,' said Pantagruel, 'I counsel you to marry.' 'But,' said
> Panurge, 'if you knew that it was better for me to stay as I am, and not
> undertake anything new, I would much rather not marry.'
> 'Then don't marry,' answered Pantagruel.
> 'But,' said Panurge, 'would you want me to remain single like this for the
> whole of my life, without conjugal company? You know that it is written,
> *Vae soli.* A man on his own has never the comforts that you see married
> people have.'
> 'For God's sake marry then,' replied Pantagruel. ...
>
> (III Chap. 9, trans. Cohen)

Like January, Panurge wants the *illusion* of dialogue, although, unlike January,
he is perturbed to find it nothing other than a monologue with an echo.

In both Rabelais and Chaucer, comedy is founded on a perception of the
redundancy of the dissuasion within the decision-making process. And this
perception is likewise evident in Chaucer's one essay at an independent dissuasion, the *Envoy to Bukton*, which is worth quoting in its entirety:

> My maister Bukton, whan of Crist our kyng
> Was axed what is trouthe or sothfastnesse,
> He nat a word answerde to that axing,
> As who saith, 'No man is al trewe,' I gesse.
> And therfore, though I highte to expresse
> The sorwe and wo that is in mariage,
> I dar not writen of it no wikkednesse,
> Lest I myself falle eft in swich dotage.
>
> I wol nat seyn how that yt is the cheyne
> Of Sathanas, on which he gnaweth evere,
> But I dar seyn, were he out of his peyne,
> As by his wille he wolde be bounde nevere.
> But thilke doted fool that eft hath levere
> Ycheyned be than out of prison crepe,
> God lete him never fro his wo dissevere,
> Ne no man him bewayle, though he wepe.
>
> But yet, lest thow do worse, take a wyf;
> Bet ys to wedde than brenne in worse wise.

But thow shal have sorwe on thy flessh, thy lyf,
And ben thy wives thral, as seyn these wise;
And yf that hooly writ may nat suffyse,
Experience shal the teche, so may happe,
That the were lever to be take in Frise
Than eft to falle of weddynge in the trappe.

This lytel writ, proverbes, or figure
I sende yow; take kepe of yt, I rede;
Unwys is he that kan no wele endure.
If thow be siker, put the nat in drede.
The Wyf of Bath I pray yow that ye rede
Of this matere that we have on honde.
God graunte yow your lyf frely to lede
In fredam, for ful hard is to be bonde.

As a *dissuasio*, this poem is self-destructing. Not only does the dissuader assume that it will be disregarded by the person to whom it is addressed, he himself has no confidence in his ability to put his own advice into practice. The dissuasion thus seems strangled by an awareness of its own pointlessness, shuffling on stage with its back to the audience ('I dar nat writen ...'; 'I wol nat seyn ...'). The relationship between the experienced speaker and the inexperienced listener is destabilized by the acknowledgement that the lessons of experience are anything but indelible, so that they could change places at any moment: the imprecations on 'thilke doted fool' who allows himself to marry a second time diverts the *dissuasio* away from Bukton to Chaucer himself – a future Chaucer whose ears will be as closed to it as Bukton's are now. The redundancy of the *dissuasio* appears above all in the fact that conviction of its truth depends, paradoxically, on its being ignored ('Experience shal the teche'). The *dissuasio* thus thwarted of its effect, the ostensible subject of the discourse, the 'sorwe and wo that is in mariage', is submerged beneath our sense of the complex relations that speaker and listener have to it; indeed, these relations become an essential part of what is being said.

The *Envoy to Bukton* suggests that, although innocence may be qualified by experience, experience is qualified by the perpetual resurgence of innocence. In the *Merchant's Tale*, we find innocence and experience similarly implicated in each other, in one of the strangest transformations ever undergone by the *dissuasio* – for this (although not to my knowledge hitherto recognized) is the determining form of the long encomium on marriage that occurs immediately after the opening of the tale, and just before the dramatized *dissuasio* I examined earlier. The dissuasion here disguises itself as *per*suasion. After a mere twenty lines of narrative in which we are introduced to the old knight January and informed of his decision to get married after sixty years of lecherous bachelordom, we are suddenly launched into a eulogy of the married state which is well over a hundred lines long.

> And certeinly, as sooth as God is kyng,
> To take a wyf it is a glorious thyng,
> And namely whan a man is oold and hoor;
> Thanne is a wyf the fruyt of his tresor.
> Thanne sholde he take a yong wyf and a feir,
> On which he myghte engendren hym an heir,
> And lede his lyf in joye and in solas,
> Where as thise bacheleris synge 'allas,'
> Whan that they fynden any adversitee
> In love, which nys but childyssh vanitee. (1267–76)

The reader's willingness to share the enthusiasm of the tone here is dampened by disquiet about what is being recommended: the marriage of an old man and a young wife does not *ipso facto* seem an ideal situation. And the disquiet finds a position to lodge in with the sudden appearance of Theophrastus, whose cynical view is briefly allowed to punctuate the rapture:

> For who kan be so buxom as a wyf?
> Who is so trewe, and eek so ententyf
> To kepe hym, syk and hool, as is his make?
> For wele or wo she wole hym not forsake;
> She nys nat wery hym to love and serve,
> Though that he lye bedrede til he sterve.
> And yet somme clerkes seyn it nys nat so,
> Of whiche he Theofraste is oon of tho.
> What force though Theofraste liste lye?
> 'Ne take no wyf,' quod he, 'for housbondrye,
> As for to spare in houshold thy dispence.
> A trewe servant dooth moore diligence
> Thy good to kepe than thyn owene wyf,
> For she wol clayme half part al hir lyf.
> And if [that] thou be syk, so God me save,
> Thy verray freendes, or a trewe knave,
> Wol kepe thee bet than she that waiteth ay
> After thy good and hath doon many a day.
> And if thou take a wyf unto thyn hoold
> Ful lightly maystow been a cokewold.'
> This sentence, and an hundred thynges worse,
> Writeth this man, ther God his bones corse!
> But take no kep of al swich vanytee;
> Deffie Theofraste, and herke me. (1287–1310)

Although dismissed, the Theophrastan view refuses to go away: it flashes out momentarily in the wry addition to the assurance that a wife, unlike the transitory gifts of Fortune, is a gift that will last and endure – longer than you wish, perhaps (1318). It thus casts the shadow of deep irony over the idyllic picture of marital harmony which follows:

> A wyf! a, Seinte Marie, benedicite!
> How myghte a man han any adversitee
> That hath a wyf? Certes, I kan nat seye.
> The blisse which that is bitwixe hem tweye
> Ther may no tonge telle, or herte thynke.
> If he be povre, she helpeth hym to swynke;
> She kepeth his good, and wasteth never a deel;
> Al that hire housbonde lust, hire liketh weel;
> She seith nat ones 'nay,' whan he seith 'ye.'
> 'Do this,' seith he; 'Al redy, sire,' seith she.
> O blisful ordre of wedlok precious,
> Thou art so murye, and eek so vertuous,
> And so commended and appreved eek
> That every man that halt hym worth a leek
> Upon his bare knees oughte al his lyf
> Thanken his God that hym hath sent a wyf,
> Or elles preye to God hym for to sende
> A wyf to last unto his lyves ende. (1337–54)

Perplexingly, however, the shadow lifts in the immediately succeeding examples of the value of woman's counsel – Rebecca, Judith, Abigail, Esther – which can be ironically interpreted only by the most violent kind of exegetical strait-jacketing; that there is nothing inherently suspicious in citing them as positive examples is shown by their being repeated almost verbatim in the sober earnest of Prudence's arguments in Chaucer's own tale of *Melibee*.[12]

There is no difficulty, however, in identifying the irony in the concluding advice on how to treat one's wife:

> Suffre thy wyves tonge, as Catoun bit;
> She shal comande, and thou shalt suffren it,
> And yet she wole obeye of curteisye ...

---

[12] Brown's attempt (1974, 391) to demonstrate ironic intent in the *Merchant's Tale* from minor verbal variations between it and the *Melibee* fails to convince. Otten (1970–1) points out that the claims for irony advanced by Tatlock (1935–6, 373, 376) and Turner (1965) are supported only by their own slanted summaries of the biblical sources, and marshals evidence to show that medieval typology interpreted these women as 'Deliverance types', foreshadowing Christ's role as Deliverer. It is in this role that they appear in both the *Merchant's Tale* and the *Melibee*. Bronson's citation (1961, 591) of Lydgate's 'Examples against Women' for a negative view of Judith simply shows yet again that medieval poets can use the same *exempla* in different ways; Brown (1974, n. 12) gives numerous medieval examples of the 'extremely widespread traditions' that presented these women in a positive light.

> No man hateth his flessh, but in his lyf
> He fostreth it, and therfore bidde I thee
> Cherisshe thy wyf, or thou shalt nevere thee.
> Housbonde and wyf, what so men jape or pleye,
> Of worldly folk holden the siker weye;
> They been so knyt ther may noon harm bityde,
> And namely upon the wyves syde. (1377–9, 1386–92)

This conclusion is representative of the passage as a whole in its liberal use of I/you pronouns, imperative verbs and conversational emphases ('I seye nat this for noght') to create a vivid sense of intimate relationship between speaker and listener. But disconcertingly at odds with this sense of intimacy is the reader's uncertainty as to who exactly the speaker is – who is the 'me' in 'Deffie Theofraste, and herke me'? Are we to read the passage as a kind of *style indirect libre* representing January's stream of consciousness (whence, then, its sardonic asides?), as a sarcastic *tour de force* on the part of the Merchant (whence, then, the passages that resist an ironic reading?), or as an intrusion by Chaucer himself (whence, then, the oscillations in its irony?)? A critic who has reviewed the various arguments put forward for each of these alternatives concludes helplessly that 'we can only accept the passage as a major Chaucerian crux, a tantalizing anomaly' (Benson, 1979–80, p. 59). The difficulties disappear, however, with the realisation that they are both caused and resolved by the ironic mode of the passage – a mode specifically designed to allow us to hear two voices speaking at the same time. Thus the critics who do best with the encomium are those who see it as simultaneously representing the Merchant and January:

> the Merchant ... speaks in a sort of double-talk ... beneath the obvious savagery runs an undercurrent of which he seems at best half-conscious, for the curses fall on himself as well as on January. The stream of consciousness we see flow by was the Merchant's own, two months ago. (Sedgewick, 1947–8, 342; cf. Elliott, 1964; Brown, 1978–9, 143 and n. 7)

The Merchant's experience speaks through January's innocence.

But what is at stake here is more than a comment on two fictional characters. In the first place, the ironic mode also involves the second-person listener/reader, on whose tacit collaboration the irony of the passage depends, and in whom its strange fusion of innocence and experience is replicated. It is the listener who supplies from a store of personal experience the sarcastic answer to the rhetorical question 'How myghte a man han any adversitee/That hath a wyf?' Antifeminism becomes the responsibility of the reader, not of the poet; if we relish the comic vignette of wifely obedience – ' "Do this," seith he; "Al redy, sire," seith she' – then we do so because we know how far removed it is from the everyday realities of married life. Chaucer's reliance on the reader's collaboration at this point can be seen if we set the rhetorical question quoted above alongside the formally similar rhetorical question which is posed to very different effect in the *Franklin's Tale*:

> Who koude telle, but he hadde wedded be,
> The joye, the ese, and the prosperitee
> That is bitwixe an housbonde and his wyf? (803–5)

Here the question calls forth a quite different area of 'knowledge', and the tacit understanding between speaker and listener creates, not a wry knowingness, but the secret thrill of shared intimacy: private happiness can be communicated only to those who have also experienced it.

Yet the voice of innocence is not entirely drowned out by the voice of experience. However different the responses to these two rhetorical questions, the fact that they meet at the formal level is a sign that the ironic picture of marital bliss in the mock-encomium gestures, however distantly, towards a true ideal. Its ludicrously comic picture of marital unanimity – ' "Do this," seith he; "Al redy, sire", seith she' – caricatures the genuine ideal of harmonious unity in love that we have already seen in Chaucer's Cleopatra, and that we see again in the speech of the abandoned female falcon in the *Squire's Tale*.

> 'And I so loved hym for his obeisaunce,
> And for the trouthe I demed in his herte,
> That if so were that any thyng hym smerte,
> Al were it never so lite, and I it wiste,
> Me thoughte I felte deeth myn herte twiste.
> And shortly, so ferforth this thyng is went
> That my wyl was his willes instrument;
> This is to seyn, my wyl obeyed his wyl
> In alle thyng, as fer as reson fil,
> Kepynge the boundes of my worshipe evere.
> Ne nevere hadde I thyng so lief, ne levere,
> As hym, God woot, ne nevere shal namo.' (562–73)

'Obeisaunce' here is not a matter of orders issued and executed; it is a spontaneous fusion of two wills into one, as two lovers instinctively take each other's desires and feelings as their own. The man's 'obeisaunce' to his mistress calls forth her own 'obeisaunce' to him, as each adapts to the contours of the other's existence. In the parodied version of the *Merchant's Tale*, this mutual yielding is replaced by a robot-like execution of commands, but even here there lingers a dim memory of the original.

The ironic mode of the passage is thus a way of holding in focus a double vision of marriage; it plays off the reader's knowledge of what marriage all too often *is*, against his or her vision of what marriage *ought* to be ('a ful greet sacrament') or hopes it to be ('paradys terrestre'). The non-ironic passages quite naturally take their place in this vision, without needing to have an ironic interpretation forced upon them.[13] But 'his or her' is in this case, strictly speaking, inaccurate. For as we focus squarely on the rapturous vision conjured up by the 'voice of innocence', we realize that this 'idiot's view of marriage' is in fact a *man's* view of marriage. It is the man's naively selfish expectations of married life that are here so enthusiastically elaborated, and the comedy of the passage plays around these expectations even more than around the shrewishness of real-life wives. What is more, on this view the shrewishness of wives is welcomed as being the only way of bringing these masculine fantasies safely down to earth. The comedy rests on the secure confidence that the naive illusions will be rapidly dispelled. The 'voice of experience' reassures us that real-life women refuse to behave like the marionette figures of male dreams.

The usual view of the mock-encomium is that it is 'antifeminist'. But if we switch our attention from spoken content to speaking subject, we see that it is much more accurate to call it anti-male.[14] The antifeminist view of wives is not introduced for its own sake; rather, it is an instrument with which to reveal and puncture selfish male illusions. The 'voice of experience' is the voice of a man who has, one might say, gone through the puncturing process, and who now looks back with wry amusement at his own innocence. The ironic mode of the passage thus constitutes the major part of its meaning: it conjures up for us a classic vision of masculine consciousness perennially condemned by its own selfishness to shuttle back and forth between two stereotypes of woman – as purveyor of 'paradys terrestre' or purgatorial shrew. And the ironic simultaneity of this passage also enables us to perceive that female shrewishness is the inevitable corrective to masculine selfishness because it is its inevitable *consequence*. The selfish husband creates the rebellious scold who is his daily punishment.

The implication of a causal relationship between male selfishness and female shrewishness in this opening passage is reinforced by its dramatic representation in the figures of Pluto and Proserpina at the other end of the tale. As Chaucer himself makes clear ('In Claudyan ye may the stories rede'; 2232), this married couple have stepped straight from the pages of Claudian's *De Raptu Proserpinae*, which relates the rape that initiated their marriage; Pluto 'ravysshed' Proserpina as she gathered flowers on the slopes of Etna (2230). If the 'ravishing' is represented in Claudian as abduction rather than forcible intercourse (the term *raptus* covers both),[15] it is no less violent and horrific for that, and Chaucer's reference to Pluto's 'grisely carte' evokes the terror of the

---

13   There is thus no need for Emerson Brown's subtle attempt (1974) to read the passage as ironic on the personal level of the Merchant's intentions, but also as ultimately serious, since God uses even women's treachery for good ends.

14   Shores (1970, 125–6) makes the point that 'the digressive panegyric is not merely antifeministic', but is a way of representing January's folly. Donaldson (1970, 38) sees the wider implications: 'The masculine selfishness latent in the whole antifeminist tradition reaches its clearest expression in the Merchant's praise of matrimony: not "he for God only, she for God in him", but he for himself, she for him.'

15   On the legal and social complexities of *raptus*, see Cannon, 1993 and 2000, and Kelly, 1998.

scene. Pluto with Proserpina in his clutches is compared by Claudian to a lion standing defiantly over a mangled heifer, dripping with its blood. Proserpina, her hair streaming in the wind, wailing and lamenting the loss of her virginity, is the archetype of the helpless victim (II 209–13, 247–72). Tereus and Philomel, we might think, repeated yet again. Yet it soon becomes clear that this recollection of Claudian is merely the preface to an ironic reversal in the relation of predator and victim. Pluto, observing May's preparations to commit adultery with Damian in the pear-tree, seizes the opportunity to deliver himself of some pompous antifeminist clichés:

> 'My wyf,' quod he, 'ther may no wight seye nay;
> Th'experience so preveth every day
> The tresons whiche that wommen doon to man.
> Ten hondred thousand [tales] tellen I kan
> Notable of youre untrouthe and brotilnesse.' (2237–41)

This is a rapist talking. The superb blandness of the irony here seems to have kept it hidden from almost all Chaucer critics so far;[16] only David Aers seems to have noticed 'the double-think and dishonesty' revealed in the 'picture of a male who "ravysshed" a female accusing her of "tresons" '(1980, 225, n. 27). But once the ironic contradiction between speaker and speech strikes one, Chaucer's relish in its comic aspect becomes blindingly obvious. Secure in his male complacency, Pluto continues with the conventional appeal to Solomon, 'Fulfild of sapience', and to his oft-quoted dictum:

> 'Thus preiseth he yet the bountee of man:
> "Amonges a thousand men yet foond I oon,
> But of wommen alle foond I noon."
>   Thus seith the kyng that knoweth youre wikkednesse.'
> $\qquad\qquad\qquad\qquad\qquad\qquad$ (2246–9)

He will redress this deplorable situation, he sanctimoniously concludes, by restoring January's sight at the crucial moment so that his wife's 'harlotrye' will be apparent to him.

---

16   The comments of J. S. P. Tatlock (1935–6, 372–3) are a beautiful example of the masculine bias that blinds the critic to the irony: 'Proserpina is the tart feminist who to win equality with man will use the most feminine of methods, and by all means has the last word. The deceitful and the unfair in the feminine is indeed eternal; heaven does not redress the balance of earth.' Pluto, on the other hand, is 'the man of power who tolerates with amusement and possibly a dash of admiration his wife's irrational and immoral tactics, because he values peace more than trivial victory'. Donovan (1957) discusses every possible aspect of the Pluto-Proserpina episode *except* the rape and the ironies attendant on it; Wentersdorf (1965, 526) comments on the rape only as a parallel to January's quasi-rape of May. Murtaugh, in a generally illuminating article (1971, 482), seems to perceive the ironic relation of rape and antifeminist comment, but does not make it fully explicit.

When Proserpina replies to this speech, we realize with a shock that she is no longer the innocent young victim who was carried off on the slopes of Etna. Instead, she speaks with the shrill stridency of the shrew:

> 'Ye shal?' quod Proserpyne, 'wol ye so?
> Now by my moodres sires soule I swere
> That I shal yeven hire suffisant answere,
> And alle wommen after, for hir sake,
> That, though they be in any gilt ytake,
> With face boold they shulle hemself excuse,
> And bere hem doun that wolden hem accuse.
> For lak of answere noon of hem shal dyen.
> Al hadde man seyn a thyng with bothe his yen,
> Yit shul we wommen visage it hardily,
> And wepe, and swere, and chyde subtilly,
> So that ye men shul been as lewed as gees.' (2264–75)

Proserpina has not finished yet; she goes on to launch a vigorous attack on the whole foundation of her husband's antifeminism:

> 'What rekketh me of youre auctoritees?
> I woot wel that this Jew, this Salomon,
> Foond of us wommen fooles many oon.
> But though that he ne foond no good womman,
> Yet hath ther founde many another man
> Wommen ful trewe, ful goode, and vertuous.' (2276–81)

Or else Solomon's 'sentence' was simply that no one is truly good but God. In any case, why does Pluto make so much of Solomon, rich and glorious though he was?

> 'Pardee, as faire as ye his name emplastre,
> He was a lecchour and an ydolastre,
> And in his elde he verray God forsook...' (2297–9)

By the end of this long tirade, Pluto is reduced to weary submission:

> 'Dame,' quod this Pluto, 'be no lenger wrooth;
> I yeve it up!' (2311–12)

Pluto is probably the only example in literature of a henpecked rapist. The role of this paradoxical figure is not only to provide comic delight in its absurdity, but to show once again, and this time in terms of a personal history, that female shrewishness is both the inevitable response to male aggression and its proper punishment.

What, then, of January and May – of the story proper in this tale? It is tempting to say that they illustrate the same point: January's selfish indifference to his own sexual unattractiveness turns his young wife to adultery. Tempting, but not true; the relation between male selfishness and female shrewishness is here given a different twist, one that blocks off the temptations to easy sentimental generalisations about woman's oppression. For May's responsiveness to Damian's advances reveals not a tender young maiden seeking balm for her bruised sensibilities, but a woman both hard-headed and hard-hearted, ready to seize any opportunity for her own advantage. It is, indeed, in this revelation that the tender, innocent victim is in fact a self-possessed manipulator of events that the story of January and May makes contact with that of Pluto and Proserpina. And it is at this moment that the reader discovers that the stereotyped thinking so brilliantly anatomized in this tale is also at work in her interpretation of it. It is easy to observe January falling in love with a stereotyped vision of womanly perfection that he creates in his own mind, 'For love is blynd alday, and may nat see' (1598):

> He purtreyed in his herte and in his thoght
> Hir fresshe beautee and hir age tendre,
> Hir myddel smal, hire armes longe and sklendre.
> Hire wise governaunce, hir gentillesse,
> Hir wommanly berynge, and hire sadnesse.
> And whan that he on hire was condescended,
> Hym thoughte his choys myghte nat ben amended. (1600–6)

It takes rather longer to see how we too are taken in by May's youth and beauty to the point where we automatically cast her in the role of the victimized young girl forced into marriage with an older man (cf. Schleusener, 1979–80, 241–2). We suffer through the repellent account of January's love-making with all the sensitivity we attribute to his bride. It is only as we see the swift decisiveness with which she stage-manages her sexual encounter with Damian and the lack of sentimentality with which she throws his letter in the privy, and as we hear the shrill vulgarity with which she speaks – 'I have ... a soule for to kepe/As wel as ye' (2188–9) – that we are embarrassed into revising our view. If we then put together January's assurances that he will settle his entire inheritance on her (2172–5) with such earlier, neglected, clues as the mention of May's lowly rank ('of smal degree'; 1625), and of her being 'feffed in his lond' (1698) on marriage, it becomes clear that so far from being forced into wedlock, she has willingly married this old fool for his money, trusting that she will not have to wait too long for it to come into her hands. If it still remains true that male selfishness creates the female shrew, this is on the general rather than the individual level; the social configurations that produce May's character and marital role far ante-date her marriage to January.

Seen from one perspective, January's naive illusions are the expression and the instrument of male selfishness and sexual aggression; seen from another, they are the beneficent veil that keeps him from perceiving his own role as pawn in a female game. His physical blindness is merely the outward symbol of a general ability to shut his eyes to reality; when Pluto miraculously restores his sight, the miracle is instantly negated by his willingness to disbelieve the evidence of his own eyes. Innocence does *not*, in his case, give way to experience; he retreats into the fool's paradise he has constructed for himself. If his naivety prompts January to enter the marital purgatory threatened by Justinus, it at least also protects him from the knowledge that he is in it. And the reader is uncertain whether to deplore this wilful blindness or be thankful for it; if it curtails female freedom in one direction, it at least opens up room for manoeuvre in another.

The tale eschews the easy pleasure of punishing January with marital misery in favour of testifying to the irrepressible human urge towards blindness. And it is our stereotyped illusions about May that show this blindness to be a general one. The romantic high-flown language which Chaucer ironically applies to the urgings of physical appetite in Damian and 'fresshe May' reproaches us with our earlier romantic belief in May as sweet innocent victim. But it also nags us (like the *Manciple's Tale*) with the sense that our attitude to the story depends on the way it is told; romance is in the eye of the beholder or the tongue of the narrator. January's self-delusion partakes of the general human urge to sublimate reality into the forms of desire – 'For love is blynd alday and may nat se.' In the tale's comic and compassionate anatomisation of this blindness, May's metamorphosis from romantic heroine into adulterous shrew plays an important part; it is not aimed at the downgrading of women, but at revealing the reader's stereotyped expectations of them, and the way these stereotyped expectations can govern feminist responses as much as antifeminist ones.

But if Chaucer chooses to dissolve the romantic picture of Isolde into the cynical outline of the fabliau adulteress, it is not just for the pleasure of unmasking the sentimentality of our response; it is also a means of making the point that women can manage without our sympathy. That is, it is a means of fending off the danger incurred in representing women as the helpless victim of oppression, the danger of *patronizing* women. May, like Proserpina, testifies to the ability of women to look after themselves. So it is that shrewishness comes not as a disappointment, but as a relief. January's willingness to substitute fictions about women for reality is exploited by May for her own advantage. And the irony of Pluto's blinkered pomposities about the treachery of women is matched by the irony in the way May cunningly allows her protestations of honesty to devolve into pathetic whimperings about men's infidelity even as she signals to her lover:

> 'Why speke ye thus? But men been evere untrewe,
> And wommen have repreve of yow ay newe.
> Ye han noon oother contenance, I leeve,
> But speke to us of untrust and repreeve.'
>   And with that word she saugh wher Damyan

Sat in the bussh, and coughen she bigan,
And with hir fynger signes made she
That Damyan sholde clymbe upon a tree. (2203–10)

May's resourcefulness turns the victimisation of women into a weapon for manipulating men. It is a lesson the Wife of Bath has also learned well, as we shall see.

With the Wife of Bath Chaucer sets himself a new problem: the problem of speaking in the voice of a woman. How is he to achieve some kind of authenticity without incurring the charge of male ventriloquism? How is the woman who has been spoken *about* for centuries to be represented as speaking *for* herself? Chaucer's way of dealing with this problem is to meet it head on: what comes out of the Wife's mouth is not a naive attempt at an unprejudiced representation of 'how women feel', but rather the most extensive and unadulterated body of traditional antifeminist commonplace in the whole of the *Canterbury Tales*. Chaucer renounces the attempt to invent radically new material; he does not even juxtapose with the antifeminist stereotypes any of the contrasting stereotypes that would counteract their effect. He does not, that is, take the easy and obvious way out by having the Wife, like Jean de Meun's La Vieille (her most obvious literary ancestor), justify herself by reference to Ovid's abandoned heroines – Dido, Phyllis, Ariadne – or by an appeal to examples of good women – Penelope, Alcestis, Griselda. Instead, he plots speaker against speech, in the paradoxical mode of the Abelard-Heloise correspondence, by giving the antifeminist material to the Wife, and the tale of Griselda, supreme example of the good woman, to the Clerk, representative of the class whom the Wife accuses of never having anything favourable to say about the female sex. The antifeminist material appears in different guise in each of the Prologue's three main sections: Jerome's arguments in favour of virginity form the basis of the first part; the second part dramatizes Theophrastus's account of female vices into the Wife's account of how she scolded her husbands; and the third part reproduces the sample miscellany of antifeminist proverbs and anecdotes contained in Jankin's 'book of wikked wyves'. Jerome has the starring role as arch-representative of antifeminist writing, but the *Epistola Valerii*, the *Romance of the Rose*, Deschamps's *Miroir de Mariage*, Matheolus's *Lamentations* and the Solomonic proverbs provide a strong supporting cast.

The prominence of this traditional antifeminist material finds its justification in the fact that the Wife of Bath is locked into a continuing struggle not so much with men as with their stereotypes of her sex – or, as she would put it, with 'auctoritee' (Hanning, 1985, 16–18). In her final quarrel with Jankin, it is not the man she goes for, but the book. The motivating force behind the first part of her Prologue, which subverts Jerome's arguments against multiple marriage without ever actually naming him, becomes clear in her account of the contents of this book, in which Jerome figures as arch-representative of the clerical antifeminism embodied in Jankin himself.

> He hadde a book that gladly, nyght and day,
> For his desport he wolde rede alway;
> He cleped it Valerie and Theofraste,
> At which book he lough alwey ful faste.
> And eek ther was somtyme a clerk at Rome,
> A cardinal, that highte Seint Jerome,
> That made a book agayn Jovinian ...
> Ana alle thise were bounden in o volume.
> And every nyght and day was his custume,
> Whan he hadde leyser and vacacioun
> From oother worldly occupacioun,
> To reden on this book of wikked wyves.
> He knew of hem mo legendes and lyves
> Than been of goode wyves in the Bible.
> For trusteth wel, it is an impossible
> That any clerk wol speke good of wyves,
> But if it be of hooly seintes lyves,
> Ne of noon oother womman never the mo.
> Who peyntede the leon, tel me who?
> By God, if wommen hadde writen stories,
> As clerkes han withinne hire oratories,
> They wolde han writen of men moore wikkednesse
> Than al the mark of Adam may redresse. (669–75, 681–96)

'Who painted the lion?' The Wife is referring to the well-known fable which relates how a lion and a man argued over which of them was superior to the other.[17] When the man attempted to prove his case by pointing to a picture of a man overcoming a lion, the lion asked who painted the picture, and on receiving the obvious reply – 'A man' – commented that if lions could paint, then the picture would be very different. Women, for the Wife of Bath, are in the same position as the lion: they are powerless to correct the distorted image of themselves produced by clerical misogynists and given all the weight of bookish authority.[18] The Wife's concern is to strip off the impersonal disguise of 'auctoritee' and to reveal the biassed individual behind the mask.

As David Aers has noted, there is no essential difference between the Wife of Bath's manipulation of 'auctoritees' and that of the clerics she attacks; 'the standard practices of medieval exegesis included the sustained pulverization and fragmentation of Biblical texts, the utter dissolution of their existential and historical meanings, and the imposition of pre-determined dogmatic

---

[17]   The fable is number 24 in Avianus's collection (though here it is a sculpted tombstone rather than a painting that is in question), and also appears, for example, in the *Romulus Vulgaris* and the *Romulus Nilantinus* (ed. Hervieux, 2^2: 231, 544), in Marie de France's *Fables* (no. 37) and their Latin derivative (ed. Hervieux, 2^2: 623–4).

[18]   For evidence of clerical antifeminism in medieval Oxford, see Pratt (1962).

propositions' (1980, 86; cf. Donaldson, 1977, 5–7). The battle between Jovinian and Jerome is a battle for possession of biblical texts, which each in turn selects, interprets and synthesizes in the construction of his own argument. Each appeals to the biblical texts as fixed and unalterable reference-points, investing the argument with impersonal authority,[19] yet each interprets them according to his own bias, using them as fluid elements in a personal discourse. 'Authority has a waxen nose: that is, it can be turned in either direction' ('Auctoritas cereum habet nasum: id est, in diversum potest flecti sensum'), as Alan of Lille sagely observes.[20] For Jovinian, God's command to 'increase and multiply' is to be taken literally; for Jerome, it must be read in the light of Paul's recommendations of virginity. Marriage is to be praised, but virginity is to be preferred (*Adv. Jov.* I.2, I.16). The Wife of Bath's contribution to the debate makes fluidity even more fluid by virtue of the simple but confusing fact that it draws on both disputants at once: if, like Jovinian, she clings to the literal 'text' of God's command to 'wexe and multiplye' (28–9), she is equally happy to appropriate Jerome. She serenely grants the superiority he claims for virginity, repeating his metaphor of the different vessels in a lord's household – some of gold, some of wood – whose equal serviceableness but differing dignity is representative of the relationship between virginity and marriage (91–104; cf. *Adv. Jov.* I. 3, I. 8). But the affective power of the metaphor disappears under the Wife's cheerful renunciation of spiritual ambition. Jerome's arguments merge with her own purposes; rebellion speaks with the voice of orthodoxy.

If the Wife asserts her 'experience' against written 'auctoritee', she does not therefore abandon the verbal world, but rather adapts its techniques to her own ends. Jerome's triple comparison of virginity, marriage and lechery to wheatbread, barley-bread and dung (*Adv. Jov.* I.7) opens up alarmingly to new meaning as the Wife subjects it to the same sort of close reading as the exegetes apply to biblical texts.

> I nyl envye no virginitee.
> Lat hem be breed of pured whete-seed,
> And lat us wyves hoten barly-breed;
> And yet with barly-breed, Mark telle kan,
> Oure Lord Jhesu refresshed many a man. (142–6)

The comparison loses its original meaning under the pressure of lateral thinking: function is substituted for hierarchical ranking. Yet the ingenuity practised here is close kin to that evident in the way Jerome finally disposes of the command to 'increase and multiply and fill the earth' by focussing on the word 'earth': 'marriage fills the earth, virginity fills heaven' (I.16). The comic play of the Wife's arguments is thus ballasted with a serious point: the stability of

---

[19] *Adv. Jov.* I.4: 'adversus singulas propositiones ejus, Scripturarum vel maxime nitor testimoniis: ne querulus garriat, se eloquentia magis quam veritate superatum'.
[20] 'De Fide Catholica' I.xxx (*PL* 210, col. 333).

words lasts only as long as does the assent to the authority that fixes their meaning (Mann, 1974; Aers, 1980, 93–9).[21] The Wife sets herself up as a new 'authority' (and is meekly accepted as such by the Pardoner: 164–87); male discourse passes into female control.

The first part of the *Prologue* thus prepares for the second, in which the Wife relates how she cowed her first three husbands into submission by her lengthy tirades against them. The source-material of this whole long section (235–394) is, as I noted earlier, Jerome's citation of Theophrastus's *Golden Book*, but it also incorporates material from the *Epistola Valerii* and the vernacular texts that draw on the Theophrastan material, in particular the *Romance of the Rose* and Deschamps's *Miroir de Mariage*. But it is not only the source-material that links these latter texts to Chaucer's, it is also their common exploitation of the dialogic potential of that source-material, and their elaboration of it into ironies of different kinds (cf. Muscatine, 1957, 210–11). I shall deal with the *Miroir* first, although chronologically it is the later of the two, because its ironies are simpler in structure. They arise from the frequent use of quoted speech in the long letter from Repertoire de Science to Franc Vouloirs which occupies the bulk of the work. There is, as we might expect, a chorus of male voices reporting the faults of their wives; but we also hear a great deal from the wives themselves. First a typical wife outlines all the expensive things she needs to keep her happy: clothes, jewels, luxurious furnishings, household goods, spices and cooking materials. This is Theophrastus's third-person account of female needs, cast in first-person form (*Adv. Jov.* 1.47). A little later, we find her outlining her husband's faults:

> 'By our Lady, such-and-such a woman is publicly respected, well-dressed and well turned-out, while I, wretched creature, am poor and despised by everybody! But I see well what's at the bottom of it: you've got your eye on our neighbour when she comes to call, I can see it, because you care nothing for me. You flirt with our maid; what did you bring her back from market the other day? Unlucky was the day you married me! I have neither husband nor lover.' (1594–1608)

This speech exactly reproduces Theophrastus's example of female nagging:

> '*That* woman is better dressed when she goes out; she is respected by everyone, while I, wretched creature, am despised among women. Why were you eyeing our neighbour? What were you saying to our maid? What did you bring back from market? *I* am not allowed a male friend or acquaintance.' (*Adv. Jov.* 1.47)

---

21 The struggle for control of the text extends itself into the marginalia that accompany the *Wife of Bath's Prologue* in the manuscripts; see Caie (1975–6), answered by Schibanoff (1988).

For Repertoire de Science, as for Theophrastus, it is not necessary to demonstrate the lack of truth in these complaints: the mere voicing of them is sufficient evidence of female troublesomeness. Yet the irony by which the speeches of women attacking men are made an essential part of a male attack on women remains open to perception by the reader.

In Jean de Meun, this use of speeches-within-speeches to create a polyphonic utterance is much more complicated: the Theophrastan material forms part of a whole system of utterances working ironically against each other. Its outer framework is the speech of the lover's friend, Amis, who is warning him of the incompatibility of love and 'seigneurie' ('lordship'); to illustrate his point he invents a long speech by a jealous husband (Le Jaloux), the kind of man who wants 'mestrise' over his wife, as an example of what *not* to do (8437–9330). Le Jaloux nags his wife about her infidelities and extravagances, and recapitulates Theophrastus's warnings against women, regretting that he did not listen to them. Yet just as Jerome paradoxically precedes his quotation of Theophrastus with the exemplary stories of good women, so Le Jaloux is imperceptibly led into recounting the stories of Penelope and Lucretia. Embedded in his recital of the wrongs women inflict on men, we find clear examples of the wrongs men do to women. Le Jaloux retrieves himself by retreating to his Theophrastan material and reinforcing it from the *Epistola Valerii*, but he runs into trouble again when he tries to use Heloise's *dissuasio* as further support. For here his approval of the subject-matter forces him into admiration for the woman speaker, and he can pursue his antifeminist line only by claiming that 'no such woman has lived since' (8795–6), and that her learning enabled her to rise above the limitations of her sex.

But it is not only in its testimony to the selflessness of its author that Heloise's *dissuasio* undermines Le Jaloux's tirade: it is also in the fact that it harmonizes perfectly with the outer framing speech of Amis. For Le Jaloux fuses with Abelard's account of Heloise's dissuasion her own later comments on it in the *Letters*:

> God knows I never sought anything in you except yourself; I wanted simply you, nothing of yours. I looked for no marriage-bond, no marriage portion, and it was not my own pleasures and wishes I sought to gratify, as you well know, but yours. The name of wife may seem more sacred or more binding, but sweeter for me will always be the word mistress, or, if you will permit me, that of concubine or whore ... [In the *Historia Calamitatum*] you thought fit to set out some of the reasons I gave in trying to dissuade you from binding us together in an ill-starred marriage. But you kept silent about most of my arguments for preferring love to wedlock and freedom to chains. God is my witness that if Augustus, Emperor of the whole world, thought fit to honour me with marriage and conferred all the earth on me to possess for ever, it would be dearer and more honourable to me to be called not his Empress but your whore.
>
> (trans. Radice, 114)

Le Jaloux incorporates this passage into his account of the *dissuasio*:

> She asked him to love her but to claim no right over her except that freely
> granted by grace ['de grace et de franchise'], without lordship or mastery
> ['sanz seigneurie et sanz mestrise'], so that he could study without any
> ties, be his own person, quite free, and that she might devote herself to
> study, being not devoid of learning ... It is written in so many words in the
> letters she sent him even after she was abbess, if anyone wants to search
> through their pages: 'If the emperor of Rome, to whom all men are sub-
> ject, condescended to wish to take me to wife and make me mistress of
> the world, I would rather' she said, '– and I call God to witness – be called
> your whore than his crowned empress.' (8747–54, 8783–94)

Heloise's rejection of 'seigneurie' and 'mestrise' accords not with the speech
of Le Jaloux, who is their arch-representative, but with the outer speech of
Amis, who like her prizes 'grace' and 'franchise' (cf. Dronke [1975] 1984,
383–4; Kelly, 1975, 44–6). The voice of 'franchise' speaks not only outside the
voice of 'mestrise', but also within it, though Le Jaloux himself is deaf to it.
Monologue becomes concealed dialogue; speech works against speaker.

Chaucer's own counterpointing of speech and speaker in the *Wife of Bath's
Prologue* probably owes a general debt to both these instances, but it goes
beyond both of them in complexity. The Wife's tirade against her husbands
begins in a quite unsurprising way as a reprise of the Theophrastan sample of
female nagging:

> 'Sire olde kaynard, is this thyn array?
> Why is my neighebores wyf so gay?
> She is honoured overal ther she gooth;
> I sitte at hoom; I have no thrifty clooth.
> What dostow at my neighebores hous?
> Is she so fair? Artow so amorous?
> What rowne ye with oure mayde? Benedicite!
> Sire olde lecchour, lat thy japes be!
> And if I have a gossib or a freend,
> Withouten gilt, thou chidest as a feend,
> If that I walke or pleye unto his hous!' (235–45)

At this point, however, Theophrastus reverts to a third-person account of
female vices, and one would expect the Wife therefore to drum up further
examples of male failings from other sources. Instead, she continues to follow
the Theophrastan model, this time passing off his antifeminist observations as
quotations of what her husbands had said to her when drunk. Her phraseology
often echoes the expansions of Theophrastan material in Jean de Meun or
Deschamps or Matheolus's *Lamentations*, but comparison with the original is
the most succinct way of indicating the close relations between the Wife's
speech and this traditional material.

Theophrastus: 'To support a poor wife is hard work; to put up with a
rich one, is torment.'

The Wife: 'Thou seist to me it is a greet meschief
To wedde a povre womman, for costage;
And if that she be riche, of heigh parage,
Thanne seistow that it is a tormentrie
To suffre hire pride and hire malencolie.'
(248–52)

Theophrastus: In addition, there is no choice in the case of a wife: she must
be taken as she is. Whether she is bad-tempered, stupid, deformed, proud,
has bad breath – whatever her fault, we find out after marriage. A horse, an
ass, an ox, a dog, even the basest slaves, clothes, kettles, wooden stools,
cups, and earthenware jugs, are all tried out first and then bought; only a
wife is not displayed before she is wed, lest she fail to give satisfaction.

The Wife: 'Thou seist that oxen, asses, hors, and houndes,
They been assayed at diverse stoundes;
Bacyns, lavours, er that men hem bye,
Spoones and stooles, and al swich housbondrye,
And so been pottes, clothes, and array;
But folk of wyves maken noon assay,
Til they be wedded – olde dotard shrewe! –
And thanne, seistow, we wol oure vices shewe.'
(285–92)

Multiplying examples would only repeat the point. When the Wife has
exhausted Theophrastus, she moves on to the rest of Jerome's text, and sup-
plements it with snippets from his vernacular imitators. The exact source is not
important; what matters is that her long speech is almost entirely made up of
the commonplaces of antifeminist tradition, presented as what her husbands
allegedly said to her. This is emphasized by the obsessive repetition in varied
forms of the phrase 'thou seyst' ('seistow', 'thou seydest'); it recurs twenty-
five times in all in nearly a hundred and fifty lines. Almost all the Wife's tirade
against her husbands, apart from the first twelve lines, is reported speech –
nothing other than what *they* are supposed to have said to *her*. Male attacks on
women become the very substance of a female attack on men. The Wife uses
antifeminist satire as a blunt instrument with which to beat her husbands into
submission (Murtaugh, 1971, 476; cf. Knapp, 1986, 391).

There is no evidence, of course, that these particular husbands ever did say
any of the things the Wife puts into their mouths; her triumphant conclusion –
'And al was fals' (382) – acknowledges this. But by the same token, there is no
real evidence that the Wife actually did the things that are alleged of women.
The Wife's speech is performative rather than constative; it does not document

the realities of an individual marital relationship (as is already evident from the fact that it is addressed indifferently to *three* husbands). The Wife's constant use of the plural – 'we wyves', 'us', 'oure' – dissolves her individual situation into a general female experience, and acts as a constant reminder of the anti-feminist commonplaces on which she draws. No matter that these particular husbands never made these accusations, their hackneyed character is evidence in itself that plenty of other men did.

The double structure of the Wife's tirade, like the double structure of the encomium on marriage in the *Merchant's Tale*, thus turns out to be the most important thing about it. Within the speech of the Wife bullying her husbands, we can hear the speeches of countless husbands bullying their wives. Her tirade thus functions simultaneously as a demonstration of female bullying and a witness to masculine oppression. What is more, it suggests that female bullying and masculine oppression have a strangely symbiotic relationship: each feeds off the other. The Wife uses the traditional masculine attacks on her sex as a way of legitimizing her own tirade; her husbands (or male readers) could equally well appeal to her scolding as evidence of the contumaciousness of women.

The double structure of the Wife's speech thus has a meaning of far wider import than its role in the Wife's individual experience. And yet it plays a crucial role in creating our sense of the Wife as a living individual. For what it demonstrates is her *interaction* with the stereotypes of her sex, and it is in this interaction that we feel the three-dimensional reality of her existence. That is, she does not live in the insulated laboratory world of literature, where she is no more than a literary object, unconscious of the interpretations foisted upon her; she is conceived as a woman who lives in the real world, in full awareness of the antifeminist literature that purports to describe and criticize her behaviour, and she has an attitude to *it* just as it has an attitude to her. On a previous occasion I have commented on a similar example of individual interaction with class satire in the *General Prologue*, where we are told that the Monk doesn't give a 'pulled hen' for the proverb that declares a monk out of his cloister to be like a fish out of water. In other satirists, we find the proverb used to comment on monks; only in Chaucer does the Monk comment on the proverb (Mann, 1973, 31). Neither the Monk nor the Wife of Bath simply *is*; they are also conscious of what others suppose them to be, and their own individuality has to work itself out through this consciousness.

In the last section of the Wife's *Prologue*, however, the antifeminist stereotypes reassert their power over the woman's life, as she is forced to listen to her husband's endless readings from his 'book of wikked wyves'.[22] Like the wife of Le Jaloux, she is forced to listen to a catalogue of female vices, but here the emphasis is on the book as source of and authority for this antifeminist attack. Lee Patterson sees the Wife's attempt to put an end to this torment by tearing three

---

22   For an edition and translation of the three most important texts in Jankin's book and a detailed discussion of their medieval manuscript transmission, see Hanna and Lawler, 1997.

pages out of Jankin's book as a gallant bid for feminine freedom which is nevertheless doomed to failure: although 'in the [Wife's] Prologue clerical antifeminism is appropriated by a woman's voice in order to articulate feminist truths', nevertheless the Wife 'remains confined within the prison house of masculine language; she brilliantly rearranges and deforms her authorities to enable them to disclose new areas of experience, but she remains dependent on them for her voice' (1983, 682; cf. Gottfried, 1984–5). There is a great deal of truth in this comment – as I suggested earlier, Chaucer could not invent a new 'female language', and sensibly did not try to do so – but I think it fails to take account of the degree to which the Wife's *Prologue* is designed precisely to make the reader conscious of the confining nature of 'the prison house of masculine language'. The Wife's tirade to her old husbands, with its repeated 'thou seyest', is the first step to this end, yet it remains open to a male reading as well as a female one. Just as the marriage encomium in the *Merchant's Tale* can be read from either a male or a female point of view, so in the Wife's speech to her old husbands we can listen to the female nagging of its frame or the male nagging of its content, as our bias leads us. But when she recounts Jankin's readings from his antifeminist book, there is no choice and no escape: we listen to these readings in the Wife's position – that is, *as a woman*. The repeated phrases here are 'Tho redde he me', 'tolde he me', 'he tolde me it', all emphasizing the presence of the listening woman.

> 'Tho redde he me how Sampson loste his heres:
> Slepynge, his lemman kitte it with hire sheres;
> Thurgh which treson loste he bothe his yen.
>   Tho redde he me, if that I shal nat lyen,
> Of Hercules and of his Dianyre,
> That caused hym to sette hymself afyre ...
>   He tolde me eek for what occasioun
> Amphiorax at Thebes loste his lyf ...
> Of Lyvia tolde he me, and of Lucye ...
> Thanne tolde he me how oon Latumyus
> Compleyned unto his felawe Arrius ... .'
>   (721–6, 740–1, 747, 757–8)

In this string of narrative *exempla* and proverbs, second-person invective disguises itself as third-person statement; phrases such as 'a womman', 'an angry wyf', claim the authority of impersonal generalisation, but they mean '*you*', as their effect on the Wife indicates.

> 'Bet is,' quod he, 'thyn habitacioun
> Be with a leon or a foul dragoun,
> Than with a womman usynge for to chyde.
> Bet is,' quod he, 'hye in the roof abyde,
> Than with an angry wyf doun in the hous;
> They been so wikked and contrarious,

> They haten that hir housbondes loven ay.'
> He seyde, 'A womman cast hir shame away,
> Whan she cast of hir smok'; and forthermo,
> 'A fair womman, but she be chaast also,
> Is lyk a gold ryng in a sowes nose.'
> Who wolde wene, or who wolde suppose,
> The wo that in myn herte was, and pyne? (775–87)

With her three old husbands, the Wife was in control, manipulating antifeminist satire to serve her own ends; here she is reduced to its helpless object. The point about this passage is that it forces us to *experience* the 'prison house of masculine language'; vain attempts to fantasize about life outside the prison walls are beside the point until the key is turned.

Chaucer's master-stroke in demonstrating the absoluteness of this confinement is his dramatisation of the fact that the more vigorously the Wife asserts herself in opposition to traditional antifeminism, the more she conforms to its stereotyped image of her. As she gleefully uses it to berate her old husbands, she appears before us as its typical representative: rebellious, nagging, domineering. Similarly, Jankin's stream of antifeminist abuse succeeds in *provoking* a violent outburst of the anger which antifeminist satire insists is a particular failing of women. In both cases antifeminist literature becomes a dynamic element in the very situations it purports to observe dispassionately from the outside. Jerome might well protest that what he meant by his work was simply to defend virginity, but such protests would be futile; the meaning of his work is fixed in the 'gloss' his male readers bring to it.

If, therefore, the *Wife of Bath's Prologue* is largely constructed of antifeminist satire, this in no way implies Chaucer's endorsement of it. A lesser writer than Chaucer might have attempted to ignore the antifeminist stereotypes, to imagine a female experience as yet unrecorded in literature. But the attempt to escape stereotypes – as Chaucer must have known – leads only to different stereotypes, created in the mirror-image of their predecessors, as the Ovidian heroines reverse the picture of the shrew. The process is evident in the way that feminism has rejected the old stereotypes, only to lend its energies to the identification of 'role-models', which are, as Christopher Ricks points out, merely stereotypes you approve of (1988, 118). Ricks's further remarks on the place of stereotypes in art are highly pertinent to what I have been arguing about their role in the *Wife of Bath's Prologue*:

> It is true that art, being fine, cannot be simply crude, but it would not follow from this that stereotypes should not have a place in art in their crude state, since there is no reason why the stereotyping should not itself then be 'placed' by the work of art, contemplated with 'a suspicious and interrogating eye' and understood. This would not be the same as making the state of the stereotype itself uncrude, but would be the provision of an uncrude setting, context, or ethos. This would be to engage something

intrinsic not only to the stereotyped character but also to our own ways with stereotypes. (118–19)

Writing the truth of woman's existence, in the *Wife of Bath's Prologue*, means not turning one's back on stereotypes, but accepting that their existence is the centrally important and interesting fact to be confronted. It means acknowledging the power they exert even as they are resisted, because they will define the form of the resistance (Hanning, 1985, 19). Chaucer could not plumb the unrecorded secrets of woman's existence, but he *could* anatomize the literary stereotypes which set the terms in which male–female relationships were played out, and he could question the male writer's role as the 'auctoritee' that supports them. And he could, in the Wife of Bath, give us the imagined representation of an individual engagement with these stereotypes and their absorption into an individual life.

The *Wife of Bath's Prologue* does not, however, end in this state of unresolved hostility. The quarrel that breaks out when the Wife attacks Jankin's book ends in his capitulation and the establishment of marital harmony. The suspicion of sentimentality in this unexpected 'happy ending' is hard to avoid, and it is worth quoting the passage in its entirety so that the mechanisms by which the final accord is reached can be seen in detail.

> And whan I saugh he wolde nevere fyne
> To reden on this cursed book al nyght,
> Al sodeynly thre leves have I plyght
> Out of his book, right as he radde, and eke
> I with my fest so took hym on the cheke
> That in oure fyr he fil bakward adoun.
> And he up stirte as dooth a wood leoun,
> And with his fest he smoot me on the heed
> That in the floor I lay as I were deed.
> And whan he saugh how stille that I lay,
> He was agast and wolde han fled his way,
> Til atte laste out of my swogh I breyde.
> 'O! hastow slayn me, false theef?' I seyde,
> 'And for my land thus hastow mordred me?
> Er I be deed, yet wol I kisse thee.'
> And neer he cam, and kneled faire adoun,
> And seyde, 'Deere suster Alisoun,
> As help me God, I shal thee nevere smyte!
> That I have doon, it is thyself to wyte.
> Foryeve it me, and that I thee biseke!'
> And yet eftsoones I hitte hym on the cheke,
> And seyde, 'Theef, thus muchel am I wreke;
> Now wol I dye, I may no lenger speke.'

> But atte laste, with muchel care and wo,
> We fille acorded by us selven two.
> He yaf me al the bridel in myn hond,
> To han the governance of hous and lond,
> And of his tonge, and of his hond also;
> And made hym brenne his book anon right tho.
> And whan that I hadde geten unto me,
> By maistrie, al the soveraynetee,
> And that he seyde, 'Myn owene trewe wyf,
> Do as thee lust the terme of al thy lyf;
> Keep thyn honour, and keep eek myn estaat' –
> After that day we hadden never debaat.
> God help me so, I was to hym as kynde
> As any wyf from Denmark unto Ynde,
> And also trewe, and so was he to me. (788–825)

The first observation to be made about this quarrel is that it is completely convincing *as* a quarrel, and what makes it so is its sense of emotional flux, which manifests itself as a constant modulation between aggression and pathos. Finding herself prone on the floor, the Wife abandons belligerence for plaintiveness; she seizes the chance to exercise the moral superiority of the obvious victim, which Jankin, aghast at the effects of his own violence, is obliged to recognize. But he cannot resist inserting into his apology the defence that she has brought his attack upon herself ('it is thyself to wyte'). In retaliation the Wife briefly reasserts her rights in the quarrel by means of the token blow on the cheek which acts as an emblematic form of vengeance ('thus muchel am I wreke'), although immediately indicating her reluctance to revive hostilities by lapsing back into pathos ('Now wol I dye').

The same alternation of assertiveness and conciliation marks the resolution of the quarrel between Pluto and Proserpina in the *Merchant's Tale*. Proserpina's long harangue having worn Pluto into submission, he nevertheless feels obliged to salvage some remnants of his dignity by asserting that his original decree shall stand:

> 'Dame,' quod this Pluto, 'be no lenger wrooth;
> I yeve it up! But sith I swoor myn ooth
> That I wolde graunten hym his sighte ageyn,
> My word shal stonde, I warne yow certeyn.
> I am a kyng; it sit me noght to lye.' (2311–15)

Proserpina responds with a matching assertion of her own dignity and a reaffirmation of her determination to nullify Pluto's decree by her own assistance to May:

> 'And I,' quod she, 'a queene of Fayerye!
> Hir answere shal she have, I undertake.' (2316–17)

But honour thus satisfied, she shows that she too knows the advantages of appeasement:

> 'Lat us namoore wordes heerof make;
> For sothe, I wol no lenger yow contrarie.' (2318–19)

Like the quarrel between Jankin and the Wife of Bath, this quarrel shows an instinctive oscillation between self-vindication and placatory assuagement. Mutual peace is achieved by a delicate process of attunement which calibrates defence of one's own wounded feelings with an acknowledgement of the other's peaceable overtures.

The second notable thing about the quarrel between the Wife of Bath and Jankin is that the Wife's victory is won not by aggression but by pathos. It is her plaintive speech of martyred affection – 'Er I be deed, yet wol I kisse thee' – that opens the way for Jankin's apology and acknowledgement of answering affection. Sentimentality is again excluded by the comic aspects of this plangency; not only is she clearly milking the pathos for all it is worth, she is also sufficiently in command of her wits to increase the moral superiority she has already won by reminding Jankin of the material benefits that her death will bring him. But the knowingness behind the pathos simply reinforces the point: the power of the underdog is real enough to be exploited by a good tactician. And what is acted – even what is over-acted – can nevertheless correspond to a real feeling: the extremity of the situation allows the Wife and Jankin the relief of abandoning confrontation for their own version of tenderness.

It is this relief that makes Jankin's final surrender into something other than a simple example of triumph for the shrew. His surrender of 'maistrye' is met by the Wife's subsequent fidelity and kindness. We may be tempted to write this off as a travestied version of marital harmony which goes against all medieval orthodoxy on the rightful and necessary ascendancy of the husband. Yet if this is a comic version of marital happiness, it is not *ipso facto* a travesty: elsewhere in Chaucer's works, we find the same surrender of masculine 'maistrye' presented in all seriousness as the foundation on which conjugal harmony is built. It is to Chaucer's various attempts to envisage what form an ideal relationship between a man and a woman would take, that I shall turn in the next chapter.

3

The Surrender of *Maistrye*

Love is a thyng as any spirit free.
Wommen, of kynde, desiren libertee,
And nat to been constreyned as a thral;
And so doon men, if I sooth seyen shal.
(*Franklin's Tale* 767–70)

The tale that the Wife of Bath goes on to tell repeats on a larger scale the pattern of surrender and reconciliation which is traced in miniature form at the end of her *Prologue*. It begins with a manifestation of masculine 'maistrye' in its ugliest form: the knight's casual rape of a young girl. It ends with the rapist's humble surrender of 'maistrye' to the old wife who has been inflicted on him as punishment:

'Thanne have I gete of yow maistrie,' quod she,
'Syn I may chese and governe as me lest?'
'Ye, certes, wyf,' quod he, 'I holde it best.' (1236–8)

This time, male surrender leads not only to marital peace and harmony, but also to the magical transformation of the ugly old hag into a beautiful young wife. Miraculous as it is, this transformation is no whit more miraculous than the transformation of a rapist into a meekly submissive husband; the magical change in the woman is merely the external projection of this even more magical change in the man.

The transformation of the rapist into an obedient husband is something that *can* only be told as fairy-tale (unless, as with Pluto and Proserpina, it is told with a comedy that likewise places it beyond the reach of serious representationalism). That is to say, the tale is not to be interpreted in realistic terms as a serious proposal for the rehabilitation of sexual offenders; rather it is (like all good fairy-tales) the imaginative embodiment of aspirations towards a transfigured reality, a vision of the way things might be. It addresses itself not to the pathology of rape, but to the imaginative representation of the processes which male psychology (in its social rather than individual form) would have to undergo to purge itself of the drive towards 'oppressioun' (889). It moves beyond the stories of rape in the *Legend of Good Women* by widening its vision beyond the horror of the crime to ask in what way men would have to change for rape to cease to exist.

The essential element in the process of transformation is the knight's subjection to female power, which begins when he is handed over to the queen
'al at hir wille,/To chese wheither she wolde hym save or spille' (897–8). It is
suggested less often nowadays than used to be the case – one is glad to note –
that the pleas of the queen and the ladies for the knight's life represent
Chaucer's acquiescence in the view that 'every woman secretly loves a rapist';
but it is a suggestion worth recording precisely because it reveals the power of
the male fantasy with which the tale contends. It is a fantasy both demonstrated and encouraged in the medieval French pastourelle, in which knights
similarly rape passing country-girls with surprising frequency: once the act is
accomplished, the girl's screams and struggles turn into sighs of pleasure and
requests to come back soon (Gravdal, 1991, 104–21). The *Wife of Bath's Tale*
deliberately overturns this male fantasy, shattering the pornographic dream of
the woman who craves sexual enslavement with the queen's retributory assertion of control over the knight. The punishment she devises is not designed
to 'let him off lightly', but to act as an educative process which will eradicate
the male mentality that produced the crime; it initiates, that is, a relentless
'feminization' of the knight that continues to the very end of the tale. For the
queen grants him only a temporary stay of execution, unless he can tell her
'What thyng is it that wommen moost desiren' (905). It is a punishment that
fits the knight's crime, since the question of what women desire is presumably
something that never enters a rapist's head. As Marshall Leicester has pointed
out, it also puts the knight 'in a position more familiar to women, who have to
cater to male desires' (1984, 160). The logic which shapes the plot of this tale
already begins to be apparent, and becomes even clearer if it is compared with
the different versions represented in its analogues, where the task imposed on
the hero follows from no original fault on his part. 'The fact that only in [the
Wife's] version is the knight a rapist means that only in her version is the quest
for what women most desire linked specifically and logically to the knight's
character and to the question of male–female relations' (ibid.).

For a whole year, the knight is compelled to search for the answer to the
queen's question, and when he finds it, it turns out to run completely counter
to his masculine self-interest:

> 'My lige lady, generally,' quod he,
> 'Wommen desiren to have sovereynetee
> As wel over hir housbond as hir love,
> And for to been in maistrie hym above.
> This is youre mooste desir, thogh ye me kille.
> Dooth as yow list; I am heer at youre wille.' (1037–42)

The knight's acknowledgement of the female desire for 'maistrye' saves his
life, but does not win him his freedom, for he has bought his knowledge at the
price of his surrender to another woman – the ugly old lady who has told him
the answer on condition that he promises to grant her whatever request she

makes once he is released. When she requires the knight to fulfil this promise by marrying her, he is subjected to a punishment that fits his crime even more closely: the forced marriage with the foul old hag is a fantasy realisation of rape-in-reverse. Like the maiden he violated, the knight is 'constreyned' (1071) to sexual congress (although, since his promise was voluntarily made, female domination allows his will a greater role than he allowed his female victim). Yet this is not all: he must also bring himself to *accept* his undesirable partner, and to yield himself to her 'governance' with a speech fit for an adoring lover addressing his mistress:

> 'My lady and my love, and wyf so deere,
> I put me in youre wise governance;
> Cheseth youreself which may be moost plesance
> And moost honour to yow and me also.
> I do no fors the wheither of the two,
> For as yow liketh, it suffiseth me.' (1230–5)

It is a speech that represents the internalisation of the answer he gave in the queen's court. Verbal repetition is not enough; it is an answer he has to live out experientially for the full release of its salvific power.

Fairy-tale though it is, this tale avoids the temptation to dilute or sentimentalize reality. Not only does it show us, on the male side, an Arthurian knight who is capable of rape; on the female side too there is an unromantic candour in admitting the full range of possible answers to the question of what women want. The suggestions made in answer to the knight's enquiries would not look out of place in Jankyn's 'book of wikked wyves':

> Somme seyde wommen loven best richesse,
> Somme seyde honour, somme seyde jolynesse,
> Somme riche array, somme seyden lust abedde,
> And oftetyme to be wydwe and wedde.
> Somme seyde that oure hertes been moost esed
> Whan that we been yflatered and yplesed.
> He gooth ful ny the sothe, I wol nat lye,
> A man shal wynne us best with flaterye,
> And with attendance and with bisynesse
> Been we ylymed, bothe moore and lesse.
>   And somme seyen that we loven best
> For to be free and do right as us lest,
> And that no man repreve us of oure vice ... (925–37)

The only suggestion flattering to women – that they love to be 'stable' and to keep secrets (945–7) – is clearly ironical, and is indignantly rejected as untrue by the Wife herself (949–50). The successful answer by which the knight saves his life would be equally at home in antifeminist literature, the very aim of which is to unmask and repudiate the female desire for 'maistrye'.

Yet the surprise of this tale – a surprise from which a large part of its power derives – is that these cynical answers to the question of what women desire are *not* introduced in order to be derided and dismissed. On the contrary, the tale legitimizes the female desire for 'maistrye' which the antifeminist writers view with such fear and hostility, by making it the just response to male 'oppressioun'. The story obliges the reader to endorse the knight's surrender to female 'maistrye' as the condition of his transformation and the tale's happy ending. And just as the fairy-tale task of finding out what women most desire is rooted in a realistic sense of the nature of his crime, so the fairy-tale choice which his new wife presents to him is an emblematized version of a *real* choice that confronts men: will he have his wife old, ugly and faithful, or young, beautiful and attractive to other men? Again, these are alternatives that are glumly rehearsed in antifeminist literature from Theophrastus onwards, as the Wife of Bath makes clear in her Prologue:

> And if that she be fair, thou verray knave,
> Thou seyst that every holour wol hire have;
> She may no while in chastitee abyde,
> That is assailled upon ech a syde ...
> And if that she be foul, thou seist that she
> Coveiteth every man that she may se,
> For as a spanyel she wol on hym lepe,
> Til that she fynde som man hire to chepe ...
> And seyst it is an hard thing for to welde
> A thyng that no man wole, his thankes, helde.
> (253–6, 265–8, 271–2; cf. *Adv. Jov.* I.47)

In the Wife's tale, however, the male egoism that generates these petulant complaints is summoned to acknowledge them as a derivative of its own selfishness by having them presented as a *choice* – a choice that forces the man to take responsibility for its results, rather than shifting the blame on to women. The only security lies in possession of that which neither he nor anyone else desires; otherwise, to accept possession means to accept risk. Acceptance of happiness is acceptance of its possible loss; 'Whoso wol han lief, he lief moot lete', in the words of the medieval proverb quoted by Criseyde (IV 1585). The problem of female fidelity is redefined as the problem of male possessiveness, and the male protagonist is forced to confront it on behalf of his sex.

The 'antifeminist' elements in the tale, then, so far from undermining its seriousness, are the most convincing testimony to it; they constitute the force behind the tale's challenge to male domination. When the knight surrenders to female 'maistrye', he surrenders not to the romanticized woman projected by male desire, but to woman conceived in the pessimistic terms of antifeminism. If he then finds, to his amazed delight, that his wife will be 'bothe fair and good' (1241), the route to this discovery is designed to underline the fact that this good fortune comes gratuitously, as a gift; it lies beyond what can be claimed as a right. The transformation also implies that the condition for the

fulfilment of male desires is their relinquishment: it is the knight's renunciation of his own demands that magically releases his bride's transformation
into a form that satisfies his desires.

The ending of the tale has been accused of wish-fulfilment in two diametric-
ally opposite directions. On the one hand, it is often said to be a fictional sublimation of the Wife's own desire for 'maistrye', the tale as a whole functioning
as a subterfuge by which she legitimates her own domineering impulses.[1] More
recently, the final transformation has been interpreted as a gratification of *male*
desires: the knight surrenders 'maistrye' only to have it promptly handed back
again, in the willing obedience of his wife. Masculine surrender creates, not the
'new woman', but a perfect incarnation of the conventional feminine ideal as
defined by man (Patterson, 1983, 682–3). What makes these contradictory
interpretations possible is also what makes them inaccurate: the magical happy
ending is a visionary glimpse of *mutuality* in male-female relationships. If male
surrender is the condition of female obedience, then the whole meaning of
'obedience' is transformed. It becomes an emotional response rather than a
formal obligation. The change is marked by the use of the word 'obeyed' in
a sexual context that gives it wholly new connotations:

> A thousand tyme a-rewe he gan hire kisse,
> And she obeyed hym in every thyng
> That myghte doon hym plesance or likyng. (1254–6)

'Obedience' here is not a response to directives, but an expression of the
instinctive desire to give pleasure, as it is in the love-making of Troilus and
Criseyde, where 'ech of hem gan otheres lust obeye' (III 1690). The pleasure
taken in the lover's body is a pleasure given *to* the lover's body; the other's
pleasure becomes one's own desire.

The female struggle for 'maistrye' (in both *Prologue* and tale) is a struggle
towards this vision of mutuality, which strips obedience of its oppression by
making it an emotional response which matches and balances male surrender.
It is a vision that cannot be reduced to a personal manifesto of the Wife's, as is
apparent when her voice makes itself unmistakably heard in the brisk reduc-
tion of it to one more female victory in the battle between the sexes:

> And thus they lyve unto hir lyves ende
> In parfit joye; and Jhesu Crist us sende
> Housbondes meeke, yonge, and fressh abedde,
> And grace t'overbyde hem that we wedde;
> And eek I praye Jhesu shorte hir lyves
> That noght wol be governed by hir wyves;
> And olde and angry nygardes of dispence,
> God sende hem soone verray pestilence! (1257–64)

---

1   See the references assembled by Leicester (1984, n. 2).

This robust epilogue divides the Wife from the tale, pointing up its existence as an autonomously coherent entity. Yet in one important sense it is incomplete: its 'happy ending' is only a 'happy beginning'. The surrender of 'maistrye', as Marshall Leicester observes, 'is where everything that is important about marriage begins, not where it ends' (1984, 173). It is in the *Franklin's Tale* that Chaucer attempts to carry the story further by placing the surrender of 'maistrye' at the beginning of the tale and asking what happens next. But in order to understand its picture of marriage, we need to give some attention to courtship, where the problem of working out a relation free of 'maistrye' is first faced. It is in *Troilus and Criseyde* that we can see Chaucer's attempt to give imaginative embodiment to the solving of that problem.

The problem of courtship is precisely a problem of mutuality: if the impetus towards the avowal and consummation of love is not exactly equal on both sides, one or other of the lovers must assume the initiative and thus run the risk of coercion, of imposing desire on the other, instead of meeting it in the other. Modern eroticism submerges this problem in the myth of the Simultaneous Kiss (bowdlerized correlative of the Simultaneous Orgasm), a familiar cliché of the movies. A sudden silence falls in conversation (best of all in a quarrel, which creates an appropriate emotional intensity); from opposite sides of the screen, male and female faces move slowly and in perfect synchronisation to its centre, where they meet in a long kiss. The kiss functions simultaneously as avowal and consummation; one-sided advances, clumsy gestures, embarrassment, the threat of rejection, are bypassed in one simple moment of physical contact. The silence of the kiss is essential to sustaining the fiction of equality: the perfect balance of physical conjunction is unsullied by the possible imbalances in its meaning – invitation to a one-night stand? confession of undying love? The verbal exchanges necessary to clarify such questions are relegated to an off-screen existence.

It is important to distinguish this strategic wordlessness, which reduces the scene to a mere icon of consummated desire, from the wordlessness that is in itself an index of feeling and depth of commitment, a tribute to the awesomeness of the revelatory moment. This is, for example, its function in the scene which represents the nearest approach in medieval literature to the Simultaneous Kiss, the kiss that seals the love between Dante's famous lovers, Paolo and Francesca.

'One day we were reading for our delight of Lancelot, how love held him bound. We were alone, without foreboding. Several times did that reading cause our eyes to meet, and take the colour from our faces, but one moment alone it was that overcame us; when we read that the longed-for smile was kissed by so great a lover, this one, who never shall be parted from me, kissed my mouth all trembling. A Galehaut was the book and he that wrote it; that day we read in it no farther.'   (*Inferno* V 127–38)

Francesca's story is an answer to Dante's question: 'how and by what means did love grant you to know your uncertain ('dubbiosi') desires?' – that is, their desires were 'dubbiosi' to themselves as well as hidden from the other. The agent of revelation is the book, which works simultaneously on both; it assumes the coercive role of pandar (Galehaut being the intermediary between Lancelot and Guinevere), and places both lovers in an equivalent position, 'conquered' ('ci vinse') by the love that the narrative discovers within them. What confirms this equivalence is the phrase 'tutto tremante', grammatically suspended between Paolo and Francesca like the vibrating current of their desires: 'la bocca mi baciò tutto tremante'. Female trembling realizes itself in the man, emptying the kiss of sexual aggression and making it instead a testimony of vulnerability equal to the woman's. Yet the initiatory step remains the man's; Dante has even altered his source, where it is Guinevere who kisses Lancelot (Perella, 1969, 153), so as to make it conform to the 'normal' pattern of male action and female response. Chaucer, like the author of the *Lancelot*, eliminates even this last vestige of masculine predominance; Criseyde, like Guinevere, takes the lead in her role as 'lady', and shows no embarrassment in sealing the new relationship with her lover with a kiss (III 182).

The reverent humility which Lancelot and Troilus manifest towards their ladies is often ascribed to adherence to the so-called 'code of courtly love'. This is misleading in two respects: first, it transposes the knight's subservience to the living woman who is his mistress into his subservience to an impersonal (and mythical) code. His behaviour is seen as dictated by rules rather than by emotion, so that what it implies about male–female relationships can be safely ignored, relegated to merely antiquarian interest. Second, in the text where this 'courtly code' is supposed to be embodied, Andreas Capellanus's treatise *On Love*, the male lover shows none of the awed bashfulness of his romance counterpart. His mental contemplation of his beloved's beauty leads rapidly to action: he enlists the help of a go-between and thinks up ways to meet and talk with his lady (I.i). The model dialogues which demonstrate how to woo women of different social classes also show the male lover in an unabashed and active role, articulate and urgent in pressing his case (cf. Moi, 1986, 23–5). Expression of emotion is conspicuous by its absence: there are no sighs, tears, tremblings, swoons, no singing of songs or writing of poems – none of the behaviour which is now routinely ascribed to 'the medieval code of courtly love'. The distribution of roles in Andreas's picture of courtship in fact follows a conventional pattern: active male, passive female. Desire is masculine; woman is its object. Male humility before the female is either a passing initial phase or a polite form in which desire masks itself.

To see how the mask is thrown off, we can look to one of the best-known narratives of courtship in the Middle Ages, the *Pamphilus*. Written on the threshold of the twelfth century, this dramatized narrative, telling of Pamphilus's wooing of the beautiful Galatea, was read as a Latin school-text throughout the medieval period, and it was certainly known to Chaucer (cf. *Franklin's Tale* 1110). At the opening of the action, Pamphilus conforms to the typical image of

romantic love: he is overwhelmed by his passion, full of querulous lamentations, rendered awestruck and speechless at the sight of Galatea's beauty. Nevertheless, like Andreas's typical lover, he speedily recovers himself, urges his suit
on her, and finds a go-between who will aid his cause. The go-between arranges
a meeting between the young couple at her house, and then invents a pretext for
going out and leaving them alone together. At this point all Pamphilus's awe
and hesitancy disappear, and he declares that the time has come to enjoy the
pleasures of love. 'Why do I delay?' he asks, and pausing only long enough to
request Galatea to submit to his wishes, he proceeds briskly to action, as we can
gather from Galatea's ensuing monologue.

> Pamphilus, take your hands away! ... your efforts are useless! They won't
> get you anywhere! ... what you want, cannot be! Pamphilus, take your
> hands away! ... you're hurting your sweetheart. The old woman will come
> back any minute. – Pamphilus, take your hands away! Alas! what little
> strength women have – how easily you imprison my hands! Pamphilus,
> you're squashing my chest with yours. It's wicked and wrong to treat me
> like this. Stop! I'll scream! What are you doing? You shouldn't undress
> me! Wretch that I am, when will that treacherous old woman come back?
> *Please* get up! The whole neighbourhood will hear our struggle. That old
> woman did wrong to entrust me to you. I'll never come here again, and
> she won't deceive me a second time the way she has now. You *may* win
> the struggle, despite my resistance, but all love is at an end between us
> from now on! (681–96)

Too busy to reply, Pamphilus speaks only when it is clear that his desires have
been accomplished:

> Now let's both have a little rest, and allow our horse to pant a little after
> the race. What a black look you turn on your beloved! Why do you weep
> and wet your face with tears? I'm entirely to blame; give me whatever
> punishment you will, And let the punishment be even worse than I've
> deserved! (697–702)

There is nothing very romantic about *this* consummation. It is not, of course,
a scene of outright rape, as Galatea's protestation that she *will* scream makes
clear (why not simply scream?).[2] Pamphilus's forcefulness is based on the
familiar assumption that decorum obliges a woman to say no even when she
means yes, and that it is therefore a man's duty to save her face by taking on
himself the responsibility and guilt of copulation – as Pamphilus does. But he

---

2   This is perhaps to yield too much to the author's point of view, however; since Galatea's
precise state of mind is not of much interest to him, we are not given enough information
to form a judgement. It is certainly the case that the male attitude exhibited here by both
Pamphilus and the author is one that frequently results in rape.

takes care to implicate her in his guilt also, by blaming her beauty as the power that drove him on (703–16). And Pamphilus's resumption of humility, in his offer to bear patiently whatever punishment she gives him (703), cannot obscure the fact that with the loss of Galatea's virginity, the balance of power between them has irreversibly shifted; it is no longer for him to beg and for her to choose whether to grant or to deny. Her loss of virginity coerces her into accepting her seducer as a husband, and even into being grateful to him for marrying her – a gratitude that retrospectively legitimates male desire.

The ritually codified sexual roles observable in the *Pamphilus* – male aggression, female reluctance – do not only have a social function; they also become in themselves a source of sexual pleasure. Female reluctance feeds and heightens male desire. A poem of Peter of Blois, which is included in the fourteenth-century manuscript collection known as the Arundel Lyrics, shows sexual aggression in a form barely distinguishable from rape: not only does the male lover resort to physical force to achieve his desires, he also finds that his mistress's tears and struggles enhance his pleasure.

> Kisses wet with salty dew
> have a more exciting taste;
> they inflame me through and through,
> firing me with urgent haste.
> Thus her weeping stokes the fires
>   as my desire's
> fed by her teardrops' flavour.
> But my darling's too distressed –
>   her heaving breast
> racked with sobs – to yield to me
>   and hear my plea
>   with favour.
>
> I redouble my appeals,
> backed with kisses by the score;
> she weeps twice as hard, and deals
> more reproaches than before.
> She regards me with an eye
>   now coldly dry,
> now moist with anxious pleading.
> First she battles for release,
>   then begs for peace.
> But when I cajole and pray
>   she turns away
>   unheeding.
>
> I boldly bring some force to bear;
> it doesn't work: she grabs my hair

and beats me back;
her nails attack
        viciously.
She grimly blocks
my access, locks
        knee with knee,
and will not free
the gateway to her treasure.

But nonetheless I soldier on;
at last her opposition's gone!
        With tighter hold
my arms enfold
        hers; I pin
her down, and kiss
my captive. This
        lets me in;
and so I win
admission to love's pleasure.

Both of us enjoy the act;
and my love, with gentle tact,
doesn't chide, but kisses me
        deliciously,
                sweet and deep.

Then she offers me a smile,
somewhat tremblingly; and while
leaning back with half-closed eyes
        she faintly sighs,
                falls asleep. (trans. Adcock, no. XII, stanzas 5–10)

Like the French pastourelle, this poem feeds a male fantasy: female acquiescence retrospectively sanctions male coercion, and reveals reluctance to have been a merely ritual female role.[3]

There is thus plenty of evidence that the 'conventional' pattern of male aggression and female submission was a familiar one in medieval literature, as doubtless also in life. The reverential, hesitant lover who meets us in courtly romance is not, that is, a mere reflex of medieval social practice; he is the

---

[3]   Cf. Gravdal's quotation (1991, 167, n. 8) from a thirteenth-century book of instruction in the art of love, which teaches the young male protégé 'that young women are so well-bred that they must be taken by force because they are too ashamed to make their desires known'. Christine de Pisan protests against the male claim 'that many women want to be raped and that it does not bother them at all to be raped by men even when they verbally protest' (*City of Ladies*, trans. Richards, 161–2).

product of conscious authorial choice – a choice dictated, in Chaucer's case at least, by the desire to purge the process of courtship of its coercive elements. For Chaucer, the aggressive male wooer belongs in fabliau, not in romance (unless he is, as Diomede is, an anti-hero). It is in the *Miller's Tale*, not in *Troilus and Criseyde*, that the influence of the *Pamphilus* is most clearly perceptible: Nicholas's first approach to Alison is founded on the same paradoxical combination of physical aggression and verbal romanticism that Pamphilus shows to Galatea:[4]

> And prively he caughte hire by the queynte,
> And seyde, 'Ywis, but if ich have my wille,
> For deerne love of thee, lemman, I spille.'
> And heeld hire harde by the haunchebones,
> And seyde, 'Lemman, love me al atones,
> Or I wol dyen, also God me save!'
> And she sproong as a colt dooth in the trave,
> And with hir heed she wryed faste awey,
> And seyde, 'I wol nat kisse thee, by my fey!
> Why, lat be!' quod she. 'Lat be, Nicholas,
> Or I wol crie "out, harrow" and "allas"!
> Do wey youre handes, for youre curteisye!'
>   This Nicholas gan mercy for to crye,
> And spak so faire, and profred him so faste,
> That she hir love hym graunted atte laste. (3276–90)

Although Chaucer criticism has never taken note of the fact, Alison's shrill 'Do wey youre handes' is an exact replica of Galatea's repeated 'take your hands away' ('tolle manus'). Like Galatea, Alison threatens that she *will* cry 'out, harrow' and 'allas', without immediately doing so. Ritualized male aggression meets ritualized female reluctance – indeed, with its own distorted chivalrousness, it is designed to allow that reluctance expression and so preserve the fiction that the woman yields to the man's sexual desire, not her own. The flowery language with which Nicholas's physical aggression is accompanied is also designed to support this fiction: it is the condition that 'nice' women exact as a sign that they are not easy game. But flowery language is not enough on its own, as Absalon finds out later in the tale; male desire must at the same time express itself with an insistence strong enough to carry the burden of responsibility for the sexual act.

This brilliant little scene in the *Miller's Tale* shows Chaucer's shrewd awareness of the sexual games people play. In *Troilus and Criseyde*, he sets himself the far harder task of plotting the development of a relationship which is liberated from these ritually codified sexual roles, and yet at the same time

4   Donaldson ([1951] 1970) shows that Nicholas's speech draws on conventional romantic phraseology.

sensitive to the real power-structures they embody.[5] In the early part of the poem, Criseyde is shown as fully alive to her vulnerability to male coercion – not only the general vulnerability of a woman to the physically and socially more powerful male, but also the special vulnerability created by her position as a traitor's daughter whose security in Troy depends on Hector's protection. As we have already seen, she is conscious that one of the arguments against rejecting Troilus's love out of hand is the danger of making an enemy of the king's son (II 708–14). But the most potent argument against yielding to love is her fear of losing the liberty from male control which she currently enjoys: complacent satisfaction in her independence of choice and action leads directly to her alarm at the possibility of its loss.

> 'I am myn owne womman, wel at ese –
> I thank it God – as after myn estat,
> Right yong, and stonde unteyd in lusty leese,
> Withouten jalousie or swich debat:
> Shal noon housbonde seyn to me "Chek mat!"
> For either they ben ful of jalousie,
> Or maisterfull, or loven novelrie ...
>
> ... 'Allas! Syn I am free,
> Sholde I now love, and put in jupartie
> My sikernesse, and thrallen libertee?
> Allas, how dorst I thenken that folie?' (750–6, 771–4)

For Criseyde at this point, surrendering to love means surrendering to male power.

The immediate answer to her fears is the song sung by her niece Antigone – a song composed by 'the goodlieste mayde/Of gret estat in al the town of Troye' (880–1) – which proclaims that love seems to be 'thraldom' only to those who have not experienced it (855–61). But Chaucer has already taken pains to show that such fears are, in this case, groundless; so far from aiming to 'thrallen' Criseyde's liberty, Troilus is himself held as 'thral lowe in destresse' by 'the fyr of love', which knows no respect for his 'blood roial', 'His vertu or his excellent prowesse' (I 435–41). Love has dissolved everyday power-structures and replaced them with its own:

> And to the God of Love thus seyde he
> With pitous vois, 'O lord, now youres is
> My spirit, which that oughte youres be.
> Yow thanke I, lord, that han me brought to this.
> But wheither goddesse or womman, iwis,
> She be, I not, which that ye do me serve;
> But as hire man I wol ay lyve and sterve.

---

[5]   The following analysis covers some of the same ground as my article 'Troilus' Swoon' (1980).

> Ye stonden in hire eighen myghtily,
> As in a place unto youre vertu digne;
> Wherfore, lord, if my service or I
> May liken yow, so beth to me benigne;
> For myn estat roial I here resigne
> Into hire hond, and with ful humble chere
> Bicome hir man, as to my lady dere.' (I 421–34)

If the language of homage and service in these lines has a history in literary convention, Chaucer nevertheless here makes plain the human feeling that this convention was devised to express: the sense of surrender, not only to the adored human being, but also to an emotional force that subsumes the individual will into its own powerful movement.

This formal surrender to the God of Love follows directly on the song which expresses Troilus's paradoxical sense of being coerced and yet willing his own coercion. If the sufferings of love are pleasurable to him, why does he lament them? How could they have so strong a hold over him unless he consents to it? And if he consents, surely he should not complain (407–15). The image in which he expresses his condition is the image of the rudderless boat, tossed endlessly on the sea.

> ... 'Thus possed to and fro,
> Al sterelees withinne a boot am I
> Amydde the see, bitwixen wyndes two,
> That in contrarie stonden evere mo.' (I 415–18)

The image, again, is a traditional one, but Chaucer's narrative shows us the lover 'rediscovering' such traditional metaphors under the impulse of feeling. And what the metaphor expresses about the experience of falling in love is not at all the sense of entering a world regulated by a 'code', by rules and social conventions; on the contrary, it is an experience that casts the lover adrift, that removes his control over his own direction even as it orients him decisively in terms of a new allegiance that carries him with the force of a current to an unknown goal. The so-called 'passivity' of Troilus is in truth a magnanimous surrender to this overwhelming experience. For Troilus, Criseyde is not a pleasure-object, to be enjoyed as quickly as possible; she is a quasi-divinity who exerts power over his life by virtue of her simple existence (432–4). Thus if, like the lover in Andreas Capellanus's treatise, he re-creates his mistress's beauty in his mind and ponders how he may constrain ('arten') her to love him (386–8), these meditations do not result, as they do with Andreas's lover, in a brisk search for a go-between, but in the expressions of surrender we have just examined. When he is first brought face-to-face with Criseyde, Troilus does not woo her with the articulate urgency of a Pamphilus or one of Andreas's model lovers; although he has a carefully prepared speech in readiness, he forgets it all under the emotional shock of hearing his lady refer to *his* 'lordshipe' over *her*, and beg him for continuance of it (III 76–84). Nothing could be farther from his mind than the notion that he might hold a dominant position in their relationship; his highest ambition is to be allowed 'to don yow my servise' (III 133). It is on this basis that their relationship is formally established, with Criseyde's stipulation that although he is a king's son, he 'shal namore han sovereignete/Of me in love, than right in that cas is', and that she is to have the right to reprove and correct him if he offends her (III 169–75).

It may appear that Chaucer achieves this admirably non-dominant role for Troilus only by a sleight of hand – that is, by transferring the coercive elements in the wooing to Pandarus, who manipulates, coaxes, threatens and deceives with unflagging energy. On this view of the narrative, Pandarus manifests the sexual aggression carefully concealed behind the rhetoric of servitude and adoration. But such a view ignores the important fact that it is only through comparing the separate roles played by Pandarus and Troilus that we can gauge the extent to which Pandarus's practical manipulations are both external and superfluous to the emotional realities of the love-affair as it develops. It is not Pandarus's threats and pleas, but the sight of Troilus and the qualities manifested in his bearing, that first stirs an *emotional* response in Criseyde; this first, accidental sight of Troilus from her window is introduced by Chaucer in *addition* to the later window-scene stage-managed by Pandarus, precisely in order to demonstrate the superfluousness of his machinations (Mann, 1986, 75–7). What he aims to create has already been created. In the scene in Deiphebus's house, Troilus's blushing speechlessness, so far from telling against him, works in his favour: Criseyde is 'wis' enough to love him 'nevere the lasse' for his inability to pour forth well-turned phrases (III 85–8). She perceives that his strangled confusion is in fact the most eloquent testimony to the depth and sincerity of his feelings that she could wish – and it is to these feelings that she responds.

Nevertheless, Troilus's non-coercive role does raise an interesting question: how is this love ever to be sexually consummated? Or more precisely, how can it be consummated without the implication that the previous structure of the relationship has been no more than a ritual sham? If Criseyde initiates the consummation from her commanding position as her lover's 'lady', she in effect acknowledges that her previous reluctance to grant any more than permission for her lover to 'serve' her was only a disguise, throwing the mantle of respectability over female desire. If, on the other hand, Troilus casts off his subservient role to claim sexual satisfaction as Pamphilus does, he in effect acknowledges that his earlier protestations of wishing no more than the right to serve Criseyde were only a temporary expedient by which he could work his way towards his desire. What enables these apparently inescapable alternatives to be bypassed is Chaucer's acute perception that human emotions and relationships are never static; the changeability that for him is, as we have seen, the most fundamental of human characteristics is ceaselessly at work to transform them. The word that Chaucer associates with this imperceptible but ceaseless movement is 'proces', the word he uses to describe how Troilus slowly won Criseyde's love:

> For I sey nought that she so sodeynly
> Yaf hym hire love, but that she gan enclyne
> To like hym first, and I have told yow whi;
> And after that, his manhod and his pyne
> Made love withinne hire [herte] for to myne,
> For which by proces and by good servyse
> He gat hire love, and in no sodeyn wyse. (II 673–9)

The minute and constant movement that constitutes the 'proces' of love makes it possible for another alternative structure of emotion to grow up alongside the acknowledged structure of sovereignty and subjection, and thus makes it possible also for the consummation to be a liberation, the emergence into recognition of a slowly enacted transition, rather than an abrupt abandonment of hypocrisy.

The place where Chaucer shows us this alternative structure coming into being is his summary of the developing relationship between Troilus and Criseyde after their first meeting at Deiphebus's house. Again he refers to this development as a 'proces' (III 470). He emphasizes in this summary Criseyde's surprised delight at Troilus's ability to anticipate her wishes before they are expressed; commands and prohibitions are redundant, since Troilus is instinctively in tune with her desires (463–9). Here again, that is, we have the miraculous fusion of two wills into one that we have already seen in Antony and Cleopatra or the avian lovers of the *Squire's Tale* – a fusion which makes obedience not a matter of the execution of commands, but the spontaneous moulding of oneself to the other, so that it is no longer possible to say whose will dominates and whose is subjected.

And in both the *Squire's Tale* and *Troilus*, it is masculine 'obeisaunce' which initiates this spontaneous fusion of wills, as we can see if we look at the details of the 'proces':

> And shortly of this proces for to pace,
> So wel his werk and wordes he bisette,
> That he so ful stood in his lady grace,
> That twenty thousand tymes, er she lette,
> She thonked God that evere she with hym mette.
> So koude he hym governe in swich servyse,
> That al the world ne myght it bet devyse.
>
> For whi she fond hym so discret in al,
> So secret, and of swich obëisaunce,
> That wel she felte he was to hire a wal
> Of stiel, and sheld from every displesaunce;

That to ben in his goode governaunce,
So wis he was, she was namore afered –
I mene, as fer as oughte ben requered. (III 470–83)

The transformation in the relationship is enacted both lexically and syntactically in this passage. Lexically, in the transformation of 'hym governe' into 'his
goode governaunce'; Troilus's subjection of himself to Criseyde produces, like
a mirror-image, her willingness to subject herself to him. And syntactically, in
the repeated 'so's – 'so discret ... So secret ... of swich obeisaunce' – which
appear at the outset merely to lend emphasis, but which suddenly attach themselves to a 'that' and release their pressure into a clause of result: 'That to ben
in his goode governaunce/... she was namore afered' (my italics). The sudden
withdrawal after this result-clause – 'I mene, as fer as oughte ben requered' –
mimics the movement in Criseyde's mind: the sudden realisation of the point to
which her feelings have led her, and a retreat to the decorum of the publicly
acknowledged situation. What the forward movement and withdrawal in these
lines reveals is precisely the growth of an implicit trust, behind the formal structure of the relationship, which reverses that structure and prepares Criseyde to
find herself in Troilus's power without feeling this as 'thraldom', for the simple
reason that her lover has made her will identical with his own.

The importance of these stanzas is that they show us that Criseyde's willingness to surrender is created by Troilus's 'obeisaunce', not by Pandarus's
coercive manipulation. Pandarus, indeed, arrives like a superfluous extra in the
following stanza ('And Pandarus, to quike alwey the fir,/Was evere ylike prest
and diligent'), his frenzied activity quite external to the slow and intimate
growth of feeling just depicted. Indeed, his engineering of the consummation,
so far from being essential to its success, threatens to destroy the whole love-
affair. For he is completely blind to the fact that his invented story of Troilus's
jealousy of one 'Horaste' alarmingly suggests that this is the moment when the
'obeisaunt' male lover throws off his subservient role to claim rights of possession over his so-called mistress. Criseyde's fears of jealousy have not lessened
over time, as her vigorous declamation against it makes clear (III 1023–9). It
is her knowledge of Troilus that carries her through the crisis, giving her assurance that *his* jealousy will be of the suffering rather than the aggressive kind
(1030–43). And of course her knowledge of Troilus is sound. Troilus's swoon
when admitted to her bedroom is not, as it is so often misrepresented as being,
the result merely of his helpless awe at Criseyde's presence; rather, it is a direct
response to the horrifying situation in which Pandarus has placed him, unable
either to reject or identify with his fictive role as the bully who has reduced
Criseyde to tears. It is the swoon that provides the surest possible demonstration that Troilus is not, in fact, the jealous bully of Pandarus's story.

When he revives, therefore, it is taken for granted that the old relationship –
Criseyde as 'lady', Troilus as servant – still holds good. Criseyde, in accordance
with their agreement, scolds him for his suspicions; Troilus begs forgiveness;
she grants it. And then a totally unexpected consequence follows: she begs *his*

forgiveness for having caused him pain. That is, she abandons her superior position and takes on the role of suppliant in her turn, acknowledging for the first time that her emotional commitment to Troilus constitutes a *claim* on her. It is this implicit act of surrender on Criseyde's part that prompts Troilus's sudden seizing of the initiative, as Chaucer makes clear:

> This Troilus, *with blisse of that supprised*,
> Putte al in Goddes hand, as he that mente
> Nothyng but wel; and sodeynly avysed,
> He hire in armes faste to hym hente. (III 1184–7; my italics)

Troilus at last takes up the role of sexual aggressor: Criseyde in his arms is compared to the lark in the grip of the sparrowhawk, and trembles like an aspen leaf (1191–2, 1198–1201). For the first time their relationship conforms to the conventional pattern of sexual roles: the man confident and demanding, the woman trembling and yielding. But the transition does not represent – as it does in *Pamphilus* – the banal inevitability with which romantic rhetoric dissolves under the pressure of male desire. Troilus exerts his dominance only because Criseyde has freely yielded, and her submission to him is balanced and supported by the submission he has already made to her. The new pattern of their relationship does not supersede the old one, but is based on it and co-exists with it.

It is in this light that we should read Criseyde's response to Troilus's claim of her surrender:

> This Troilus in armes gan hire streyne,
> And seyde, 'O swete, as evere mot I gon,
> Now be ye kaught; now is ther but we tweyne!
> Now yeldeth yow, for other bote is non!'
> To that Criseyde answerde thus anon,
> 'Ne hadde I er now, my swete herte deere,
> Ben yolde, ywis, I were now nought heere!' (III 1205–11)

Criseyde's words are often taken to be the dropping of a mask – an admission that at some earlier date she took a conscious decision to yield to Troilus, although this decision has been coyly concealed from him as from the reader. But read in context, her use of the past tense makes perfect sense without recourse to imputations of sexual hypocrisy. First of all, Criseyde is retrospectively acknowledging to *herself* a surrender to Troilus that she can recognize as having taken place by virtue of her delight in the present moment. She recognizes, that is, that the pressures that have brought her to the consummation scene have been inner as well as outer, and that these inner pressures are now strong enough to bear the whole responsibility of her surrender; coercion is overtaken and swallowed up in the full tide of her volition. Secondly, she teasingly makes clear to Troilus that she is well aware that his sudden 'aggression' is the *result* of her surrender, not its cause; what is being claimed physically is something that already exists in the emotional structure of their relationship. Her words reach behind the formal claim of surrender to the intimate understanding between Troilus and herself that empties that claim of its potential aggression. Lastly, Criseyde's words add a generosity to her surrender. She does not yield grudgingly, making the consummation a favour granted and received, rather than a mutual expression of love; she meets Troilus's desire with her own.

Comparison with Boccaccio's version of the consummation scene reveals how hard Chaucer worked to achieve this vision of sexual mutuality. Boccaccio's Criseida, so far from assuming a superior role as Troiolo's 'lady', shows him all the deference due to his rank; when he comes to her house for the consummation, she apologizes for having kept so august a personage skulking in hiding until it is safe for him to emerge (III. 28). Troiolo, unlike his English counterpart, is quite unembarrassed by his lady's humility; with a lordly graciousness, he makes light of the matter, and again without embarrassment, takes her in his arms and kisses her (III. 29). They proceed to bed, where Criseida coyly asks if she should remove her shift, which Troiolo begs her to do (III. 31–2). Her question elicits the expression of masculine desire as justification for her own relinquishment of modesty. Contrast with this Criseyde's candour, and the unembarrassed confidence with which she writhes her body around Troilus's, like 'the swote wodebynde' around a tree (1230–2). Her trembling 'as an aspes leef' must thus be seen as the emotional trepidation felt before her own final commitment, not as the conventional coy reluctance that gratifies masculinity's pleasure in its own potency. The commitment made, her fear vanishes, to be replaced by a sense of a newly liberated self that makes mock of all her old worries about 'thraldom':

> And as the newe abaysed nyghtyngale,
> That stynteth first whan she bygynneth to synge,
> Whan that she hereth any herde tale,
> Or in the hegges any wyght stirynge,
> And after siker doth hire vois out rynge,
> Right so Criseyde, whan hire drede stente,
> Opned hire herte and tolde hym hire entente. (1233–9)

The cruel irony, of course, is that it is *because* Troilus is not a coercive or possessive lover that he is obliged to acquiesce in the plan that will lead to his loss of Criseyde. Despite all counsels of wisdom, Troilus cannot in the last resort resist suggesting to Criseyde that they elope together before she is exchanged. Criseyde cannot see the need for such drastic action, since she relies on the simple fact that she has no desire to do anything other than return to Troy and to Troilus as soon as possible. Why, then, adopt a plan that seems to assume that, once in the Greek camp, she is bound to stay there – and, even worse, bound to *want* to stay? Troilus's further urging produces a distraught outburst: if he insists on an elopement, it can only be because he does not trust her (IV 1604–10). To this, Troilus can have no answer but assent to her departure. He must allow her the freedom to *choose* to be faithful to him. Had he overridden her protests and insisted on elopement, he might to all intents and purposes have secured her fidelity, but it would have been at the cost of taking on a coercive role alien to their relationship as we have seen it. He would have taken on the role of the fabliau-husband, such as the carpenter in the *Miller's Tale*: 'Jalous he was, and heeld hire narwe in cage' (3224). He allows her to go, not out of 'his general and deplorable passivity' (Delany, 1981, 53), but out of a reverence for her freedom of being and action. If the plan fails, it is not because of Troilus's inertia, but because of Criseyde's.

When one compares the complexity and sensitivity with which Chaucer works out his vision of a relationship freed of male coercion and female hypocrisy, with the irritable and reductive complaints about Troilus's inertia and weakness so familiar on the lips of Chaucer critics and students, one can measure the hold that the conventional notion of sexual roles still has over modern culture, and the distance we still have to travel before we can match the fourteenth century in seeing male 'obeisaunce' as admirable. So long as we admire Diomede instead of Troilus, we should not be surprised if that is what we get.

Such claims as Troilus has on Criseyde are, however, only those of a lover:[6] how if he were her husband? Could he then allow her the same freedom of choice? Would he not be *obliged* to insist on his own rights over her? And would not his 'obeisaunce' contradict orthodox medieval teaching on the rightful supremacy of the husband in marriage? It is the *Franklin's Tale* that provides the answer to these questions. The courtship between Arveragus and Dorigen is elided into an introductory paragraph; this is a tale that attempts to open up the 'happy ever after' ending of the *Wife of Bath's Tale* for exploration. As with Troilus and Criseyde, it is Arveragus's 'meke obeysaunce' (739) which wins him Dorigen's love, but here it seems that this 'obeysaunce' will of necessity be replaced by 'swich lordshipe as men han over hir wyves' (743). But Arveragus 'Of his free wyl' prolongs the relationship of courtship into marriage: he promises Dorigen to 'take no maistrie/Agayn hir wyl', nor to show her jealousy, 'But hire obeye, and folwe hir wyl in al,/As any lovere to his lady shal' (745–50). The only qualification is his retention of 'the name of soveraynetee' so as to preserve his social dignity (751–2). As in the *Wife of Bath's Prologue* and the *Wife of Bath's Tale*, the male surrender of 'maistrye' is reciprocated by female fidelity and humility: Dorigen promises to be his 'humble trewe wyf' (757).

That this marital accord is the subject of approval, rather than to be interpreted as a wilful subversion of orthodox marital relations, is made clear in the long and eloquent celebration of it that follows.

> For o thyng, sires, saufly dar I seye,
> That freendes everych oother moot obeye,

6   Kelly (1975, 217–42) argues that Troilus and Criseyde contract a clandestine marriage, but even if his argument is accepted, my point is unaffected, since the 'marriage' is not publicly acknowledged and thus gives Troilus no obvious rights or duties in the question of whether Criseyde should leave Troy.

If they wol longe holden compaignye.
Love wol nat been constreyned by maistrye.
Whan maistrie comth, the God of Love anon
Beteth his wynges, and farewel, he is gon!
Love is a thyng as any spirit free.
Wommen, of kynde, desiren libertee,
And nat to been constreyned as a thral;
And so doon men, if I sooth seyen shal. (761–70)

What is important here is the natural connection established between liberty and obedience. Each sex is obliged to acknowledge the other's desire for liberty as the just counterpart of its own: the men who might be preparing a knowing smile at woman's natural resistance to constraint are brought up short by their own swift assimilation into the women's condition – '*And so doon men*' (my italics). They must then measure the reasonableness of the female desire for liberty against their own desire for it. But if each sex is to have this desired liberty, then each must in turn 'obeye', so as to create it for the other. The threat of 'maistrye' is averted not by equality – the modern watchword – but by 'patience', a concept which Chaucer endows with a special depth of meaning in his long account of its workings:

Looke who that is moost pacient in love,
He is at his avantage al above.
Pacience is an heigh vertu, certeyn,
For it venquysseth, as thise clerkes seyn,
Thynges that rigour sholde nevere atteyne.
For every word men may nat chide or pleyne.
Lerneth to suffre, or elles, so moot I goon,
Ye shul it lerne, wher so ye wole or noon;
For in this world, certein, ther no wight is,
That he ne dooth or seith somtyme amys.
Ire, siknesse, or constellacioun,
Wyn, wo, or chaungynge of complexioun
Causeth ful ofte to doon amys or speken.
On every wrong a man may nat be wreken.
After the tyme moste be temperaunce
To every wight that kan on governaunce.
And therfore hath this wise, worthy knyght,
To lyve in ese, suffrance hire bihight,
And she to him ful wisly gan to swere
That nevere sholde ther be defaute in here. (771–90)

For us, patience is an essentially static quality: it is a matter of gritting one's teeth and holding on, of suppressing responses rather than cultivating them. The concept of patience described in these lines is the exact opposite of this: its very essence is in movement and change. In the first place, it is because human beings are subject to constant change, not just from day to day but from moment to moment, that patience is needed to harmonize their relationships. A whole miscellany of physical and emotional disturbances – anger, sickness, astral influence, wine, and all the rest – destabilize mood, feelings or behaviour, threatening the balance of a relationship. The only way that harmony can be preserved is through constant adaptation, as each partner responds to change in the other. It is rather like the constant but invisible movement needed to keep one's balance in a ship. Patience is thus not merely a response to change: it *embodies* change in itself (cf. Hanna, 1978, 77). 'Governaunce' incorporates 'suffrance', a tempering of behaviour according to the changing needs and restrictions of the moment ('After the tyme...'). The polar opposite of patience is 'rigour' (775); so far from implying frozen immobility, patience expresses itself as flexibility, pliability.

What this means for the marriage of Arveragus and Dorigen is that there are no fixed roles, no unalterable distribution of power; instead there is a ceaseless alternation of 'lordshipe' and 'servage', as the final lines of this passage make clear.

> Heere may men seen an humble, wys accord;
> Thus hath she take hir servant and hir lord –
> Servant in love, and lord in mariage.
> Thanne was he bothe in lordshipe and servage.
> Servage? Nay, but in lordshipe above,
> Sith he hath bothe his lady and his love;
> His lady, certes, and his wyf also,
> The which that lawe of love acordeth to. (791–8)

The constant shifts in the relationship of Dorigen and Arveragus are enacted in the vocabulary: 'servant ... lord ... servant ... lord ... lordshipe ... servage ... servage ... lordshipe ... lady ... love ... lady ... wyf'. The frequently encountered view that this is a marriage founded on 'equality' does not accurately reflect the complexity of the relationship described. What these lines show us is not sameness, but a doubling of roles: their constant alternation shows that each partner is *simultaneously* both dominant and subservient in the relationship (as are Troilus and Criseyde in the consummation scene).[7] I would venture to say that this seems to me a more realistic notion on which to ground a relationship than 'equality', which ignores the difficulty of settling matters by vote in a democracy of two, and also seems to require a quite unrealistic 'sameness' between partners. Yet the distinction is perhaps important only at

---

7   Crane (1994, 93) objects that 'these lines may strive toward an idea of equivalence between Dorigen and Arveragus, but that idea, if it is even latent, finds expression only by juxtaposing two conditions in which male and female have reversed hierarchical relations', and thus shows that 'gender is a system of difference that entails inequivalence'. Cf. Weisl, 1995, 108. In answer to this objection, I would add to my comments above that the importance of the alternating hierarchies is that they emphasize *change*, harnessing the constant fluctuations in human emotion and behaviour to the service of something positive.

the level of mental image: the *result* of the doubled roles in the *Franklin's Tale* could be described as equality. It is simply that the ideal of patience offers not only a goal to be achieved but also an idea of the means of achieving it.

The tale itself shows us this idea in practice. It shows us, first of all, the threat to a marriage posed by change, both external and internal. External change comes with Arveragus's departure to England for 'a yeer or tweyne' in pursuit of knightly 'worshipe and honour' (809–11). Internal change comes with the slow erosion of Dorigen's first intensities of suffering at his absence, under the influence of the passage of time and the persuasion of her friends. The danger lies in the possibility that these changes might coalesce with the 'aventure' of Aurelius's love for Dorigen (940), to create a fundamental reorientation of her affections. The 'proces' that leads her to gradual acceptance of Arveragus's absence (829) *could* also lead her to transfer her love to the handsome young squire who is near at hand. Dorigen, that is, is a potential Criseyde. But there are other potentialities too in this narrative: Dorigen's vivid fears that Arveragus will be shipwrecked on the 'grisly rokkes blake' brings this possibility into the story immediately before we hear of Aurelius's love. Dorigen decisively rejects the possibility of betrayal; Arveragus is still too important a presence in her emotions to be displaced. But had he indeed been shipwrecked on the way home, we can see that her grief at his death must inevitably have slackened over time as did her grief at his absence, and that Aurelius's declaration of love could well then provoke a different emotional response. Remarriage is not betrayal, but the same 'proces' can lead to both.

Neither of these possibilities is, however, realized; Dorigen's determined response closes off the possibility of betrayal. Or does it? Aurelius understands perfectly well that her meaning is uncompromisingly negative, but the 'impossible condition' through which she chooses to express it raises the possibility that the idea of loving Aurelius might gain a foothold in her mind by entering it in negative form, as the idea of loving Troilus entered Criseyde's. Is her condition perhaps even an appeal for the male coercion which would relieve her of responsibility? – a kind of emotional strip poker in which the rules of the game substitute for acknowledged volition? Yet the very nature of the condition refutes this interpretation of it: the removal of the rocks from the coast of Brittany looms large in Dorigen's mind only because of her love and concern for her husband. Moreover, when Dorigen is confronted with the fulfilment of her 'impossible' condition, the exemplary stories to which she looks for analogues to her own condition show that she thinks of the performance of her promise as nothing other than a rape; the narratives she desperately rehearses are tales of women who killed themselves either to avert rape or as a result of it.

It is here that we become aware of yet another potentiality that could be realized in the narrative – one that would assimilate it to the pattern of the Lucretia-legend (one of those that Dorigen recalls) and the static pathos of the *Legend of Good Women*. For Dorigen's long soliloquy (1355–1456) halts the narrative before the contemplation of two possible endings, both of them gloomy: either Dorigen will renege on her promise (an alternative she herself does not consider), or else she will kill herself to avoid fulfilling it. Critics, indeed, often find fault with Dorigen for failing to carry out her projected suicide. But Dorigen's reluctance to end her life seems less a sign of weakness than of the human resistance to stasis, to finality. What suggests this is the parallel resistance we feel on the narrative level to accept the ending of the story at this point: we do not want the forward trajectory of curiosity in 'what happened next?' simply to run itself against the blank wall of 'and so she killed herself'. Commitment to the story is, like patience, a commitment to *movement*, a commitment to follow events rather than force them into a pre-determined shape.

Narrative curiosity thus does duty for a motive: Dorigen, while intending to die, lives, for no other reason than the human refusal of stasis. And this allows space for Arveragus to find out from her the reason for her grief, and to urge her, against all narrative expectation, to keep her promise to Aurelius. It is often said that at this point the special structure of the marriage relationship collapses into the traditional pattern of male dominance and female subservience; Arveragus is forced to reassume the 'maistrye' he has surrendered, and Dorigen is forced to obey him. Such an interpretation ignores the care with which the narrative is constructed so as to exemplify the doubling of roles intimated in the opening passage. If Arveragus insists that Dorigen keep her promise, it is nevertheless *her* promise to whose claims he subordinates his own feelings and wishes. The duality is evident when Dorigen tells Aurelius she is going 'Unto the gardyn, *as myn housbonde bad,/My trouthe for to holde*' (1512–13; my italics). If Dorigen obeys her husband's command, it is a command that she should live out the implications of her independent action. The fact that disaster seems the inevitable result simply makes Arveragus's action all the more impressive, inasmuch as it increases the pressures on him to assume control, to 'rescue the little woman' from the mess she has got herself into. Like Troilus, he will not compromise her autonomy by stepping in to take charge when disaster threatens; Dorigen, like Criseyde on her departure from Troy, is allowed to exercise the autonomy of action she has claimed. Arveragus relinquishes his own claims so that she may meet the ones she has created. So far from depriving her of her freedom, Arveragus's action means that she must take full responsibility for it; her husband's refusal to forbid her to keep her promise deprives her of the alibi of male coercion.

Arveragus also honours another clause in his initial offer to Dorigen: that he should show her no jealousy (748). In this respect, the importance of his response to Dorigen's revelation of her promise, and the fulfilment of its condition, has not been fully appreciated. It becomes clear if we stop to think of the most likely responses that an average husband would make: 'what exactly went on between you and this young man while I was away? in what circumstances did you manage to make him such an extraordinary promise? are you sure you weren't flirting with him? how do I know this isn't a trumped-up story to get me to agree to my own cuckolding?' What Arveragus actually says is simply: 'Is ther oght elles, Dorigen, but this?' (1469). The interesting thing about this question is that it *could* be read as an invitation to further confessions – 'have you anything *else* to tell me?' – and if Dorigen *had* a guilty conscience, she would surely project this interpretation on to it. It is a testimony to the purity of her motives, and to her rock-sure sense of Arveragus's generosity, that her answer makes clear that she unhesitatingly interprets it in the sense that Arveragus surely intends it – 'is the matter no more serious than that?': 'Nay, nay …/This is to muche' (1470–1). It is in this question, with its quiet relinquishing of interrogation and of anger, that we can feel Arveragus's 'patience' and its absorption of the crisis.

Arveragus's 'suffrance' reveals the completeness of his *trust* in Dorigen. The reader knows that the story of the promise is a true one, but Arveragus has no way of being sure of this. In accepting it, he might be as foolishly deluded as January is when he accepts May's equally improbable account of what was going on in the pear-tree.[8] It is only his trust in Dorigen that assures him he is assenting to a harsh necessity rather than being the dupe of a plot. This is the reason, I think, why he stipulates that Dorigen should tell no one of what happens: since rape, in the last resort, is distinguished from voluntary copulation by affective state rather than by physical fact, Dorigen's yielding to Aurelius must be kept within the private understanding which alone can interpret it aright.

Arveragus and Dorigen thus surrender to the 'aventure' that confronts them, and surrender to each other's will in doing so. It is at this point that we can see what is meant by patience, and by the injunction 'Lerneth to suffre'. But just as patience is not simply stony endurance, so 'suffering' is not simply a matter of bearing pain. It carries with it, in Middle English, the sense of *allowing* (*OED* 12–18) – allowing space for events to develop in ways beyond the scope of one's ability to foresee or control them. Arveragus's surrender appears foolish in the light of what seems inevitable at the time – as Chaucer acknowledges in his appeal to the reader to suspend judgement (1493–8). But the point of the tale is that the inevitable does not happen; 'suffrance' makes room for unexpected narrative potentialities to realize themselves, and it is only when they have been taken account of that Arveragus should be judged ('whan that ye han herd the tale, demeth': 1498). Indeed 'suffrance' creates these potentialities: Arveragus's surrender is the direct cause of Aurelius's capitulation. The reciprocal surrender that characterizes the marriage extends itself outwards into society. For Aurelius is as non-coercive a lover as Arveragus. His attempt to win Dorigen by removing the rocks seems to represent a rather desperate gamble on the possibility that its 'impossible condition' represents a yes hidden somewhere in her no, rather than a decision to have by coercion what he cannot have voluntarily. His non-coerciveness is clearly evident in the speech by which he informs Dorigen that the rocks have gone: ducking and weaving, taking refuge in subjunctives and subordinate clauses, parentheses and qualifications, he is quite unable to bring himself to the point – unable, that is, to tell Dorigen that she must keep her promise. The most he can manage is to remind her of it, with the exhortation 'Dooth as yow list' (1335); if this was the alibi she needed, he has provided it. In this brilliantly imagined speech, we see that Aurelius is a true lover; he wants Dorigen, not the empty enjoyment of her body. So it is that when her distracted

---

8   I owe this point to a former student, Tim Melley.

answer to his enquiry as to where she is going – 'Unto the gardyn, as myn housbonde bad,/My trouthe for to holde – allas, allas!' (1512–13) – reveals the promise as coercion, and also reveals by contrast Arveragus's *non*-coerciveness, his submission to his wife's 'trouthe', Aurelius's immediate response is to release her from the bonds in which he holds her.

The quality that moves him to do so is pity – 'compassioun' and 'routhe' for both Dorigen and Arveragus (1515, 1520). Pity is no longer the static emotion of the *Legend of Good Women*, but a dynamic force capable of opening up the narrative in unforeseen directions. Like patience, it becomes the agent and expression of change, and particularly of change in its benign form. It is patience and pity that open up the narrative possibilities for a happy ending. As Arveragus's surrender is met by Aurelius's, so Aurelius's in its turn is reciprocated by the clerk's generosity in releasing him from his debt. Patience works itself out in a sequence of change; the opening vision of balance and harmony as the result of constant shifts and adaptations is endorsed and illustrated in the tale. And it is the tale that also demonstrates the meaning of the proverb 'Patience conquers', whose paradoxical structure mimics the paradoxical simultaneity of 'lordshipe' and 'servage' in marriage.

The idea that patience conquers is no doubt comforting, but is it true? Is the happy ending that justifies Arveragus's surrender of 'maistrye' merely wishful thinking? It might be a sufficient answer to this question to say that it *can* be true; it is one of the versions of experience that has a right to be recognized and recorded. In the *Canterbury Tales* it is set alongside other versions of experience; in the fabliau-world of the *Miller's Tale*, for example, patience is reduced to a kind of animal stoicism – 'He moste endure, as oother folk, his care' (3232) – in which its transforming power disappears. In the *Wife of Bath's Prologue*, it is comically travestied into an instrument for cowing one's husband into submission:

> 'Ye sholde been al pacient and meke,
> And han a sweete spiced conscience,
> Sith ye so preche of Jobes pacience.
> Suffreth alwey, syn ye so wel kan preche;
> And but ye do, certein we shal yow teche
> That it is fair to have a wyf in pees.
> Oon of us two moste bowen, doutelees,
> And sith a man is moore resonable
> Than womman is, ye moste been suffrable.' (434–42)

The *Franklin's Tale* shows the grander and more serious conception of patience that lies behind such mundane manifestations, and with which even they make some faint contact, as it in turn is irrigated by memories of such humdrum experience.

What refutes the charge of wishful thinking within the *Franklin's Tale* itself, however, is the tale's demonstration that the very definition of patience is acceptance of the worst. Arveragus and Dorigen have 'nothing to lose' in hazarding themselves to the development of events, because they have already accepted loss. The narrative embraces the potentiality of Dorigen's rape, of her suicide, of the life-long stain on marital happiness, as it embraces the possibility of Arveragus's shipwreck, or Dorigen's betrayal. It is indeed the sense of these 'alternative versions' to the story that lends authenticity to what does happen, by virtue of the acknowledgement that it does not always happen. They lie like a dark shadow that throws into relief the gratuitousness of happiness – the fact that (as the choice offered to the knight at the end of the *Wife of Bath's Tale* makes clear) it comes as a gift, carrying with it the risk of its loss. It is not because it is a certain route to a happy ending, but on the contrary because *un*happy endings are so common, that patience is a necessary ideal.

The *Franklin's Tale* offers a vision of patience, and the surrender of male 'maistrye', as a marital ideal. But is this ideal also Chaucer's? Should it rather be attributed to the Franklin's individual notion of 'gentillesse', as the *Wife of Bath's Tale* has been seen as the wishful thinking of the Wife of Bath? That this is not so, and that both the Franklin and the Wife speak for Chaucer in this respect, can I think be seen from examination of his own tale in the Canterbury collection, the tale of *Melibee*. It is a tale which critics and readers usually pass over, but which is, in fact, a keystone in the structure of the *Canterbury Tales* – precisely because of the importance of the role it gives to patience and to women. Its soberness of intent can be measured in the fact that it is in prose, and that its narrative element is minimal, most of it being devoted to a long argument between Melibee and his wife Prudence. Its susceptibility to being read as the individualized utterance of an identifiable speaker is also minimized by virtue of the fact that it is an almost word-for-word translation of a pre-existing work, Renaud de Louens's French version of the *Liber Consolationis et Consilii* of Albertano of Brescia. The significance it acquires in the *Canterbury Tales* is not the result of any major alterations to this original, but resides rather in its silent interaction with the tales that take up its themes and modulate them into other forms. Critics have often privileged the *Parson's Tale* as the non-fictional 'core' of the *Canterbury Tales*, the centre to whose values all the other tales must be related. If there is a centre of this sort, a far better case could be made for identifying it with the *Melibee*. For the *Parson's Tale* is, after all, told by the Parson, and in that respect can claim no privileges over the tales told by the other pilgrims, whereas the *Melibee* is given special authority by being told by Chaucer himself – likewise one of the Canterbury pilgrims on the level of fiction, to be sure, but also one who has links with the plane of reality outside the work that the other pilgrims lack. 'Chaucer the pilgrim' is the fictional projection of the poet Chaucer, whose authority is lent to the values of the *Melibee*. For all these reasons, it is the *Melibee* that enables us to answer the question of whether it was possible for the masculine surrender of 'maistrye' in marriage to be seriously approved of, by Chaucer and by medieval society, instead of seen as the overthrow of rightful hierarchy.

The numerous points of contact with other tales that precede it in the Canterbury collection give the reader of the *Melibee* a strange sense of *déjà vu*. Prudence, 'suffering' her husband's anguished grief over the injuries inflicted by his enemies on herself and their daughter, until she 'saugh hir tyme' (979–80), reminds us of the *Franklin's Tale*'s notion of patience governing itself 'After the tyme'. Melibee, like January, summons a council not so much to tell him what to do as to endorse what he has already decided upon. Melibee rejects Prudence's first attempt to offer advice with reference to the dictum of Solomon quoted by Pluto in the *Merchant's Tale*: 'alle wommen been wikke, and noon good of hem alle' (1057). Furthermore, 'if I governed me by thy conseil, it sholde seme that I hadde yeve to thee over me the maistrie, and God forbede that it so weere!/For Jhesus Syrak seith that "if the wyf have maistrie, she is contrarious to hir housbonde"' (1058–9). He also cites the female propensity to gossip, illustrated in the *Wife of Bath's Tale* by the story of Midas, which would, he says, make Prudence incapable of keeping his 'conseil' secret. These familiar charges are rejected by Prudence with the same arguments as are used by Proserpina in the *Merchant's Tale* (2277–90): though Solomon never found a good woman, other men have certainly done so. Or perhaps what he meant was that no one is perfectly good save God alone (1076–9). As for 'maistrye', in accepting 'conseil' a man does not yield 'lordshipe and maistrie of his persone' to his counsellor (1082). Melibee knows her well enough to know she is no 'jangleresse', and has experience of her 'grete pacience' (1085–9). Nor is it true that women always counsel men to evil – and here she cites as proof of the value of women's counsel the examples of Rebecca, Judith, Abigail and Esther that we have already encountered in the marriage encomium of the *Merchant's Tale* (1096–1101). Prudence concludes with a stirring affirmation of woman's value as testified by the proverbial verses: 'What is bettre than gold? Jaspre. What is bettre than jaspre? Wisedoom./And what is better than wisedoom? Womman. And what is bettre than a good womman? Nothyng' (1107–8).

Convinced by these arguments, Melibee promises Prudence 'I wol governe me by thy conseil in alle thyng' (1114). This masculine submission cannot be attributed to romantic gallantry, neither is it the weary capitulation of a henpecked fabliau-husband; it is an act of sober earnest, prompted by the claims of morality and reason. But how much, it may be asked, is here conceded? – since, as Prudence has pointed out, acceptance of counsel does not imply surrender of 'lordshipe'. Has she won no more than permission to be the 'power behind the throne'? The proverbial verses quoted by Prudence on the excellence of woman over all things are glossed in a fourteenth-century Latin text along just these lines: 'A woman is good in that she does good to her husband (and he to her), and is able not only to counsel him, but even to rule over him. So the wise would often say: A chaste matron rules her husband by obeying him.'[9] Is the

---

9   The text in question is the translation of *Kalila and Dimna* by Raymond of Béziers, ed. Hervieux, 5: 622.

ideal enshrined in 'Patience conquers' to be reduced to nothing more than this sort of traditional domestic manipulation?

What saves it, I think, from this fate, is that the tale extends the notion of patience beyond the marital context in ways that make it clear that 'ruling by obeying', here as in the *Franklin's Tale*, is a role to be assumed by men as well as women. Melibee's submission to Prudence is but the first step in a much larger submission to his enemies and to the evils they have inflicted on him. Prudence urges him not to take revenge, as he had planned, but instead to show 'suffraunce': 'it is good as now that ye suffre and be pacient' (1480). She rehearses at length all the reasons that may 'make yow for to enclyne to suffre, and for to han pacience in the wronges that han been doon to yow' (1493). High on the list is the need to imitate 'the pacience of oure Lord Jhesu Crist, as seith Seint Peter in his Epistles./"Jhesu Crist," he seith, "hath suffred for us and yeven ensample to every man to folwe and sewe hym,/for he dide nevere synne, ne nevere cam ther a vileyns word out of his mouth./Whan men cursed hym, he cursed hem noght, and whan men betten hym, he manaced hem noght"' (1501–4). The saints too suffered their tribulations with 'grete pacience' (1505–6). Solomon praised patience, saying *inter alia* that ' "It is moore worth to be pacient than for to be right strong;/and he that may have the lordshipe of his owene herte is moore to preyse than he that by his force or strengthe taketh grete citees."/And therfore seith Seint Jame in his Epistle that "patience is a greet vertu of perfeccioun" ' (1515–17).

Melibee needs a lot of convincing, but eventually he yields to Prudence's arguments. Interestingly, his submission is finally achieved by a 'semblant of wratthe' in Prudence (1687) which induces a placatory attitude in him; patience is not all saccharine sweetness but includes 'seeing the time' for sterner measures. Melibee's agreement to submit to his enemies is a reaffirmation of his former surrender to Prudence's counsel: 'Seyeth shortly youre wyl and youre conseil, and I am al redy to fulfille and parfourne it' (1712). Prudence proposes that he empower her to speak privately with his enemies so that she may ascertain what is best for him to do. Melibee responds with an even stronger expression of submission: 'Dame, ... dooth youre wil and youre likynge;/for I putte me hoolly in youre disposicioun and ordinaunce' (1724–5). The Wife of Bath herself could hardly ask for more.

This submissiveness on Melibee's part is reciprocated by a similar submissiveness on the part of his enemies, who respond to Prudence's overtures with similar words: 'we putten oure dede and al oure matere and cause al hoolly in youre good wyl/and been redy to obeye to the speche and comandement of my lord Melibee' (1741–2). To Prudence's proposal that they yield themselves into Melibee's power, they reply: 'Worshipful lady, we putten us and oure goodes al fully in youre wil and disposicioun,/and been redy to comen .../for to maken oure obligacioun and boond as strong as it liketh unto youre goodnesse;/that we mowe fulfille the wille of yow and of my lord Melibee' (1765–8). Prudence's final task is to persuade Melibee to respond to his enemies' submission, not by inflicting punishment on them, but instead by showing them 'pitee' and 'mercy' (1864). In one of his rare expansions of his source, Chaucer describes Melibee's last capitulation to his wife: 'his herte gan enclyne to the wil of his wif, considerynge hire trewe entente,/and conformed hym anon and assented fully to werken after hir conseil' (1871–2).

As in the *Franklin's Tale*, harmony is achieved through a chain of surrender. It begins with Prudence's 'suffraunce' of the injuries inflicted on herself and her daughter. This 'suffraunce' extends itself to Melibee, who surrenders his will to Prudence, and this wins his enemies' surrender to her and to him. Here the husband's surrender is not the lover's 'obeisaunce' to his lady but an exercise in Christian 'suffraunce' that finds its model in Christ's Passion. But this Stoico-Christian conception of patience, supported by quotations from Seneca as well as from the Bible, is not alien to the world of the *Franklin's Tale*, where Dorigen learns patience to the 'purveiaunce' that has ordained the existence of the 'grisly rokkes blake'. The *Wife of Bath's Tale*, the *Franklin's Tale* and the *Melibee* are variations on the same theme; fairy-tale makes contact with Christian myth, and both tell the same story: it is the surrender of power that creates power. What gives flesh to fairy-tale and Christian myth alike is the subtle and accurate rendering of the structure of human feeling and reaction – whether expressed in the marital squabbles of the Wife of Bath, or the romantic harmony of Troilus and Criseyde – which makes 'obeisaunce' into an ideal that is rooted in behavioural realities. And this ideal holds good throughout the *Canterbury Tales*. The dominant husband of the *Clerk's Tale* is not an orthodox riposte to the Wife of Bath's heretical rebelliousness; he is, as we shall see, himself a monstrous perversion, the caricature that confirms the ideal. 'Love wol nat been constreyned by maistrye', but 'humylitee', as Melibee tells his enemies, 'constreyneth me to doon yow grace and mercy' (1878–80). The constraining bonds of love are forged, not by 'maistrye', but by patience.

The *Melibee* inculcates the virtue of patience, and it makes of it a womanly quality, exemplified in the 'greet pacience' with which Prudence treats her husband (1064). But it is not *only* a womanly quality; it is, like pity, something that men are to learn from women. Melibee submits himself to his wife and to patience in one and the same process; his patience must match hers.

In assigning this tale to himself, Chaucer identifies himself with the values it embodies, and with the centrality of woman's role. But there is another way in which his telling of the *Melibee* identifies him with the surrender of 'maistrye', and that is in the dramatized context he creates for the tale. For it is not, of course, the only tale he tells. On being called on for his contribution, he launches into the romance of *Sir Thopas*, an excruciating stream of doggerel which is interrupted by the Host's violent protests that he can bear no more of it. Chaucer mildly excuses himself by saying that it is the best poem he knows (928), and the Host, after vehemently insisting 'Thy drasty rymyng is nat worth a toord!' (930), bids him tell a tale in prose if he knows no better poetry – a directive with which Chaucer cheerfully complies.

This sublimely comic scene is, as G. K. Chesterton long ago perceived, a brilliantly conceived articulation of Chaucer's relationship to his own poetic creation. 'The Poet is the Maker; he is the creator of a cosmos; and Chaucer is the creator of the whole world of his creatures' ([1932], 1962, 21). It might seem therefore that the creator reserves to himself the 'maistrye' whose surrender he encourages in others, concealing his personal 'auctoritee' under the mask of impartial representation. But Chaucer does not remain external to his creation, the hidden puppet-master pulling its strings. Instead, he enters it, placing himself on the same fictional level as the other pilgrims, and his authority on a level with theirs. And he enters it only to be hooted off the stage; his literary 'auctoritee' is rejected by his own literary creations. It is the *size* of this joke that Chesterton rightly stresses; the importance of *Sir Thopas* is far greater than its role as a parody of bad romances. 'Chaucer is mocking not merely bad poets, but good poets, the best poet he knows; "the best in this kind are but shadows"' (22).

In this subjection of the creator to his creation, Chesterton even sees 'some dark ray of the irony of God, who was mocked when He entered into His own world, and killed when He came among His creatures' (22). The solemnity of the one event and the comic frivolity of the other would seem to make such a comparison far-fetched, yet the careful differentiation in emotional resonance is the very sign of the Chaucerian tact that, in making the parallel, refuses to allow it to aggrandize the claims of the literary creator. Where the Crucifixion and the *Thopas–Melibee* sequence *do* make contact is in the concept of 'suffrance', in which the literary creator humbly conceives himself as following the pattern of the divine. As in the *Legend of Good Women* – but here even more decisively – Chaucer renounces authority over his literary creation. At the heart of his masterwork he places a dramatized enactment of his own surrender of 'maistrye', both masculine and poetic. The values endorsed in the tales are also embodied in his role as writer. The language in which he writes, the materials of which his writing are made, are not personal, idiosyncratic, designed to impose an individual vision on the duller herd of his readers. Instead, his poetry reveals the richness of meaning in the worn phrases of their everyday speech – 'Patience conquers', 'Make virtue of necessity', 'Time flies', 'Time heals' – and in the apparently threadbare wisdom distilled in such a work as the tale of *Melibee*. His own contributions to the Canterbury collection overtly renounce both self-aggrandizement and individual expression, the first being a garbled pastiche of the worst kind of hack verse-writing, and the second a patient and faithful translation of another's prose. It is for the pilgrims – that is, Chaucer's audience – to infuse life into the poet's contribution by their response (Mann, 1991b), as the wisdom of the *Melibee* is enlivened by the narratives that weave its commonplaces into the texture of human experience. His imagined surrender to the control of his audience is the pledge of the sincerity and the consistency of Chaucer's commitment to the surrender of 'maistrye'. And it is, by the same token, the pledge of his commitment to the female value of patience.

4

Suffering Woman, Suffering God

'Wommen are born to thraldom and penance,
And to been under mannes governance.'
                                    (*Man of Law's Tale* 286–7)

The marriage that begins the *Man of Law's Tale* is not the culmination of a romantic courtship; instead, Constance, its heroine, is the instrument of a politico-religious alliance. Although he has never set eyes on her, the Sultan of Syria falls so passionately in love with her by reputation alone that he engages that he and all his baronage will embrace Christianity if he can have her as his bride. The matter is settled, not by the delicate negotiation of feeling, but 'by tretys and embassadrie,/And by the popes mediacioun,/And al the chirche, and al the chivalrie' (233–5) – everyone, it appears, being consulted but Constance herself. She accepts her fate without protest, but also without enthusiasm. The day of her departure for Syria is a day of sorrow, for both Constance and the members of her family, which on Constance's side at least represents not only regret at what she is leaving behind, but also fear of what she is going to.

Allas, what wonder is it thogh she wepte,
That shal be sent to strange nacioun
Fro freendes that so tendrely hire kepte,
And to be bounden under subjeccioun
Of oon, she knoweth nat his condicioun?
Housbondes been alle goode, and han been yoore;
That knowen wyves; I dar sey yow na moore. (267–73)

An everyday tragedy, one might say. Constance's fate must have been the fate suffered by multitudes of medieval women (and men too) whose marriages were dictated not by individual choice but by the accumulation of landed estates or the forging of political alliances. The narratorial comment encourages us to see the situation in its most bleakly depressing aspect, but Constance herself renounces the protest for which its cynicism seems to make room, accepting her fate with Stoic resignation as the general lot of women, as she takes leave of her parents for the last time:

'Allas, unto the Barbre nacioun
I moste anoon, syn that it is youre wille;

But Crist, that starf for our redempcioun
So yeve me grace his heestes to fulfille!
I, wrecche womman, no fors though I spille!
Wommen are born to thraldom and penance,
And to been under mannes governance.' (281–7)

Constance's view of woman's fate derives from Genesis, where God decrees that as a punishment for Eve's sin in eating the apple, women should suffer the pains of childbirth and subjection to their husbands (Gen. 3: 15–16).

The mask of romantic fiction here seems to fall away, leaving the bleak visage of reality. Woman's fate is not to be the 'lady' whose word is law to her submissive lover, it is 'thraldom' to her father and her husband. The aspirations of the *Franklin's Tale* – 'Wommen, of kynde, desiren libertee,/And nat to been constreyned as a thral' – seem here to be brought down to earth. Power is male, submission and suffering are female. In this context, patience seems to dwindle into nothing more than the opium of the oppressed, a convenient means of persuading them to accept the inevitability of 'thraldom'.

And indeed such is the view of the Sultan's mother, whose vigorous resistance to her son's marriage is in marked contrast with Constance's resignation. Indignantly she protests to her council her unwavering loyalty to Mohammed:

'What sholde us tyden of this newe lawe
But thraldom to oure bodies and penance,
And afterward in helle to be drawe,
For we reneyed Mahoun oure creance?' (337–40)

The Sultaness's rejection of Christianity is also a rejection of the 'thraldom and penance' that for Constance is woman's lot. And this rejection of the womanly condition is emphasized in the narrative comment that follows:

O Sowdanesse, roote of iniquitee!
Virago, thou Semyrame the secounde!
O serpent under femynynytee,
Lik to the serpent depe in helle ybounde!
O feyned womman, al that may confounde
Vertu and innocence, thurgh thy malice,
Is bred in thee, as nest of every vice!

O Sathan, envious syn thilke day
That thou were chaced from oure heritage,
Wel knowestow to wommen the olde way!
Thou madest Eva brynge us in servage;
Thou wolt fordoon this Cristen mariage.

> Thyn instrument – so weylawey the while! –
> Makestow of wommen, whan thou wolt bigile. (358–71)[1]

The Sultaness is not only an evil woman, she is also, it seems, a *counterfeit* woman. The immediate meaning of 'feyned' is 'feigning, false' (*MED* 6b), but the pressure from 'virago', with its implications of 'mannishness', and the suggestion of counterfeit in 'serpent under femynynytee' also activate the sense 'feigned' (*MED* 5d; cf. Delany, [1974–5] 1983, 42). That this is Chaucer's intention here is confirmed by the similar outburst against Constance's second wicked mother-in-law, Donegild, who is called 'mannysh' (782). The Sultaness and Donegild are 'masculine' in their choice of action over suffering; in contrast to Constance, who suffers her fate with a Stoic dignity, they assert themselves in active opposition to whatever they do not like. The Sultaness murders her son and his guests at the wedding feast, and sends Constance out to sea in a rudderless boat; Donegild invents false letters to and from Alla, Constance's second husband, which lead to Constance being set adrift a second time with her child.

The obvious cruelty of their actions seems to tip the scales unfairly against the active self-assertion that fuels them, and so to endorse Constance's passive resignation as the only acceptable feminine ideal. Yet to read the tale in this way is to endorse a simplistic opposition between 'active' and 'passive' that the tale is precisely designed to question; in context, the terms dissolve into each other, as we have seen them do in the representations of love and marriage. The active independence of the two 'mannish' women, seen from another perspective, appears as mere illusion. In imposing her will on events, the Sultaness acts as the 'instrument' of Satan's will; her independence becomes the tool of his designs. Donegild likewise is presented as a mere receptacle for the 'feendlych spirit' that makes use of her body ('Thogh thou heere walke, thy spirit is in helle!': 784). What makes this more than a dramatically articulated endorsement of feminine submissiveness is that it is not only female power that is presented as illusory and limited in this way, it is also the 'mannes governance' to which Constance is subjected. Immediately after the expression of resignation to her father's will, there follows an extraordinary passage of cosmic vision which represents him as a helpless pawn in the play of forces far greater than his own.

> O firste moevyng! Crueel firmament,
> With thy diurnal sweigh that crowdest ay
> And hurlest al from est til occident

---

1   *The Riverside Chaucer* puts the 'so' in line 370 outside the parenthetical exclamation, but comparison with other uses of this traditional formula in Chaucer (e.g., line 632) show that it is an integral part of it; I have emended the punctuation accordingly. (As does the *Riverside Canterbury Tales*.)

That naturelly wolde holde another way,
Thy crowdyng set the hevene in swich array
At the bigynnyng of this fiers viage,
That crueel Mars hath slayn this mariage.

Infortunat ascendent tortuous,
Of which the lord is helplees falle, allas,
Out of his angle into the derkeste hous!
O Mars, o atazir, as in this cas!
O fieble moone, unhappy been thy paas!
Thou knyttest thee ther thou art nat receyved;
Ther thou were weel, fro thennes artow weyved.

Imprudent Emperour of Rome, allas!
Was ther no philosophre in al thy toun?
Is no tyme bet than oother in swich cas?
Of viage is ther noon eleccioun,
Namely to folk of heigh condicioun?
Noght whan a roote is of a burthe yknowe?
Allas, we been to lewed or to slowe! (295–315)

The power of the Emperor is annihilated beneath the crushing weight of astral influence. The summit of human power is merely the lowest rung on the ladder of cosmic hierarchy.

But there is more to this passage than that, for the vision of the cosmos in these stanzas is of a quite extraordinary character. The mechanics of it are orthodox enough: the 'natural' movement of the planetary spheres from West to East is counteracted by the East–West movement of the Primum Mobile, the 'first moving' sphere whose outermost position in the system gives it greatest influence, so that it imposes its own motion on the heavenly bodies beneath it. Scientifically, this theory of a double motion in the cosmos accounted for the precession of the equinoxes – that is, the slight shift to the east in the annual return of the stars to their original position in relation to the sun. Poetically, the double motion was often interpreted as a reflection of moral hierarchy – for example, of the proper subjection of the senses to reason (Mann, 1983a, 170–1). In striking contrast to other medieval writers, Chaucer makes it expressive of a violence and cruelty in the cosmos as a whole. The Primum Mobile is a 'crueel firmament'; it 'crowds' and 'hurls' the planets away from their natural course. The planets whose influence blights Constance's marriage are thus themselves helpless victims of a greater force; their power, like the Emperor's, is limited and thwarted of its effect. The 'lord of the ascendant' is not powerful but 'helplees', the moon is 'fieble'. Images of power ('crueel Mars') resolve themselves strangely into images of impotence. When probed for precise scientific information on the state of the heavens, this passage is revealed as 'technical but unspecific' (Eade, 1982, 82) – suggesting that

Chaucer chose such technical terms as 'tortuous' and 'derkeste hous' less for their informative value than for their emotional colouring. The universe we see here is not a harmoniously ordered whole; it is crooked, awry, at odds with itself, held together only by violence.

The question of 'mannes governance' is thus no sooner introduced than it is expanded on to a cosmic scale. Woman is subject to man; man is subject to the planets, the planets to the Primum Mobile. And the Primum Mobile –? Beyond the first moving sphere, there is only the First Mover – that is, God, the invisible presence behind this cosmic scheme. Silently but inexorably this passage raises the question of God's 'governance' of the cosmos, which seems, like that of man over woman, to express itself as cruelty and tyranny. This is a question that is central to Boethius's *Consolation of Philosophy*, in translating which Chaucer constantly used the words 'governance' and its associates – 'governe', 'government', 'governor' – to express God's control over his creation. Boethius's crushing personal misfortunes cause him to doubt the divine governance that seems to punish the innocent and allow the guilty to go free: 'O thou governour, governynge alle thynges by certein ende, whi refusestow oonly to governe the werkes of men by duwe manere?' (I m.5.31–3). Philosophy diagnoses Boethius as having 'foryeten by which governementz the werld is governed, forthy weenestow that thise mutacions of fortunes fleten withouten governour'; she undertakes to bring him to 'the sothe sentence of governance of the world, that thou bylevest that the governynge of it nis nat subgit ne underput to the folye of thise happes aventurous, but to the resoun of God' (I pr.6.79–92). But for Boethius, the ordered governance of the heavens – the regular motions of the wheeling stars, the waxing and waning of the moon, and the unfailing succession of day and night, summer and winter – is precisely the criterion against which the anarchy in human affairs can be measured (I m.5). In the *Man of Law's Tale*, the operations of the cosmos provide no such reassuring vision of governance; instead they repeat and intensify the human sense of 'thraldom and penance', of helpless subjection to powerful cruelty. Woman's subjection to 'mannes governance' thus becomes in this tale a paradigm of the human condition. Woman's 'thraldom' to man is replicated in man's 'thraldom' to God.

The parallel has been recognized by Sheila Delany: Chaucer, she says, represents through Constance's marriage 'the relation of humanity at large to an apparently arbitrary and inscrutable God'. Constance 'suffers because that is the human condition. Her passivity is what orthodox Christianity of the period recommended as a response to the human condition' ([1974–5] 1983, 37). But it is perhaps already apparent here that for Delany, 'the human condition' is equivalent to the social status quo; she sees Constance's 'extreme humility and silent endurance' (36) as designed to encourage an attitude of passive acceptance in the victims of social injustice. 'Constance seems to exist in order to suffer; yet it is unclear why she suffers', she protests, with the confidence of one who is sure the answer to such questions can be found in an inadequate social welfare programme or a lack of revolutionary commitment. The 'why' that Chaucer turns on the problem of suffering in the *Man of Law's Tale* is larger than that. And so far from trying to suppress this question, it is the function of the tale to raise it. Constance's bleak obedience to her father's will focusses the human sense of pain and bewilderment in the recognition that the power exercised by a supposedly loving Father should make itself felt as cruelty (Kirk, 1978, 96–7). It raises the question of whether fatherhood is simply a mask worn by tyranny; whether human beings are not God's children but his thralls (Mann, 1983a, 171).

There is, of course, no final answer to the 'why' of suffering on a metaphysical level, and Chaucer does not try to give one. Faith in the 'purveiaunce' of God does nothing to dispel or deny the darkness of man's 'ignorance' (479–83). The *Man of Law's Tale* 'answers' the question it so movingly raises only on the emotional, experiential level of Christianity itself, by locating God *in* the suffering. Boethius's question about divine justice is echoed by the constable who is charged with sending Constance out to sea for the second time:

> 'O myghty God, if that it be thy wille,
> Sith thou art rightful juge, how may it be
> That thou wolt suffren innocentz to spille,
> And wikked folk regne in prosperitee?' (813–16)

Like the Emperor of Rome and the planetary bodies, the constable is a figure who unites power and impotence:

> 'O goode Custance, allas, so wo is me
> That I moot be thy tormentour, or deye
> On shames deeth; ther is noon oother weye.' (817–19)

And the same combination of power and helplessness is found in the God he assumes to be all-powerful, as we see in Constance's immediately following prayer to Mary; the ruler of the cosmos is incarnated in the child slain on the cross.

> 'Mooder,' quod she, 'and mayde bright, Marie,
> Sooth is that thurgh wommanes eggement
> Mankynde was lorn, and damned ay to dye,
> For which thy child was on a croys yrent.
> Thy blisful eyen sawe al his torment;
> Thanne is ther no comparison bitwene
> Thy wo and any wo man may sustene.' (841–7)

Divine power dissolves into powerlessness; the human victim becomes the tormentor. In the Crucifixion, the 'why' of human suffering is turned back on human kind: it is to mankind and not to God that the 'why' of divine suffering is to be addressed.

The cruelty of which mankind complains in the divine Father is nowhere more apparent than in the Crucifixion of his own Son. Constance's identification with Mary's maternal sufferings teaches us to see that her sorrowful questioning of Alla's paternal cruelty would fit equally well on the lips of Mary at the foot of the cross (Mann, 1983a, 174):[2]

> 'O litel child, allas! What is thy gilt,
> That nevere wroghtest synne as yet, pardee?
> Why wil thyn harde fader han thee spilt?' (855–7)

Deguileville's 'Piteous complaint of the Virgin Mary for the death and passion of her son', which I quote in Hoccleve's translation, makes the implicit parallel evident:[3]

> 'O fadir god, how fers & how cruel,
> In whom thee list or wilt, canst thow thee make.
> Whom wilt thow spare, ne wot I neuere a deel,
> Syn thow thy sone hast to the deeth betake,
> That the offendid neuere, ne dide wrake,
> Or mystook him to the, or disobeyde,
> Ne to noon othere dide he harm or seide.'
>
> (ed. Seymour, 1–7)

Yet the very framing of this question is enough to make it clear that the division between cruel Father and suffering Son is, once again, an illusion; the Father *is* the Son who suffers, united in singleness of godhead. The Father's cruelty is the vehicle for the Son's love. And just as power dissolves into powerlessness, so powerlessness assumes power; it is through the suffering of the cross that mankind is redeemed. Thus Constance invokes the 'hooly croys', not only as symbol of suffering, 'reed of the Lambes blood', but also as a source of strength and power, 'Victorious tree, proteccioun of trewe' (451–62).

The *Man of Law's Tale* deconstructs power, showing that it does not exist as a separate, self-contained entity, like a parcel that can be transferred from one possessor to another. Instead, it is diffused into its operations, where it is qualified by the complex relationships of which it forms part. The tale contemplates the question of what power is or could be – a question that feminism, in the struggle for urgent and immediate objectives, sometimes fails to bring into focus. I quote a recent example, which there is no advantage in attributing: 'What the women's movement wanted (and still wants) is for

---

2   The Marian parallel is recognized (with illustration from the Pseudo-Bonaventuran *Meditations*) by Weissman (1979, 151–2), but is interpreted as an instance of Chaucer's ridicule of 'late Gothic piety' in the tale.
3   The lament forms part of the debate between the green tree and the dry tree in Deguileville's *Pèlerinage de l'ame* (6353ff.), the continuation of the *Pèlerinage de la vie humaine*, from which Chaucer translated a hymn to the Virgin (*An ABC*).

women themselves to have power so that they do not need to depend on men granting it to them.' It is hard to disagree with this. But then we may ask: power over whom? over what? If women identify male power as repression, how can they wish to acquire such power? 'Power over their own lives' might be the safe answer; the question is, how great can that power be? The cosmic scale of the *Man of Law's Tale* means that it moves on the plane where the writ of human power over human lives ceases to run. To ignore the existence of this plane is to fall prey to delusions about power whose function is precisely to foster masculine self-importance. There is a telling moment in the *Second Nun's Tale* where the Roman prefect Almachius attempts to subdue Cecilia by boasting of his power:

> 'Han noght oure myghty princes to me yiven,
> Ye, bothe power and auctoritee
> To maken folk to dyen or to lyven?
> Why spekestow so proudly thanne to me?' (470–3)

Unimpressed, Cecilia reveals the hollowness of this claim:

> 'Thou seyst thy princes han thee yeven myght
> Bothe for to sleen and for to quyken a wight;
> Thou, that ne mayst but oonly lyf bireve,
> Thou hast noon oother power ne no leve.' (480–3)

Almachius is no more than a 'ministre of deeth' (485); his vaunted power is only the power to destroy. This is a power already available to women, as the Sultaness and Donegild show. The *Man of Law's Tale*, so far from endorsing this kind of power, turns against it the full force of its indignation, calling it 'tirannye' (779).

Constance's 'silent endurance' does not imply limpness or inertia; when attacked on board ship by a would-be rapist, she resists so vigorously that she throws him overboard 'with hir struglyng wel and myghtily', so that he is drowned (921–2) – the only instance, this, in Chaucer, of a woman fending off rape by her own physical efforts. Still less does it imply masochism, as Delany suggests; there is no sign that she takes pleasure in the sufferings inflicted on her. As Eugene Clasby puts it:

Her acceptance of what she cannot change is not to be construed as submission to the rule of those who have contrived her situation. Her womanhood is not a sign of human bondage, but an image of human freedom. It is an image of independence from circumstances and worldly authority, of the human capacity to live and to give life, even in the most desperate of situations. (1976–9, 225–6)

For Chaucer, this Boethian freedom from the bondage of Fortune was the highest ideal of Christian philosophy, and it is a sign of the importance he gives to women that it is not in a man, but in two women – Constance and Griselda – that he embodies this ideal.

The operations of power in this tale are not, however, restricted to the machinations of the destructive figures – the Sultaness, Donegild, and the knight who engineers Constance's accusation for murder. Power is manifested in a very different way in pity, which works throughout the tale to counteract the machinations of 'tirannye'. It prompts the constable and Hermengild to take Constance in and shelter her (528–9). It is likewise the agent of Constance's release from the charge of murdering Hermengild, when her plight arouses the pity of her judge, King Alla:

> The kynges herte of pitee gan agryse,
> Whan he saugh so benigne a creature
> Falle in disese and in mysaventure ...
>
> This Alla kyng hath swich compassioun,
> As gentil herte is fulfild of pitee,
> That from his eyen ran the water doun. (614–16, 659–61)

Pity is the pressure brought to bear by the sufferer on the beholder; it is the invisible strength which acts as the 'champioun' Constance lacks (631). The appeal to Christ to be her 'stronge champion' (635) is answered by Alla's pity, which is the vehicle for God's power as the Sultaness's intransigence is the vehicle for Satan's: he makes the knight swear the truth of his accusation on the Gospels, provoking the hand of heaven to strike him down and a divine voice to proclaim Constance's innocence. Here as in the *Franklin's Tale* pity is a *dynamic* power.

Alla's power to save Constance is thus qualified on the one hand by its role as a surrogate for God's power, and on the other by the fact that it is pity for Constance's suffering that calls it into action. Pity cancels power, uniting beholder with sufferer – a union enacted in the Middle English word 'pitous' itself, which means both 'pitiable' and 'pitying'. It is a union we can see also in the language of Constance's prayer to the Virgin:

> 'Thou glorie of wommanhede, thow faire may,
> Thow haven of refut, brighte sterre of day,
> Rewe on my child, that of thy gentillesse
> Rewest on every reweful in distresse.' (851–4)

'Rewe' and 'rewest' are called into existence as a response to 'reweful', but are also presupposed by it; the pitier is absorbed into the state of the pitied, the pitiable create pity. Pity submerges the Creator in his creation, uniting power and suffering in the image of the cross, 'Reed of the Lambes blood ful of pitee' (452). It unites Mary with the suffering of her child, in fulfilment of Simeon's prophecy that 'a sword shall pierce through thy own soul also' (Luke 2:35).

The Middle English lyric 'Stond well, moder, under Rode' (ed. Davies, no. 24) reflects the common belief that the pains Mary suffered at her son's Crucifixion stood in place of the pangs of childbirth that she had been spared at the Nativity (Keiser, 1985, 171):

> 'Moder, now thou might well leren
> Whet sorewe haveth that children beren,
> Whet sorewe it is with childe gon.' (37–9)

Her pain is the common pain of women. So Constance sees in Mary's pain the mirror of her own; the community of suffering creates the community of pity. Constance's support is not in the bland assurance of a divine plan, but in her imagined identification with another woman's pain. The *Man of Law's Tale* does not produce Christianity like a rabbit out of a hat to 'answer' the problems of human existence; instead, it grounds Christianity in human experience, painfully feeling its way through cruelty to the pity that beholds and suffers.

Most important of all, the circle of pity reaches beyond the bounds of the story to embrace the reader (Gray, 1979, 185). The *Man of Law's Tale* is, one might say, the literary counterpart of the Pietà – a form developed in the visual arts at exactly this period, and for which the Middle English name was 'a pite' (*MED* 5)[4] – in which Mary's pity for her dead son, Christ's pity for mankind, and the beholder's pity for their suffering, are realized as a single emotion.[5] Nothing could be further from the truth than Morton Bloomfield's claim that 'the tragedy of victimization' represented in this tale distances the reader from the narrative because we 'perpetually feel superior to' the suffering victim (1972, 385). On the contrary, Chaucer appeals to the power of pity to work on the reader as it does on Alla, obliterating distance in an intense identification of feeling:

> Have ye nat seyn somtyme a pale face,
> Among a prees, of hym that hath be lad
> Toward his deeth, wher as hym gat no grace,
> And swich a colour in his face hath had
> Men myghte knowe his face that was bistad
> Amonges alle the faces in that route?
> So stant Custance, and looketh hire aboute. (645–51)

---

[4]   The earliest examples are early fifteenth-century, but there is no reason to suppose that the term is not as old as the form itself, which developed in late fourteenth-century Germany. Pinder (1920) argues that the roots of the Pietà are literary; the *Man of Law's Tale* is a good example of the general sensibility that stimulated its development.

[5]   The Pietà is an example of the pictorial aids to devotion to which art historians apply the term 'Andachtsbild' ('meditational image'); Panofsky comments on such images that they encourage in the beholder a contemplative immersion in the subject represented, a spiritual fusion of subject and object (1927, 264).

The appeal in the next stanza to 'queenes, lyvynge in prosperitee,/Duchesses, and ye ladyes everichone' to have 'som routhe' on Constance (652–4), is an appeal to submerge the difference represented by their own 'prosperitee' in an imaginative identification with the fate threatening this 'Emperoures doghter'. The pathetic mode of the tale is thus a means by which the reader can be 'educated' into pity, can relinquish neutrality and independence in an imaginative surrender to the story.

Precisely because it asks for such a surrender, the power of pathos is often resisted by modern readers (e.g. Weissman, 1979), but it is for all that a power of which the women's movement has freely availed itself. What legitimates its use here is the tale's representation of the *strength* necessary to surrender. It is a strength we feel in Constance's unshaken dignity, in her equally calm acceptance of disaster and of good fortune, in her unconscious influence on those around her. The twice-repeated motif of the rudderless boat is at the heart of this tale because it expresses the courage needed to hazard the self to the flux of events, bereft of all supports to selfhood save selfhood alone. And it also expresses the power that is released as a result of this surrender, in the shape of the mysterious force that preserves Constance from death and carries her to unforeseen destinations. This is a power that is guaranteed poetically, as the fussy machinations of 'tirannye' are not, in the two great series of rhetorical questions which confront the miracle of Constance's preservation. I quote only a part:

> Now sith she was nat at the feeste yslawe,
> Who kepte hire fro the drenchyng in the see?
> Who kepte Jonas in the fisshes mawe
> Til he was spouted up at Nynyvee?
> Wel may men knowe it was no wight but he
> That kepte peple Ebrayk from hir drenchynge,
> With drye feet thurghout the see passynge.
>
> Who bad the foure spirites of tempest
> That power han t'anoyen lond and see,
> Bothe north and south, and also west and est,
> 'Anoyeth neither see, ne land, ne tree'?
> Soothly, the comandour of that was he
> That fro the tempest ay this womman kepte
> As wel whan she wook as whan she slepte.
>
> Where myghte this womman mete and drynke have
> Thre yeer and moore? How lasteth hire vitaille?
> Who fedde the Egipcien Marie in the cave,
> Or in desert? No wight but Crist, sanz faille.
> Fyve thousand folk it was as greet mervaille
> With loves fyve and fisshes two to feede.
> God sente his foyson at hir grete neede. (484–504)

The brilliance of this lies in the way that the continuity of form disguises a reversal of function: as the flow of questions extends itself, we realize that they are coming back to us as answers, like a wave breaking and returning on itself. Like the 'why' of suffering, the 'why' of salvation is answered only by multiplied images of itself. It is a tautology that constitutes a frank acknowledgement that to answer either question by saying 'it is God's will' is to reformulate the enigma without solving it. But if the questions multiply enigma, they turn it into a source of strength; the confidence that sustains their rhetoric lifts and carries the reader forward on its billowing waves as Constance is lifted and carried on the sea. The reader is summoned to surrender to the tale, to be carried by it rather than to resist it with sceptical interrogation, and to feel this surrender not as cowardly inertia but as the absorption into the movement of a greater power. Constance's surrender to God is re-enacted as literary experience in our own surrender to Chaucer.

The surrender is not, however, rewarded by easy reassurance, and the withholding of this reassurance is another source of the tale's strength. As the tale deconstructs power, so it deconstructs the 'happy ending'; the points where Constance seems to have come finally to an end of suffering – her peaceful life with Hermengild and the constable, her marriage with Alla – prove to be only temporary halting-places before the turbulent movement of events carries her on again. Even at the end of the tale, finality is resisted; no sooner has the joyful reunion between Constance, her father and her husband knotted up the narrative threads into a happy conclusion than Chaucer sets to work to unravel it:

> This kyng Alla, whan he his tyme say,
> With his Custance, his hooly wyf so sweete,
> To Engelond been they come the righte way,
> Wher as they lyve in joye and in quiete.
> But litel while it lasteth, I yow heete,
> Joye of this world, for tyme wol nat abyde;
> Fro day to nyght it changeth as the tyde.
>
> Who lyved euere in swich delit o day
> That hym ne moeved outher conscience,
> Or ire, or talent, or som kynnes affray,
> Envye, or pride, or passion, or offence?
> I ne seye but for this ende this sentence,
> That litel while in joye or in plesance
> Lasteth the blisse of Alla with Custance. (1128–41)

These beautiful and moving lines – some of the most moving in Chaucer's poetry – dissolve the illusion of the 'happy ending' into the momentary fluctuations of lived existence; happiness is not a fixed state but a series of discrete moments brought on the tide of life, with 'sodeyn wo' always hard behind (421–7). This time the rhetorical question is not a dramatic challenge, but a quiet appeal to the common knowledge that comes from a shared humanity – a knowledge of the inevitable instabilities of mood and feeling that make change an ineradicable part of human experience, and patience, here as in the *Franklin's Tale*, a necessary response. Resignation is not a matter of pious platitudes that blanket out the realities of suffering; rather, it lies in the matter-of-fact simplicity of tone in these lines, in the unblinking steadiness of vision with which they focus on the inevitability of change. The possibility of suffering disappears only with the possibility of happiness; it is only when Constance returns to her father after Alla's death, in a circular movement that shows her life to have run its worldly course, that she is said to have 'scaped al hire aventure' (1151). To live in the world is to be borne on the flux of 'aventure'; patience and pity follow its movement.

The *Physician's Tale* is closely linked to the *Man of Law's Tale*. It too is a tale of pathos, focussing on suffering. Virginius feels himself obliged to kill his daughter Virginia, in order to save her from becoming the sexual prey of the false judge Apius. And it too has met with suspicious hostility and with attempts to deal with the problem of suffering by denying its necessity. Virginius is blamed for having acted rashly, for having prized his daughter's virginity above her life, for having failed to appeal to the 'freendes' whose support we are told he enjoys (4), or to the 'thousand peple' who arrive in time to reveal Apius's villainy and save Virginius from punishment (260–1). But it is not just Virginius who shows no interest in these practical possibilities, it is also the tale itself. The 'why' of suffering is not addressed to the question of how it can be avoided, but to the question of its meaning. Thus the *raison d'être* of the tale, as Chaucer tells it, is its focussing of two major paradoxes: first, that Virginia's 'beautee was hire deth', as the Host puts it, and second, that Virginius's cruelty to his daughter is the expression of his love.

As in the *Man of Law's Tale*, human suffering mirrors divine suffering. Like Christ, Virginia has not deserved to die (216–17); like Christ, she is slain by her father, 'For love, and nat for hate' (225). Pity wears the visage of cruelty: 'My pitous hand moot smyten of thyn heed' (226). Virginia compares herself with Jephtha's daughter, allegorized in medieval exegesis as a type of Christ's sacrifice (Hoffman, 1967–8). Her submission to her father – 'Dooth with youre child youre wyl, a Goddes name!' (250) – echoes Christ's agony in the garden: 'Father, if thou be willing, remove this cup from me: nevertheless not my will, but thine, be done' (Luke 22: 42; cf. Matt. 26: 39, 42). In Virginius, the suffering of God the Father is united with the suffering of Mary: the 'fadres pitee stikynge thurgh his herte' (211) echoes the metaphor of the sword piercing Mary's heart at the death of her son. In the light of these thickly concentrated allusions, Sheila Delany's statement that this tale lacks 'redeeming symbolic depth' is little short of astonishing ([1981], 1990, 130). It is almost *all* symbol; the tale converges on the central emblematic scene in which the father kills his daughter, on the event that unites human experience with divine.

Like the *Man of Law's Tale*, this is also a tale about 'governance' and 'thral-dom' (Mann, 1983a, 176). It begins with a long address to those who have 'governaunce' over children (73, 96) – 'maistresses', fathers and mothers; Virginia's virtue, which means that she stands in no need of a 'maistresse', seems to set her free even from benign 'governance'. But, like Constance, she is threatened with 'thraldom': the churl Claudius, at Apius's prompting, claims she is his 'thral' (183, 189), not Virginius's daughter. Virginia chooses to die as a daughter rather than to live as a thrall; of the two alternatives confronting her, she chooses 'deeth' rather than 'shame' (214, 249).

The narrative possibility that threatened Dorigen in the *Franklin's Tale* is here grimly realized. Rape – in this case, a lifetime of rape[6] – is averted by death. Bodily destruction is preferred to destruction of the self. But whereas Dorigen is accused of delay in carrying out her projected suicide, Virginius is accused of haste in killing his daughter. The problem seems to lie in the fact that the death that averts rape is administered by a man, rather than the woman herself: one form of male violence is averted by another. The point of the *Physician's Tale* is, however, to show the crucial distinction between the two parallel acts of male violence, the one informed by the desire to 'enthral' Virginia, the other by love. The one aims to extinguish her selfhood, the other to save it. The notion that Virginius acts solely out of a rigid adherence to a 'masculine-feminine ideal of virginity' (Cox, 1997, 63) finds no support in Chaucer's text – although it *is* applicable to some other versions of the tale, where Virginius and Icilius, Virginia's betrothed, assert their determination to preserve the chastity that reflects their masculine honour.[7] Chaucer, signifi-cantly, removes these assertions of masculine honour; equally significantly, his is the only version in which Virginia is told of her own death beforehand, and the only one in which she is allowed to speak about it. If her speech expresses acquiescence in her father's will, this does not represent her submis-sion to a 'tyrannical father who demands absolute control over his children's life' (Laskaya, 1995, 159), but an acknowledgement that the same external compulsion constrains both of them.

The *Physician's Tale* is not an explanatory story – it does not serve to iden-tify the cause of suffering, except as human wickedness – it is an 'enabling' story: that is, it enables us to understand how divine cruelty might be the expression of the Father's love, and how it is wickedness that calls that cruelty

---

[6]   Hoffman's high-minded criticism of the Physician for failing to understand that 'true chastity is a spiritual state' and that the sacrifice of Virginia was therefore unnecessary (1967–8, 30) shows an astounding indifference to what it is that Virginia is to be consigned to. Surprisingly, this indifference is shared by critics writing from a feminist perspective, who likewise see the question at issue as the preservation of virginity rather than the evasion of multiple rape (Bloch, 1989; Laskaya, 1995, 159; Cox, 1997, 95).

[7]   See Livy, *Ab urbe condita* III.xiv (Bryan and Dempster, 1958, 404), and Gower, *Con-fessio Amantis* VII 5247–52 ('Lo, take hir ther, thou wrongfull king,/ For me is levere upon this thing/ To be the fader of a Maide,/ Thogh sche be ded, than if men saide/ That in hir lif sche were schamed/ And I therof were evele named').

into being. Like the *Man of Law's Tale*, finally, the *Physician's Tale* is a tale of 'pitee' – 'pitee' both as *pietas*, familial love, and as compassion (Gray, 1979, 179; Mann, 1983a, 175–6). Its central scene not only shows us Virginius's fatherly pity for his daughter, it also arouses pity in the reader through its description of their tender words and embraces, Virginia's tears and swoon, and her childish request that her father should 'smyte softe' (252). The people who save Virginius from the death he must have assumed as a necessary consequence of his act are aroused by 'routhe and ... pitee' at Virginia's fate (261). Pity counteracts tyranny. Those who complain that it did not do so earlier, in time to save Virginia, make the mistake of identifying function with mimesis. If the tale represents pity as a response to tyranny, its *function* is to nurture a pity that will pre-empt tyranny.

In Virginia, Lucretia and Christ become one. The sacrificial victim who cancels death by spiritual survival takes female form; woman, like Christ, takes her death 'in pacience' (223; cf. *Melibee*). Dubious as the honour may seem to us, a Christian society had no greater to bestow. Woman's suffering is not thereby legitimized – as Christ's was not – but it acquires a centrality through being the point at which divine experience merges most fully with human. When we turn to the *Clerk's Tale*, we find that there too, woman's patient suffering elevates her to a type of Christ, with the addition that, like Christ's, it is a *powerful* suffering. The motto of the *Franklin's Tale* – 'patience conquers' – is confirmed and deepened as the marital relationship takes on a Christological dimension.

The *Clerk's Tale* has proved even harder for the modern reader to accommodate than the *Physician's Tale*. Medieval readers were uncomfortable with Walter's cruelty, but they seem to have had no difficulty in admiring Griselda, only in believing that such extreme patience could exist (Middleton, 1980). From the nineteenth century onwards, however, readers have found it difficult to give her the sympathetic approval that the tale requires (Morse, 1985, 54). And on the face of it, their response is reasonable. Griselda acquiesces not only in her own 'subjeccioun' to her husband, but also in the death which she supposes him to inflict on her children. She endures without protest his dismissal of her in favour of a new wife, and obeys his command to set the house in order for the marriage. In all this she is praised for her steadfast calm and uncomplaining patience. The *Merchant's Tale*'s conception of the ideal wife as a doormat, a creature without will or feeling of her own, here seems to be realized in the flesh.

Paying attention to the narrative detail of the tale will go some way towards avoiding misinterpretation. It is important to note, for example, that Griselda's unquestioning obedience to her husband is not the simple result of her marriage vow, but something that she takes upon herself with the unique promise that is the special condition of her marriage. It is this promise, not her wifely duty, that exacts Griselda's cheerful compliance with Walter's every wish. As in the *Franklin's Tale*, a fairy-tale promise claims an absolute adherence that the practical common-sense of everyday life could not tolerate. And as in the *Franklin's Tale*, adherence to it becomes a test of 'trouthe', of the integrity of selfhood invested in the promise; to deny one's promise is to deny oneself. It is in this steady maintenance of selfhood that Griselda's strength makes itself felt in the very act of self-denial.

The second thing that must play a part in interpretation of this tale is that this marriage, like that of Dorigen and Arveragus, is in its early stages forged by a complicated interaction of 'lordshipe' and 'servage'. Walter's marriage is not the result of his own initiative; it is imposed upon him by his tenants' wishes. To Walter, marriage appears 'servage':

> 'Ye wol,' quod he, 'myn owene peple deere,
> To that I nevere erst thoughte streyne me.
> I me rejoysed of my liberte,
> That seelde tyme is founde in mariage;
> Ther I was free, I moot been in servage.' (143–7)

His tenants represent it, however, in the terms of the *Franklin's Tale* – that is, as a paradoxical fusion of 'servage' and 'lordshipe':

> 'Boweth youre nekke under that blisful yok
> Of soveraynetee, noght of servyse,
> Which that men clepe spousaille or wedlok.' (113–15)

Despite his regret for his lost liberty, Walter assents 'of [his] free wyl' to their demands (150), but he in turn lays an imposition on them: instead of letting them find for him one of the highest-born in the land, he will choose his own wife, and whoever she may be, they are to agree to accept her with the honour and reverence fitting for an emperor's daughter, and never to grumble at his choice (162–70). To this demand, his people agree 'with hertely wyl' (176).

The process of negotiation by which the marriage is agreed on is thus a classic example of the combination of 'lordshipe' and 'servage'. Each of the parties involved yields in one respect in order to assert their will in another. The natural expectation is that the marriage will bear the same character as the negotiations that have brought it about – that it will indeed be a 'blisful yok/Of soveraynetee' for both partners. The expectation is strengthened by the fact that Walter's response to his tenants shows the 'pitee' that subordinates the wishes of a great lord to those of his inferiors:

> Hir meeke preyere and hir pitous cheere
> Made the markys herte han pitee. (141–2)

It also shows the trust that embodies a willingness to hazard the self to the control of others: 'I se youre trewe entente,/And truste upon youre wit, and have doon ay' (148–9). Trust is evident likewise in his refusal of the high-born wife that they would choose for him:

> 'For God it woot, that children ofte been
> Unlyk hir worthy eldres hem bifore;
> Bountee comth al of God, nat of the streen
> Of which they been engendred and ybore.
> I truste in Goddes bountee, and therfore
> My mariage and myn estaat and reste
> I hym bitake; he may doon as hym leste.' (155–61)

The choice of a low-born wife, which in hindsight we read as allowing Walter more room for dictatorship, appears at this moment – with perfect validity – as a surrender of the self to divine providence. It is not an insurance policy designed to minimize the loss of liberty as far as possible, but on the contrary, a leap in the dark, an act of faith in the individual virtue buried by obscure circumstances.

The promise that Walter exacts from Griselda is a call for a similar leap in the dark on her part, a similar exercise of trust. It seems, on the face of it, like the last link in the chain of acts combining 'lordshipe' and 'servage': Griselda's elevation to power and riches is twinned with her subordination to her husband. Yet from this point on, trust fails and mutuality ceases. Walter is obsessed with the desire to actualize the total commitment which has been promised, to see whether in fact it has limits or secret reservations. Mutuality is swallowed up in the one-sided exercise of his will. The marital unanimity which in the *Franklin's Tale* flows spontaneously from the shifts and adaptations of each partner to the other is here achieved by painful grinding effort, as Griselda must bend all her own desires to the shape that Walter imposes on them.

> For which it semed thus: that of hem two
> Ther nas but o wyl, for as Walter leste,
> The same lust was hire plesance also.
> And, God be thanked, al fil for the beste.
> She shewed wel, for no wordly unreste
> A wyf, as of hirself, nothing ne sholde
> Wille in effect, but as hir housbonde wolde. (715–21)

It is a picture that seems to call for the acerbic scorn with which Defoe's Roxana greets her lover's attempts to persuade her that marriage involves no loss of liberty, for 'where there was a mutual Love, there could be no Bondage; but that there was but one Interest, one Aim, one Design; and all conspir'd to make both very happy':

Ay, said I, *that is the Thing I complain of*; the Pretence of Affection, takes from a Woman every thing that can be call'd *herself*; she is to have no

Interest; no Aim; no View; but all is the Interest, Aim, and View, of the
Husband ... you, that are now upon even Terms with me, and I with you,
says I, are the next Hour sat up upon the Throne, and the humble Wife
plac'd at your Footstool; all the rest, that you call Oneness of Interest,
Mutual Affection, *and the like*, is Curtesie and Kindness then, and a
Woman is indeed, infinitely oblig'd where she meets with it; but can't
help herself where it fails. (149–51)

The *Clerk's Tale* goes beyond the picture of mutual affection presented in the
Franklin's Tale to ask, as does Roxana, what happens when it fails. In this tale,
patience is shorn of its quality of movement, its role as reciprocal response, and
is frozen into the marble stillness of endurance. Walter's summons to Griselda
to 'Shewe now youre pacience' (495) is as cynical as, if less comic than, the
Wife of Bath's exhortations to her old husbands to practise the patience they
preach (*Wife of Bath's Prologue* 434–9). He even has the audacity to *pretend* to
experience 'lordshipe' as 'servage' as a pretext for tormenting her:

> 'But now knowe I in verray soothfastnesse
> That in greet lordshipe, if I wel avyse,
> Ther is greet servitute in sondry wyse.
>
> I may nat doon as every plowman may.
> My peple me constreyneth for to take
> Another wyf, and crien day by day.' (796–801)

There is no shred of support for Walter's behaviour in the narrative; on the
contrary, Chaucer carefully adds to it explicit condemnations of his obsessive
desire to test Griselda.

> But as for me, I seye that yvele it sit
> To assaye a wyf whan that it is no nede,
> And putten hire in angwyssh and in drede ...
>
> O nedelees was she tempted in assay!
> But wedded men ne knowe no mesure,
> Whan that they fynde a pacient creature. (460–2, 621–3)

Where Petrarch asks whether the loss of her children did not sufficiently prove
Griselda's obedience and fidelity without further testing, Chaucer explicitly
refers this same question to women:

> But now of wommen wolde I axen fayn
> If thise assayes myghte nat suffise?
> What koude a sturdy housbonde moore devyse
> To preeve hir wyfhod and hir stedefastnesse,
> And he continuynge evere in sturdinesse? (696–700)

Admiration for Griselda's patience in no way implies the sanctioning of Walter's right to test her. Bernard Levy's suggestion that the test is designed 'in order to prove her worthy of complete acceptance into the royal society' by revealing her innate 'gentilesse' (1986, 403) is completely alien to the spirit of the tale, both in its complacent snobbery (what proves *Walter's* 'gentilesse'?) and in its denial of Chaucer's insistence that Walter's testing of his wife is 'nedelees'. The *Clerk's Tale*, so far from being, as Kittredge claimed ([1911–12] 1959, 198), an answer to the *Wife of Bath's Tale*, shares with it – and with the *Franklin's Tale* and the *Melibee* – the same vision of a marital ideal, founded on the surrender of masculine 'maistrye'. The monstrous perversion of this ideal created by Walter's tyranny merely proves the point from a negative direction.

We know, then, how the women will judge Walter, but how are they to judge Griselda? Whereas Roxana's imaginary wife 'can't help herself', Griselda *could* help herself but renounces the attempt. She could, that is, protest and remonstrate, or appeal to outside agencies for the protection of her children. The fairy-tale absolutes of the story of course teach the reader to renounce such impulses towards practical solutions along with the realism they imply. Yet realism is not a mode entirely alien to this tale, as Elizabeth Salter has shown (1962, 50–9); on the contrary, some of its finest moments reside in the vivid immediacy of speech and thought which realizes Griselda's sufferings as lived experience. Nor is the cynicism that pervades the comic tales entirely absent; behind the bland assurance that 'A wyf, as of hirself, nothing ne sholde/Wille in effect, but as hir housbonde wolde' (720–1), there flickers briefly the kind of irony that runs through the mock-encomium of the *Merchant's Tale* – an irony that accommodates the protest Griselda renounces. The protest suppressed throughout the tale finally breaks loose in its Envoy, where husbands are warned not to repeat Walter's experiment, for modern women are made in a different mould, and 'noble wyves' are exhorted to take care that they show no such patience and humility.

> Folweth Ekko, that holdeth no silence,
> But evere answereth at the countretaille.
> Beth nat bidaffed for youre innocence,
> But sharply taak on yow the governaille.
> Emprenteth wel this lessoun in youre mynde,
> For commune profit sith it may availle.

> Ye archewyves, stondeth at defense,
> Syn ye be strong as is a greet camaille;
> Ne suffreth nat that men yow doon offense.
> And sklendre wyves, fieble as in bataille,
> Beth egre as is a tygre yond in Ynde;
> Ay clappeth as a mille, I yow consaille.

Ne dreed hem nat; doth hem no reverence,
For though thyn housbonde armed be in maille,
The arwes of thy crabbed eloquence
Shal perce his brest and eek his aventaille.
In jalousie I rede eek thou hym bynde,
And thou shalt make hym couche as doth a quaille.

If thou be fair, ther folk been in presence,
Shewe thou thy visage and thyn apparaille;
If thou be foul, be fre of thy dispence;
To gete thee freendes ay do thy travaille;
Be ay of chiere as light as leef on lynde,
And lat hym care, and wepe, and wrynge, and waille!

(1189–1212)

As in the *Merchant's Tale* and the *Wife of Bath's Prologue*, female shrewish-ness is seen as the natural punishment for masculine bullying. But if the Envoy shows us this as the most obvious response to behaviour such as Walter's (and what else is there, given that the 'Mutual Affection' of the *Franklin's Tale* is ruled out by the very terms of the problem?), it also shows us that it leads straight back into the impasse of marital hostility: '*Oon* of us two moste bowen, doutelees', as the Wife of Bath tells her husbands (440). Mutuality dis-appears as a possibility. So the *Clerk's Tale* refuses the obvious option of Griselda's rebellion, as the *Franklin's Tale* refuses the obvious narrative option of Dorigen's suicide. And our consciousness of this refusal goes towards cre-ating our sense of the strength in Griselda's patience. 'The energy that would animate a crime is not more than is wanted to inspire a resolved submission', as George Eliot observes in *Middlemarch*. The energy released in the Envoy is our measure of the energy involved in Griselda's submission.

But the most obvious testimony to Griselda's strength is the tale's ending. It is an ending often ignored in critical accounts of the tale, yet it is crucial to its meaning. For it is not Griselda who gives way under the pressures of her trial, but Walter. As in the *Franklin's Tale*, the story does not simply illustrate the virtue of patience; it shows that patience *conquers*. And here, as there, it conquers through pity. The 'pitee' that had marked Walter at the beginning of the tale reasserts itself, already threatening to break forth as he inaugurates her final test:

But wel unnethes thilke word he spak,
But wente his wey, for routhe and for pitee. (892–3)

The 'routhe' that prompts his final change of heart ('This sturdy markys gan his herte dresse/To rewen upon hire wyfly stedfastnesse': 1049–50) blossoms into the 'pitous joye' of the reconciliation scene (1080), calling forth 'many a teere on many a pitous face' (1104).

Through pity, suffering realizes itself as power. Griselda's patience – her 'sadnesse', in Chaucer's term – constitutes an unrelenting pressure on Walter.

It is a pressure felt by the reader of the tale in the form of narrative suspense; like Walter, the reader is driven by curiosity, the desire to know at what point Griselda will give way. Thwarted of satisfaction on this side by Griselda's unvarying self-consistency ('She was ay oon in herte and in visage': 711), the forward pressure of narrative suspense turns instead to Walter for release, finding relief, as does Walter himself, in his capitulation. The 'variance' he looks for in Griselda he realizes in himself. The 'ynogh' with which he closes her trials corresponds in one sense to the 'ynogh' with which the Knight halts the unrelenting stream of woe which is the *Monk's Tale* (2768); human nature resists sameness, seeks the relief of change. It is the pressure of Griselda's sameness that eventually issues in Walter's change.

The word 'ynogh' is of central significance in this tale, as I have shown in detail elsewhere (1983b). Walter's response to Griselda's promise to obey him – 'This is ynogh, Grisilde myn' – is repeated verbatim as he puts an end to her testing. The repetition raises the question of what *is* enough; so far from being satisfied by Griselda's first promise, Walter succumbs to the insatiable desire to test her 'alwey moore and moore' (458). Walter's insatiability is answered by Griselda's 'sadnesse', a word coloured in this context by its oldest English meaning (still active in Chaucer's usage), 'satisfied, sated, full' (*MED* 1). Griselda's 'sadnesse' – steadfastness, constancy – reflects her 'suffisaunce', the Boethian self-sufficiency that creates her willingness to relinquish wealth, status, children and husband, in the knowledge that none of these things ever belonged to her of right. How deeply Boethian a heroine she is, we can see in the speech that Philosophy imagines Fortune as addressing to Boethius, for it contains the plot of the *Clerk's Tale* in embryo, with Walter as surrogate of Fortune:

> 'Whan that nature brought the foorth out of thi modir wombe, I resceyved the nakid and nedy of alle thynges, and I norissched the with my richesses, and was redy and ententyf thurwe my favour to sustene the – and that maketh the now inpacient ayens me; and I envyrounde the with al the habundance and schynynge of alle goodes that ben in my ryght. Now it liketh me to withdrawe myn hand. Thow hast had grace as he that hath used of foreyne goodes; thow hast no ryght to pleyne the, as though thou haddest outrely forlorn alle thy thynges. Why pleynestow thanne? I have doon the no wrong.' (II pr.2.14–28)

The difference is that Griselda is *not* 'inpacient' at the loss of Fortune's goods; what Philosophy teaches Boethius through Fortune's speech, she expresses in her actions. Her patience is thus not specifically or exclusively a feminine ideal, despite the special relationship women are (as we shall see) given to it. It represents the Stoic 'suffisaunce' which meets 'with evene herte' 'the strook of Fortune or of aventure' (811–12). As in the *Man of Law's Tale*, woman's subjection to man is the experience in which the human subjection to God's 'purveiaunce' is focussed and explored.

Chaucer's concluding comments on the *Clerk's Tale*, which he borrowed from Petrarch, encourage us to see this, and not a moral about proper wifely behaviour, as its true meaning. It is not designed to encourage wives to imitate Griselda, 'for it were inportable, though they wolde', but to encourage all human beings to be 'constant in adversitee'.

> For sith a womman was so pacient
> Unto a mortal man, wel moore us oghte
> Receyven al in gree that God us sent;
> For greet skile is he preeve that he wroghte.
> But he ne tempteth no man that he boghte,
> As seith Seint Jame, if ye his pistel rede;
> He preeveth folk al day, it is no drede.
>
> And suffreth us, as for oure excercise,
> With sharpe scourges of adversitee
> Ful ofte to be bete in sondry wise;
> Nat for to knowe oure wyl, for certes he,
> Er we were born, knew al oure freletee;
> And for oure beste is al his governaunce.
> Lat us thanne lyve in vertuous suffraunce. (1149–62)

Rather than solving the difficulties inherent in the *Clerk's Tale*, this reading of it has in general only been found to increase them, for in paralleling God's role with Walter's, it seems to make of God a sadistic bully. Yet it is precisely this vision of God that the tale wishes us to confront. Like the *Man of Law's Tale*, it asks if his 'governaunce' is mere tyranny, and if mankind's belief in his fatherly kindness is a mere delusion. In her challenging interpretation of the *Clerk's Tale*, Elizabeth Salter drew attention to the jarring note struck by Griselda's reference to Walter as 'benyngne fader':

> 'O tendre, o deere, o yonge children myne!
> Youre woful mooder wende stedfastly
> That crueel houndes or som foul vermyne
> Hadde eten yow; but God of his mercy
> And youre benyngne fader tendrely
> Hath doon yow kept' – and in that same stounde
> Al sodeynly she swapte adoun to grounde. (1093–9)

Griselda's thankfulness to Walter and to God would be, Salter believes, appropriate 'in isolation'; the difficulty comes in Chaucer's failure to keep the tale on the general and abstract plane of its religious meaning. Walter's actions are 'not sufficiently mysterious and inexplicable'; we know too much about his cruelty (1962, 60).

So far from representing a failure in narrative control, however, the jarring reference to Walter as 'benyngne fader' is the very nub of the tale's meaning.

For the difficulty in reconciling Walter's evident cruelty with his claimed benignity is the very problem that the tale transposes on to its religious level. If Walter appears to kill his children, God does so in sober earnest. Griselda's words of renunciation to Walter – 'Naked out of my fadres hous …/I cam, and naked moot I turne agayn' (871–2) – echo Job's response to the news of his children's death: 'Naked came I out of my mother's womb, and naked shall I return thither: the Lord gave, and the Lord hath taken away; blessed be the name of the Lord' (1: 21). Job's words are the model for the response of the earthly mother whose children are taken from her by death; like Griselda, she must trust in the benignity of the divine Father whose actions seem both senseless and cruel (Mann, 1983a, 179–80). Griselda's dignified speeches of resignation to Walter's will are, we are told, appropriate for the deity, but inappropriate for her husband. But it is this very inappropriateness that raises the question of their appropriateness for God, the question that orthodox piety effectively suppresses; it forces us to experience just what is asked of human beings in their submission to the divine will.

As in the *Man of Law's Tale*, the religious level of the *Clerk's Tale* does not 'answer' the problem of suffering but finds an imaginative form within which it can be apprehended as a mystery. The gulf between cruelty and benignity cannot be bridged by explanation; it can only be bridged by faith – the 'feith' that Griselda brought to Walter as her marriage dowry.

> 'To yow broghte I noght elles, out of drede,
> But feith, and nakednesse, and maydenhede.' (865–6)

Trust fails in Walter, but it never falters in Griselda, however sharp her awareness of the disparity between the 'gentil and kynde' aspect he wore at their wedding and his later harshness. It is in the words 'benyngne fader' that we can plumb the depth of this trust, and thus take true measure of the depth of trust needed to have faith in the benignity of the divine will. Like Arveragus's trust in Dorigen, Griselda's trust erases the need for explanations and recriminations; it finds 'suffisaunce' in the restoration of what has been lost, a restoration as gratuitous, as little to be claimed by right, as the original gift.

The 'sadnesse' that had seemed to suppress emotion in Griselda releases itself *as* emotion in the tightness of her embrace:

> And in hire swough so sadly holdeth she
> Hire children two, whan she gan hem t'embrace,
> That with greet sleighte and greet difficultee
> The children from hire arm they gonne arace. (1100–3)

The religious meaning of the *Clerk's Tale* lies not in the revelation of a sanctioning explanation for Griselda's suffering, but in the imagined participation in this ecstatic moment when it is obliterated by joy. It is a moment which is strangely and movingly illuminated by a passage in the autobiography of the nineteenth-century writer Margaret Oliphant – a passage concentrating all the sufferings she endured over the years in the loss, one by one, of the children she struggled to support. I quote it because it not only shares the same imagined vision as the end of the *Clerk's Tale*, but because it too shows the power of the feelings that can be released into the simple word 'enough'.

> Ah me, alas! pain ever, for ever, God alone knows what was the anguish of these years. And yet now I think of *ces beaux jours quand j'étais si malheureuse*, the moments of relief were so great and so sweet that they seemed compensation for the pain, – I remembered no more the anguish. Lately in my many sad musings it has been brought very clearly before my mind how often all the horrible tension, the dread, the anxiety which there are no words strong enough to describe, – which devoured me, but which I had to conceal often behind a smiling face, – would yield in a moment, in the twinkling of an eye, at the sound of a voice, at the first look, into an ineffable ease and the overwhelming happiness of relief from pain, which is, I think, our highest human sensation, higher and more exquisite than any positive enjoyment in this world. It used to sweep over me like a wave, sometimes when I opened a door, sometimes in a letter, – in all simple ways. I cannot explain, but if this should ever come to the eye of any woman in the passion and agony of motherhood, she will more or less understand. I was thinking lately, or rather, as sometimes happens, there was suddenly presented to my mind, like a suggestion from some one else, the recollection of these ineffable happinesses, and it seemed to me that it meant that which would be when one pushed through that last door and was met – oh, by what, by whom? – by instant relief. The wave of sudden ease and warmth and peace and joy. I felt, to tell the truth, that it was one of them who brought that to my mind, and I said to myself, 'I will not want any explanation, I will not ask any question, – the first touch, the first look, will be enough, as of old, yet better than of old.' (146–7)

To see Walter as an image of God's cruelty and Griselda as an image of human suffering is not, however, to exhaust the religious meaning of this tale. It is merely the first step that leads, through *engagement* with the problem of suffering, to an even deeper level of the tale, where the symbolic associations of the two central characters astonishingly reverse themselves. For as in the *Man of Law's Tale*, we see that it is not humanity only that suffers, but also God. Griselda's suffering reaches beyond the human, figuring forth the divine. It is this realisation of the divine in woman's form that is Chaucer's most original development of the meaning of this traditional story.

It is the word 'enough' that leads us on to this deeper level. Its numerous uses in the tale show Chaucer exploiting a double meaning in the Middle

English adverb 'ynogh', which means not only 'sufficiently, moderately', but also 'extremely, ... fully, completely, entirely ... as much as well could be'.[8] 'Enough', that is, does not represent merely a limited satisfaction; it also represents complete fulfilment. It is not only a mean, a half-way house between the extremes of 'too little' and 'too much', but is also itself an extreme, finding its limit only in the completeness of perfection. So the 'enough' that Griselda bestows on Walter knows no limitation; it is an inexhaustible outpouring that out-distances even his insatiability. And in this boundless will to suffer until satisfaction is reached, Griselda images the Christ who speaks in vision to Julian of Norwich, offering more and yet more:

> Then seide oure good lorde askyng: Arte thou well apayd that I sufferyd for thee? I seyde: ȝe, good lorde, gramercy; ye, good lorde, blessyd moet þow be. Then seyde Jhesu our good lord: If thou arte apayde, I am apayde. It is a joy, a blysse, an endlesse lykyng to me that evyr I sufferd passion for the; and yf I myght suffer more, I wolde suffer more ...

> And in these wordes: If I myght suffer more I wolde suffer more, I saw truly þat as often as he myght dye, as often he wolde, and loue shulde nevyr lett hym haue rest tille he hath done it. And I behelde with gret diligence for to wet how often he wolde dye yf he myght. And truly the nomber passyd my vnderstandyng and my wittes so ferre that my reson myght nott nor cold nott comprehende it ne take it.
> And whan he had thus ofte dyed or shuld die, yet he wolde sett it at nought for loue; for alle thynkyth hym but lytylle in regard of his loue.
> (Long Text, Chap. 22)

As Julian's Christ shares Griselda's limitless suffering, so Walter's desire to have 'more and more' from Griselda is paralleled in Julian's insatiable longing for the divine:

> This saw I bodely, swemly and darkely, and I desyred mor bodely light to haue seen more clerly. And I was answeryde in my reason: If god will shew thee more, he shal be thy light; thou nedyth none but him. For I saw him and sought him, for we be now so blynde and so vnwyse that we can never seke god till what tyme þat he of his goodnes shewyth hym to vs. And whan we see owght of hym graciously, then are we steryd by the same grace to seke with great desyer to see hym more blessedfully. And thus I saw him and sought him, and I had hym and wantyd hym; and this is and should be our comyn workyng in this life, as to my syght.
> (Long Text, Chap. 10)

---

8   See *OED* 1, 2a, and *MED* b, d, e. For more detailed analysis of this word and its associates in the *Clerk's Tale*, see Mann, 1983b, on which the following discussion draws.

Julian of Norwich enables us to see that the religious interpretation of the *Clerk's Tale* that identifies Walter's role with God's is only half of the picture. God is more truly imaged in Griselda's boundless suffering than in Walter's tyrannical cruelty. And in Walter we can see the image of man making endless trial of the patience of God, endlessly testing to see how far it will go. How much man asks of God – and receives from him – can be seen in Griselda's words to Walter:

> 'For wiste I that my deeth wolde do yow ese,
> Right gladly wolde I dyen, yow to plese.
>
> Deth may noght make no comparisoun
> Unto youre love.' (664–7)

Griselda's words do not figure human resignation to God – it is not man who dies to do God 'ese' – but God's self-sacrifice for love of man. In Walter's unworthiness of the flood of love here unstintingly poured out for him, we can gauge man's unworthiness of the divine love that he takes for granted. Like Griselda, God meets man's endless demands with a limitless abundance that man must finally acknowledge as satisfaction. So, like the *Clerk's Tale*, Julian of Norwich finds repose in the simple word 'enough':

> tendyrly oure lorde towchyth vs and blysydfully callyth vs, seyeng in oure soule: Lett me aloone, my derwurdy chylde, intende to me. I am inogh to þe, and enjoy in thy sauiour and in thy saluation. (Long Text, Chap. 36)

In Griselda, human suffering and divine patience are united in one person, as Christ united manhood and Godhead. And it is her 'wommanhede' that is the ground of the union. Patience, like pity, is a *womanly* quality.

> Men speke of Job, and moost for his humblesse,
> As clerkes, whan hem list, konne wel endite,
> Namely of men, but as in soothfastnesse,
> Though clerkes preise wommen but a lite,
> Ther kan no man in humblesse hym acquite
> As womman kan, ne kan been half so trewe
> As wommen been, but it be falle of newe. (932–8)

Job, type of human suffering, was also interpreted in the Middle Ages as a type of Christ. Griselda's patience, like Job's, mirrors the divine in human experience, and mirrors it in female form.

The feminist reader is immediately suspicious: is the assurance that women excel in patient suffering merely a means of confining them in their traditionally subordinate role by praising them for their meek acceptance of it?[9] Reassurance may come from the fact that patience is not, for Chaucer, a gender-specific virtue in the sense that it is a feminine ideal only; on the contrary, it is an ideal for both sexes alike. Activity is not reserved for men, passivity for women; the celebration of patience in the *Franklin's Tale* shows each sex active and passive by turns. But the ideal that governs this alternation is derived from female experience. What makes patience a specifically female quality for Chaucer is not, I think, the conventional expectations of his society about female behaviour. It is rather its intimate connection with female sexuality, and in particular with childbirth. In Latin, *patior* and *patientia* are technical terms for the female role in intercourse (Adams, 1982, 189–90), a usage that gives a punning quality to Chaucer's comments on Constance's wedding night in the *Man of Law's Tale*:

> They goon to bedde, as it was skile and right;
> For thogh that wyves be ful hooly thynges,
> They moste take in pacience at nyght
> Swiche manere necessaries as been plesynges
> To folk that han ywedded hem with rynges,
> And leye a lite hir hoolynesse aside,
> As for the tyme – it may no bet bitide. (708–14)

Constance's patience derives not only from her holiness but also from her sexuality, and it expresses both.

To object to the identification of woman's sexual role as 'passivity' is, paradoxically, to endorse the masculine ideology that defines activity as superior. Chaucer himself is free of any such ideology. For him, it is the 'passive' role that is superior; we must never forget that patience *conquers*. It is 'rigour', the attempt to dominate and control, that is impotent and sterile. So woman's sexual activity expresses itself as acceptance; she is not violated or subordinated by male penetration, but absorbs it into her own essential rhythm, making it part of her own movement.

The quality of acceptance is even more important in childbirth, the crucial demarcation between male and female. In the same passage of the *Man of Law's Tale* we can see how the processes of parturition involve the will in cooperative responsiveness rather than initiatory decision.

---

9   Lesley Johnson objects to the use of the word 'merely' here, asking 'why should the putative response of a feminist be constructed in unfairly reductive terms?' (1994, 203) So far from wishing to be 'unfairly reductive' to a putative feminist, by the 'feminist reader' here I meant *myself*; the question posed here is one I pose seriously to myself. Johnson argues that even if patience is accepted as an ideal for both sexes, 'a valuable question still remains about the masochistic qualities of the kind of spirituality on offer here and why it might be especially appropriate to realize the figure of a suffering God in female form' (ibid.). The second of these questions I try to answer above; the first would need a larger exposition of the word 'masochistic' which itself seems unfairly reductive. As I have argued in connection with Constance, there is no sign at all that Griselda *enjoys* suffering – quite the reverse.

Now faire Custance, that is so humble and meke,
So longe is goon with childe, til that stille
She halt hire chambre, abidyng Cristes wille.

The tyme is come a knave child she beer ...
(Man of Law's Tale 719–22)

The space between the stanzas enacts the quiet space in which the self is subordinated to the workings of nature. 'The tyme is come'; the moment of birth
is determined not by human decree but by natural maturation, the 'fullness of
the time' in which Mary brought forth her son (Gal. 4: 4). So Griselda's 'sadnesse', her 'fullness' of self-sufficiency, is linked with 'ripeness' ('rype and
sad courage': 220; cf. 438). The acceptance of the slow maturation of another
being within one's own is a fundamental image of patience. But the acceptance
called for in childbirth is greater than this: it is above all the acceptance of
pain. When Griselda is called upon to relinquish the second of her children,
she expresses her resignation in Petrarch's Latin version of the tale by saying
'truly, I have no part in these children beyond the bearing of them' ('preter
laborem'; Bryan and Dempster, 1941, 316). Chaucer intensifies her resignation into a strange poignancy:

'I have noght had no part of children tweyne
But first siknesse, and after, wo and peyne.' (650–1)

The strangeness lies in the first impression that Griselda is saying her children
are nothing but a nuisance, and the oddity of this response from one whom we
see elsewhere to be a tenderly loving mother concentrates attention on the
words to find their meaning and the source of their ability to move. It lies,
I think, in the acceptance of suffering that unites the bearing of children with
the endurance of their loss. The 'siknesse, wo and peyne' of pregnancy and
childbirth teach the self-surrender that is the very essence of patience.

Childbirth is not simply an image of suffering; it is an image of 'suffraunce'
in the dual Middle English sense of 'suffering-and-allowing'. The woman in
childbirth becomes the vehicle of a power that she can control only by full
identification with it, by ceasing to resist it. It is the dual sense of 'suffraunce'
that gives new meaning to the final statement that God

... *suffreth* us, as for oure excercise,
With sharpe scourges of adversitee
Ful ofte to be bete in sondry wise ...
And for oure beste is al his governaunce.
Lat us thanne lyve in vertuous *suffraunce.*
(1156–8, 1161–2; my italics)

'Allowing' here seems to be allocated to God; 'suffering' to mankind. But as in
the *Man of Law's Tale*, the tale shows that the suffering that God 'allows' is

visited on himself. Griselda, as she bids her daughter what she thinks is a last farewell, marks her with the sign of the cross 'Of thilke Fader – blessed moote he be! –/That for us deyde upon a croys of tree' (557–8). She does not refer, as she most naturally might, to the Son who died on the cross, but to the Father (Engle, 1989, 450); the Father who decreed the death of his Son is also the Son who suffered death at the will of his Father. For God to 'allow' the world to be as it is is for him also to suffer it, to endure the pain of its cruelty.

Julian of Norwich identifies the nature of the Second Person of the Trinity as 'moderhede', grounding the identification in the quality of mercy that unites Christ with human mothers, but also in the experience of suffering. The suffering of the Cross is assimilated to the pains of childbirth:

> We wytt that alle oure moders bere vs to payne and to dyeng. A,/what is that? But oure very moder Jhesu, he alone beryth vs to joye and to endlesse levyng, blessyd mot he be. Thus he susteyneth vs with in hym in loue and traveyle, in to the full tyme þat he wolde suffer the sharpyst throwes and grevous paynes that evyr were or evyr shalle be, and dyed at the last. And whan he had done, and so borne vs to blysse, yett myght nott all thys make a seeth to his mervelous loue. And that shewd he in theyse hye ovyrpassyng wordes of loue: If I myght suffer more I wold suffer more. He myght no more dye, but he wolde nott stynte werkyng. (Long Text, Chap. 60)[10]

The love that embraces the pain of birth sustains and informs the mother's 'allowing' of her child to be chastised for its own good:

> The kynde lovyng moder that woot and knowyth the neyde of hyr chylde, she kepyth it full tenderly, as the kynde and condicion of moderhed wyll. And evyr as it waxith in age and in stature, she channgyth her werkes, but nott her loue. And when it is wexid of more age, she sufferyth it that it be chastised in brekynge downe of vicis, to make the chylde receyve vertues and grace. This werkyng with all þat be feyer and good, oure lord doth it in hem by whome it is done. (ibid.)

The *Clerk's Tale* shares with Julian's *Showings* this relatively rare vision of divinity in female as well as male form.[11] For Chaucer, as for Julian, the suffering of childbirth is the mirror in which divine patience is reflected. It is the quintessential image of conquering patience, of powerful suffering, and one which validates the notion of patience as a female quality. If Walter's tyranny caricatures God's 'governaunce', Griselda's patience *truly* reflects God's suffering. Her 'vertuous suffraunce' is not opposed to God's 'governaunce'; it is one with it.

---

10   I adopt the variant reading 'throwes' in place of 'thornes'; Colledge and Walsh admit it is 'attractive', and it is in addition a clear example of *difficilior lectio*.
11   For documentation and discussion of the tradition, see Cabassut, 1949, Bynum, 1982 and Heimmel, 1982.

5

The Feminized Hero

'... pitee renneth soone in gentil herte.'

(Knight's Tale 1761)

It is nowadays a commonplace that the meaning of a term is not fixed in isolation, but only in relation to the cultural or linguistic structure of which it forms part. So the value assigned to 'woman' or 'womanhood' cannot be fully determined without reference to the values invested in the term 'man'. To make 'woman' into a moral positive is not enough, if she becomes thereby merely the 'silent bearer of ideology', as Mary Jacobus puts it (1979, 10) – if, that is, her morality acts only as a salving conscience for the men who are left free to practise the *realpolitik* required for effective action in the world. The question of how Chaucer conceives of men is thus the last and most crucial element in determining the status of women in his writing.

Male heroes are, as I have already noted, few and far between in Chaucer. In the *Canterbury Tales*, the moral high ground is occupied by Constance, Griselda, Cecilia, Prudence, and no man is accorded the central and dominating position in the narrative that they enjoy. It is only in Troilus that a single male consciousness becomes the central locus of poetic meaning; whatever the prominence given to Criseyde, the central subject of this poem is the loss of happiness, and it is to Troilus and not to Criseyde that this experience belongs. The question raised by this experience – the question of what meaning can be attached to human happiness in a mutable world – has urgency only if we believe that it was a *true* happiness, and also that its loss cannot simply be written down to failings or vices – female fickleness, male inertia – which could be avoided by those wishing for better fortune. Chaucer takes pains, therefore, to present Troilus as admirable throughout; he is 'this ilke noble knyght' to the last (V 1752). In his final emotional rejection of human love, Chaucer still speaks, not of Troilus's weakness or folly, but of his 'grete worthynesse' and his 'noblesse' (V 1829, 1831). It is to Troilus that we should look first, therefore, for evidence of Chaucer's conception of a masculine ideal.

It is in Troilus that we can first clearly perceive that the male hero in Chaucer is a *feminized* hero. I have shown in Chapter 3 that Troilus is divested of the coerciveness characteristic of the 'active' male, and that his unreserved surrender to the force of love is for Chaucer not a sign of weakness but of a generous nobility. He is feminized not only in his reverence for woman but also in his vulnerability and sensitivity of feeling. 'Feminized' is not to be equated with 'effeminate'; Troilus's physical prowess and bravery are carefully established at numerous points in the poem, most notably in the visual image created by the description of his return from the battlefield, watched by the curious Criseyde:

> So lik a man of armes and a knyght
> He was to seen, fulfilled of heigh prowesse,
> For bothe he hadde a body and a myght
> To don that thing, as wel as hardynesse;
> And ek to seen hym in his gere hym dresse,
> So fressh, so yong, so weldy semed he,
> It was an heven upon hym for to see. (II 631–7)

Troilus is not lacking in the conventional attributes of 'manhod' (II 676) – courage, strength, dignified self-restraint. It is with 'manhod' that he controls his words and deeds so as not to betray his relationship with Criseyde to anyone (III 428), and 'with mannes herte' that he suppresses his emotions when the exchange of Criseyde for Antenor is being debated in the Trojan parliament (IV 154); similarly when leading her out from Troy, he 'gan his wo ful manly for to hide' (V 30). But the domination implied in this conception of manhood is a domination of self, not a domination of others. It stands in implicit but eloquent contrast to the notion of manhood assumed in Pandarus's impatient advice on how to prevent the loss of Criseyde:

> … 'Frend, syn thow hast swych distresse,
> And syn the list myn argumentz to blame,
> Why nylt thiselven helpen don redresse
> And with thy manhod letten al this grame?
> Go ravysshe here! Ne kanstow nat, for shame?
> And other lat here out of towne fare,
> Or hold here stille, and leve thi nyce fare.
>
> Artow in Troie, and hast non hardyment
> To take a womman which that loveth the
> And wolde hireselven ben of thy assent?
> Now is nat this a nyce vanitee?
> Ris up anon, and lat this wepyng be,
> And kith thow art a man; for in this houre
> I wol ben ded, or she shal bleven oure.' (IV 526–39)

Pandarus speaks for the conventional notion of 'manhod' as aggressive egoism; 'showing oneself a man' slides with ease into 'ravishing women'. His protest that 'It is no rape' (596), because Criseyde's willingness can be presumed[1] – indeed she would probably think Troilus foolish if he did *not* assert himself in this way (598–9) – reincarnates the male assumption of female willingness, and the need to exercise responsibility on her behalf, that we saw illustrated in *Pamphilus* and Peter of Blois's lyric. Like Galatea, she will 'a lite hire greve', but allow herself to be quickly appeased (603–4). The same conception of 'manliness' is evident when Pandarus repeats his advice a little later:

> 'Forthi tak herte, and thynk right as a knyght:
> Thorugh love is broken al day every lawe.
> Kith now somwhat thi corage and thi myght;
> Have mercy on thiself for any awe.
> Lat nat this wrecched wo thyn herte gnawe,
> But manly sette the world on six and sevene;
> And if thow deye a martyr, go to hevene!' (IV 617–23)[2]

'Manliness', for Pandarus, means acting vigorously in one's own interests and letting the rest of the world go hang. This is the 'mannishness' that is repudiated in the Sultaness and Donegild in the *Man of Law's Tale*; this scene in *Troilus* shows us that it is not only in women that this kind of manliness is to be rejected, but also in men. Chaucer carefully dissociates Troilus from Pandarus's ideas of manliness, locating true manhood instead in Troilus's rejection of 'ravysshyng of wommen' (IV 548),[3] and in his 'passive' suppression of self to the interests of others – the people of Troy and Criseyde herself (McAlpine, 1978, 159–62). When Chaucer speaks of Troilus's manhood he habitually pairs it with the 'feminized' characteristics – capacity for feeling or suffering, 'gentilesse' – that cleanse it of aggression: 'his manhod and his pyne', 'manly sorwe', 'gentil herte and manhod' (II 676, III 113, IV 1674).

It is not only in his refusal of coerciveness that Troilus is a 'feminized' hero. It is also in the fact that the story in which he is set casts him in a feminine role in that it assimilates him to the women of Ovid's *Heroides* – abandoned and betrayed by his lover, immobilized, frustrated of action and movement, finding relief only in memory, lamentation and fruitless letter-writing. Roland Barthes writes of the essentially feminine nature of this situation.

> Historically, the discourse of absence is carried on by the Woman: Woman is sedentary, Man hunts, journeys; Woman is faithful (she waits),

---

[1]   In terms of fourteenth-century law, Pandarus is mistaken; the term *raptus* covered cases where the woman consented to her own abduction – i.e., what we would now call elopement (Cannon, 2000).

[2]   The repeated emphasis on 'manhood' and 'being a man' is Chaucer's own development from the single word 'virilmente' in the corresponding speeches in *Filostrato* (IV 64–5, 71–5).

[3]   This too is Chaucer's addition (cf. *Filostrato* IV 67), as is the crucial condition, 'so it were hire assent' (IV 554), attached to his consideration of the possibility of asking King Priam to grant him Criseyde in marriage.

man is fickle (he sails away, he cruises). It is Woman who gives shape to
absence, elaborates its fiction, for she has time to do so; she weaves and
she sings; the Spinning Songs express both immobility (by the hum of the
Wheel) and absence (far away, rhythms of travel, sea surges, cavalcades).
It follows that in any man who utters the other's absence *something feminine* is declared: this man who waits and who suffers from his waiting is
miraculously feminized. A man is not feminized because he is inverted
but because he is in love. (Myth and utopia: the origins have belonged, the
future will belong to the subjects *in whom there is something feminine*.)

(1979, 13–14; cf. Lipking, 1988, xix)

Whether or not this is 'historically' true, the influence of the *Heroides* fixed it
as a mental model for the Middle Ages. So Troilus finds himself in the situation of Dido, Ariadne, Penelope, endlessly yearning into a void, imprisoned
in inaction and emotional paralysis. The Ovidian lament, after centuries of history, is uttered by a male voice. It is Boccaccio, of course, who earns the credit
for first transposing this essentially feminine genre into masculine form, but in
the *Filostrato* its function is simply to add lyrical pathos to his appeal to his
mistress: 'whenever you find Troiolo weeping and grieving over the departure
of Criseida, you may understand and recognize my own words, tears, sighs,
and torments', he writes to Maria d'Aquino in his Prologue. In Chaucer, it
acquires extra significance by being linked with a distinct conception of masculinity which bears the stamp of female experience. If Constance and Griselda
are characterized by suffering, so is Troilus; there is no division between active
male and suffering female.

This is one final reason for Chaucer to tell a tale of female betrayal: that it
enables him to break down the apparently inevitable division between the active
male betrayer and the passive female sufferer. That he was conscious of the
Ovidian nature of Book V of his poem can be deduced, I think, from a typically
bland witticism which he added to Boccaccio's narrative in Book I: Pandarus,
affirming his ability to help Troilus even though he himself is unsuccessful in
love, quotes from a 'lettre' written by an 'herdesse', Oenone, to Troilus's
brother Paris, to the effect that Phoebus, inventor of medicine, was able to cure
all complaints except his own love (I 652–65). The 'lettre', as the quotation
from it shows, is nothing other than Epistle V of the *Heroides*, here treated as if
it were a historical document rather than a product of the imagination – as if,
that is, it were a real-life letter that Paris showed to some of his friends and
might well have shown to his brother Troilus. In his note on this passage, Barry
Windeatt draws attention to its submerged link with Criseyde's vow of fidelity
to Troilus in Book IV (when the River Simois flows backwards to its source,
then alone will she be untrue: 1548–54), which echoes Paris's vow of fidelity to
Oenone, quoted in the same *Heroides* epistle (V 29–30, with Xanthus in place
of Simois), and is destined to the same fate as his. The pattern of Troilus's life
merges with the pattern of Oenone's life; her 'lettre' ceases to be a mere source
of apt simile and becomes instead the mirror that reflects his own experience.

Troilus is not the only Chaucerian hero to find himself in the *Heroides* posture, abandoned and grief-stricken. *The Complaint of Mars* likewise climaxes a narrative of female betrayal with an extended lament by the betrayed male lover. If the narrative in this case is a witty astrological allegory rather than a serious exploration of human love, the complaint itself has a lyrical intensity that makes it a genuine expression of feeling. Here it is not only a male who suffers, but also a god; as in the *Man of Law's Tale*, his power is reinscribed as impotence by the planetary role that separates his heavenly course from that of his beloved Venus. The male sufferer is also the focus of attention in the *Book of the Duchess*, although in this case it is bereavement rather than betrayal that has deprived him of his mistress. Here it is the predicament of the abandoned lover that introduces the spectre of betrayal, which presents itself, as it does in the *Franklin's Tale*, as a possible result of death. To Chaucer's jocular comment that the Black Knight's long rehearsal of his love is a case of 'shryfte withoute repentaunce', the Knight makes passionate reply:

> 'Repentaunce? Nay, fy!' quod he,
> 'Shulde y now repente me
> To love? Nay, certes, than were I wel
> Wers than was Achitofel,
> Or Anthenor, so have I joye,
> The traytor that betraysed Troye,
> Or the false Genelloun,
> He that purchased the tresoun
> Of Rowland and of Olyver.
> Nay, while I am alyve her,
> I nyl foryete hir never moo.' (1115–25)

Forgetting is betrayal, but forgetfulness of the absent is, as Barthes says, 'the condition of survival': 'if I did not forget, I should die' (1979, 14). 'Hit was gret wondre that Nature/Myght suffre any creature/To have such sorwe and be nat ded', as Chaucer says of the Black Knight (467–9). Nature resists the stasis imposed by absence, pressing towards the emotional movement that is the condition of life.

Like Troilus, the Black Knight is condemned to stasis by his 'trouthe', perennially arrested by fidelity to a past that is forever sundered from the living movement of the present. Like Troilus – and like Griselda, for whom likewise the only way out of stasis is betrayal, not only of the beloved but also of the self. Chaucer's heroes share the same experiences as his heroines; the only 'active' males in the early poems are the villains of the *Legend of Good Women*, who inflict suffering without feeling it.

The *Canterbury Tales* lacks male heroes in the sense of central figures in the narrative, but it is not entirely lacking in examples of admirable male behaviour, as we have already seen in Arveragus, Aurelius, Alla, Melibee. It is however the figure of Theseus in the *Knight's Tale* that represents the fullest development of an ideal of feminized masculinity. Displaced as he is from the hero's central position by the younger knights Palamon and Arcite (whose pairing debars each of them likewise from a central heroic role), it is nevertheless to Theseus that it falls to voice and to embody the values that constitute the wisest response to their experiences. And the key element in these values is the womanly quality of pity.

At the opening of the tale Theseus, antagonist and conqueror of 'Femenye', the Amazonian land of women, seems to represent a masculinity sharply opposed to women and womanliness. But the conquest culminates not in enslavement, but in a marriage. It is the *separateness* of 'Femenye', its severance from the masculine world that is resisted; the marriage of Theseus and Hippolyta signals its reintegration. Even more important, the marriage symbolizes the union of masculinity and femininity in each partner. Hippolyta is 'The faire, hardy queene of Scithia' (882); her physical bravery is not rejected as 'unwomanly', but is as admirable as her beauty. And in Theseus, as the first scene of the narrative action makes clear, masculine prowess is infused with feminine 'pitee'. As he returns to Athens to celebrate his victory and his wedding, he is confronted by a double line of kneeling women, wailing and begging for his pity. Their leader, having first swooned so that 'it was routhe for to seen and heere' (913–14), asks for his 'mercy and socour' (918).

> 'Have mercy on oure wo and oure distresse!
> Som drope of pitee, thurgh thy gentillesse,
> Upon us wrecched wommen lat thou falle.' (919–21)

They are, she explains, the widows of the Argive leaders who fought against Creon at Thebes; Creon, 'Fulfild of ire and of iniquitee', has decreed 'for despit and for his tirannye' that their husbands' bodies should lie unburied and be eaten by dogs (934–47). Falling prostrate, she and her companions cry 'pitously':

> 'Have on us wrecched wommen som mercy,
> And lat oure sorwe synken in thyn herte.' (950–1)

As in the *Man of Law's Tale*, piteousness metamorphoses itself into pity:

> This gentil duc doun from his courser sterte
> With herte pitous, whan he herde hem speke.
> Hym thoughte that his herte wolde breke,
> Whan he saugh hem so pitous and so maat,
> That whilom weren of so greet estaat;
> And in his armes he hem alle up hente,
> And hem conforteth in ful good entente. (952–8)

Here again the dual meaning of the word 'pitous' – 'pitiable' and 'pitying' – manifests the dynamic quality of pity: cause instantaneously re-creates itself as effect. And once again it manifests the levelling, unifying nature of pity, its power to overturn and obliterate the relationship between conqueror and suppliant. Boccaccio's Teseo remains in his chariot throughout this scene (*Teseida* II 22–5, 42–3); Chaucer places his Theseus on horseback and makes him instantly dismount under his 'pitous' impulse, so as to illustrate dramatically the levelling of conqueror with victims, the abandonment of his triumph for identification with their grief (cf. Crampton, 1974, 56–8).

The carefully arranged iconography of the scene – the formal lines of kneeling women confronting the mounted conqueror – emphasizes the subjection to 'pitee' as a subjection to women. The womanliness of pity is assumed in Theseus's final appeal to Emily to show Palamon her 'wommanly pitee' (3083) by taking him for her husband. The connection between women and pity is a notion we have already seen in the *Legend of Good Women* and the *Man of Law's Tale*, and it is apposite to cite here another instance of it in the *Squire's Tale* which has a special connection with the presentation of Theseus in the *Knight's Tale*. The female falcon betrayed by her lover praises Canacee for the womanly compassion she shows in her grief:

> 'That pitee renneth soone in gentil herte,
> Feelynge his similitude in peynes smerte,
> Is preved alday, as men may it see,
> As wel by werk as by auctoritee;
> For gentil herte kitheth gentillesse.
> I se wel that ye han of my distresse
> Compassion, my faire Canacee,
> Of verray wommanly benignytee
> That Nature in youre principles hath set.' (479–87)

'Pitee renneth soone in gentil herte' is an oft-repeated maxim in Chaucer's poetry, and it is applied to Theseus in the scene where he and his retinue come upon Palamon and Arcite fighting in the grove. Theseus's first response to the discovery of their identities is angrily to condemn them to death, but he is persuaded to forgive them by the intercessory pleas of the queen and all the ladies with her.

> The queene anon, for verray wommanhede,
> Gan for to wepe, and so dide Emelye,
> And alle the ladyes in the compaignye.
> Greet pitee was it, as it thoughte hem alle,
> That evere swich a chaunce sholde falle,
> For gentil men they were of greet estaat,
> And no thyng but for love was this debaat;
> And saugh hir blody woundes wyde and soore,

> And alle crieden, bothe lasse and moore,
> 'Have mercy, Lord, upon us wommen alle!'
> And on hir bare knees adoun they falle
> And wolde have kist his feet ther as he stood. (1748–59)

It is Chaucer who introduces this second set of kneeling women into the narrative; Boccaccio's Teseo feels only a momentary anger that passes of its own accord (V 88), so that there is no need for the women to intervene. Again the visual image points up the feminine nature of pity, the 'verray wommanhede' that prompts it. And again Theseus's submission to pity is a submission to women:

> Til at the laste aslaked was his mood,
> For pitee renneth soone in gentil herte.
> And though he first for ire quook and sterte,
> He hath considered shortly, in a clause,
> The trespas of hem bothe, and eek the cause,
> And although that his ire hir gilt accused,
> Yet in his resoun he hem bothe excused,
> As thus: he thoghte wel that every man
> Wol helpe hymself in love, if that he kan,
> And eek delivere hymself out of prisoun.
> And eek his herte hadde compassioun
> Of wommen, for they wepen evere in oon. (1760–71)

The 'compassioun' Theseus feels for women is itself a womanly quality implanted in him. It feminizes him without rendering him effeminate; so far from being contradictory to his role as lord, he recognizes it (as Alceste teaches the God of Love to recognize it) as an essential part of that role ('Fy/ Upon a lord that wol have no mercy': 1773–81). As he was ready to combat 'ire' and 'tirannye' in Creon, Theseus is ready to combat them in himself, and it is through his 'womanly' qualities that he conquers them.

Theseus's 'ire', though rejected, nevertheless plays an essential role in this scene. As already noted, Chaucer diverges from his Boccaccian source in making Theseus's initial anger a much more serious and violent matter than Teseo's. Teseo's irritation subsides almost immediately, and he treats Palemone and Arcita with conciliatory courtesy; Theseus, in contrast, shakes with rage ('he first for ire quook and sterte': 1762), and summarily condemns the two Theban knights to death. Theseus's anger shows, first of all, that his capacity for 'pitee' is not the result of a constitutional lethargy or softness; the 'pitous' hero is as fiery and peremptory as other men. But even more important, it shows the dynamic power of 'pitee', its capacity to effect *change*. The importance of showing us Theseus as first violently angry, and then yielding to pity, is that it shows us Theseus changing his mind along with his mood. 'Pitee', that is, represents not only a willingness to sympathize and forgive, it also represents an openness to change – change of heart, change of plans. Having seen Palamon and Arcite as deadly enemies, Theseus looks on them with new eyes as suitors for the hand of his sister-in-law – as potential allies and kinsmen.

In the opening episode with the widow ladies as in this scene in the grove, Theseus's openness to 'pitee' was equally an openness to change, a willingness to respond and adapt to 'aventure', the unforeseen and arbitrary interventions of chance. In granting the request of the widow ladies, Theseus abandons his plans for triumph and celebration, allowing their grief to replace his own rejoicings. Having just concluded one war and turned his mind to feasting, he finds he must start all over again, leave his bride, and go to war again. His acceptance of this change in his plans is, as Chaucer emphasizes, total and immediate: he goes not a foot further towards Athens (Boccaccio's Teseo is already there when he meets the ladies), and does not rest so much as half a day, but at once sets out for Thebes (965–70). This readiness to change, to drop one set of plans or conceptions or attitudes, characterizes Theseus throughout the tale. To the two important instances already discussed, others can be added. Having decreed that Palamon and Arcite shall be perpetually imprisoned without possibility of ransom, Theseus nevertheless reverses this decree and yields to Perotheus's request for Arcite's release. Chaucer again increases the vehement implacability of Theseus's original decision in order to emphasize the change entailed by its reversal. Having determined that Emily shall marry the winner of the tournament, he has to accept the frustration of this plan by Arcite's death, and make a new plan to deal with the new situation. At the beginning of the tale he declares war on Thebes; at its end he forges a new alliance with the city. Throughout the tale, he is ready to respond to events, rather than attempting to force them into the mould of his own will. He does not arrogate to himself the decision of who shall marry Emily, but allows it to be settled by chance ('aventure'), contenting himself with providing the ordered framework of the tournament within which the random activity of chance may be invested with a determining significance. Following Charles Muscatine's brilliant study of the tale (1957, 175–90), many critics have seen Theseus as a representative of civilized order,[4] but some have suggested that his role is seriously undermined by the impossibility of maintaining this order in the face of the anarchic intrusions of chance.[5] Such a view is an almost complete reversal of the truth: Theseus's heroism consists not in his attempts to impose an ordered stasis on the flux of existence, but rather in his readiness to move with the course of events, to match their change with his own.

Chaucer's attempt to identify knightly heroism with 'suffraunce' rather than 'hardynesse' runs counter, as Alcuin Blamires (1979) has shown, to the prevailing assumptions in late medieval society and in a substantial part of its literature. But he was not alone in seeing pity as the supreme virtue of the male hero, nor

[4]   References are given in Aers (1980, 228, n. 1).
[5]   See Salter, 1962, 9–36. Aers (1980, Ch. 7) argues that Chaucer reveals the 'order' represented by Theseus as no more than legalized violence.

in his conception of the adaptibility and responsiveness that lies at its heart. Dante, in the *Convivio*, praises 'pietà' as the greatest of all virtues, and defines it in a way that illuminates what I have been suggesting about Chaucerian 'pitee':

> pity makes every other virtue shine with its own light. Wherefore Vergil, in speaking of Aeneas, as the height of his praise calls him 'piteous' [pietoso]; and pity is not what common people think it to be – that is, feeling grief at another's harm – rather, that is one of its special consequences, which is called misericord, and it is an emotion [passione]. Pity, however, is not an emotion, but a noble disposition of spirit [animo], ready to receive love, misericord, and other beneficent feelings. (II.x)

'Ready to receive...'; it is this receptivity that Chaucer sees in the 'gentil herte', its quickness to take impression from outer influences. He would have found a similar idea of nobility in Ovid's *Tristia*, in lines that read like a gloss on Theseus's behaviour in the grove.

> Quo quis enim major, magis est placabilis irae;
> Et faciles motus mens generosa capit. (III.v.31–2)

The greater anyone is, the more easily is his anger appeased; a noble mind is open to easy movements.

The *pietas* of Aeneas, which for Vergil implied his duty and affection towards family, country and gods, has by Dante's time been redefined by a shift in the meaning of the word; in medieval Latin, its primary sense was 'gentleness, mildness, mercy'.[6] For Dante, Aeneas's heroism lies not only in his military prowess, but even more in his susceptibility to tender feelings. 'Wommanly pitee' does not mark a division between female and male; it is the highest virtue of the male hero. So in *Sir Gawain and the Green Knight*, the crowning virtue among the five represented on Gawain's pentangle is 'pité þat passez alle poyntez' (654). The prominence given to pity here has caused some puzzlement, since the exercise of compassion for the weak and afflicted does not play a part in Gawain's adventures in this story. What the poet means by 'pité', I think, is rather what Dante means by 'pietà': the responsiveness, the willingness to subordinate the self to outer pressures, that characterizes Gawain as it does Theseus. Aeneas is the model for the heroes of medieval romance in this respect also. His voyage, the site of his new city, his bride, are chosen for him. He 'follows his destiny', journeying 'where fate calls him', not as he determines.[7] Just so does the romance hero surrender to the

---

6   The effects of this shift on medieval interpretations of Vergil's epic are discussed by Colin Burrow (1993).

7   Such phrases are frequent in the *Aeneid*: see I 382, 'data fata secutus'; III 7, 'incerti quo fata ferant, ubi sistere detur'; III 494, 'nos alia ex aliis in fata vocamur'; and cf. IV 340; X 472; XI 97, 112.

claims of 'aventure', putting himself at the disposal of chance (Mann, 1994). Like the golden bough that will yield itself effortlessly to Aeneas's hand 'if fate summons you' ('si te fata vocant': VI 147), the sword in the stone can be removed only by the hero whose destiny it seals. The romance hero does not choose his heroic task; it is imposed upon him – often by women. His journeyings are led by the path, not by direction towards an identified goal. Often, and most characteristically, he fights without armour, or with one hand tied behind his back; he yields his sword to his enemy or his neck to the axe of a monster. The narrative images that express his heroism are the perilous bed and the rudderless boat – not images of aggressive action, but of passive suffering, the courage to abandon the self to danger without resistance or evasion. 'Pitee' is not merely the extension of succour to the weak by the strong, it is a willingness to submerge strength in weakness in an act of imaginative identification. It is, as Robin Kirkpatrick puts it, 'the ability to respond with all one's being to another being' (1983, 248). And this responsiveness encompasses not only human beings but also events, the 'aventures' which the romance hero allows to dictate the pattern of his life, accepting the destiny they forge.[8]

Theseus's constant refashioning of his plans is thus a sign of strength rather than a betrayal of weakness. If Criseyde's 'pitee' leads to a tragic pattern of events, Theseus's 'pitee' works constantly in the opposite direction, towards justice and harmony. The difference does not lie in an act of will, but in the dual potentiality implicit in the random contingencies that can shape themselves into malign or beneficent patterns. Pity, like patience, is not an insurance policy that will guarantee happiness, but like patience it is founded on a recognition of changeability as fundamental to human existence, and meets that changeability with its own. Pity works to channel changeability in positive directions, to provide a release from the static deadlock of misery. In the *Knight's Tale*, it acts in partnership with chance as a dynamic force in the narrative, moving it forward when it seems to have ground inexorably to a halt. We can see this in the very opening of the tale, which reads like the 'happy ever after' ending to a story rather than the initiation of a developing action.

---

[8]   Space does not allow me to trace the development of this new heroic ideal in the works of Chrétien de Troyes, but I may cite, for example, the lecture delivered by King Baudemagus on the 'dolçor' and 'pitié' that are the signs of 'boens cuers' in a knightly hero (*Chevalier de la Charrete* 6308–15), and the 'pitiez' that instinctively summons Yvain to rescue the lion which becomes his grateful servant (*Yvain* 3373). Burnley, in an invaluable study of the vocabulary which articulates and defines a Christianized Stoic ethos in Middle English texts (1979), has demonstrated the central role of pity and the associated concepts of patience and 'suffraunce' in this ethos. The preference for the active hero, characterized by anger, rather than the passive hero, characterized by pity, appears to be a Renaissance creation. Crampton contrasts Chaucer and Spenser: 'Chaucer seems to place value on suffering and Spenser seems to place value on action' (1974, 180). Burrow (see note 6 above) sees the crucial divide as falling between Ariosto and Tasso, and attributes the shift from pity to anger as the defining heroic trait to the influence of the latter.

It is Theseus's pity for the widow ladies that breaks away from the finality of his celebrations and sets the action going again with the campaign against Thebes. This campaign successfully concluded, and Palamon and Arcite having been condemned to perpetual imprisonment, the story seems to have immobilized itself again; their falling in love with Emily provides a potential narrative development, but it needs Perotheus's chance arrival and Theseus's change of heart in respect of Arcite to bring about his release and a change in the status quo. With Arcite's return to serve Emily in disguise, the narrative falls into another lull, broken by Palamon's chance escape from prison. Chance likewise brings Theseus on the scene while Palamon and Arcite are engaged in combat, and it is here that the narrative threatens to be terminated once and for all by the anger that decrees their death. It is Theseus's 'pitee', as we have seen, that releases the narrative potential in the love of the two knights for Emily, and allows that potential to be realized. The death of Arcite seems to deny this potential and bring the action to a standstill once again; it is Theseus's patient acceptance of his death that leads him to see the possibility of making 'vertu of necessitee' (3042) – that is, of shaping the scattered fragments created by the blow of chance into a new and positive form. Emily's 'wommanly pitee' is the instrument for moving forward from narrative stasis and creating new possibilities for happiness out of misery.

Time and chance provide the material of change; it is pity and patience that give change a positive form. Theseus's final speech does not try to deny change by imposing order on it; on the contrary, recognition of change is the premise on which this speech is based. The tree falls, the stone wears away, the river runs dry, man dies. Nothing is odder, for Theseus, than the human blindness to these inevitable 'successiouns' of mutable things. That a man should die is not strange; what is strange is that we are always so *surprised* when a man dies. Theseus's pity and his patience embody a deep acknowledgement of the 'successiouns' of mutable things, and a willingness to move with them that is not shared by the static rigour of 'ire' and 'tirannye'. The 'happy ending' of the *Knight's Tale* is no more final than the 'happy ending' with which it began; as this story stops, another will start. It is because they embody the flexibility necessary to respond to the ceaseless movement of life that pity and patience are heroic virtues.

Emily's role in the *Knight's Tale* is a minor one, but it is nevertheless shaped in such a way as to make clear that the masculine ideal represented in Theseus does not relegate a feminine ideal to second place, but is on the contrary derived from it. The ending of the tale, as we have already seen, reaffirms the 'pitee' that characterizes Theseus as a preeminently 'wommanly' quality. It is in the description of Diana's temple, and the scene when Emily visits it, that Chaucer attaches this concept of womanliness to female experience.

The description of Diana's temple is another of Chaucer's additions to his source; Boccaccio devotes all his descriptive efforts to the temples of Mars and Venus (which are in any case conceived as the celestial destinations of the prayers of Arcita and Palemone, rather than the earthly buildings in which those prayers are uttered). In Chaucer, the three temples are incorporated into the lists where the tournament is to be fought, and each is given equivalent importance; he is therefore obliged to invent a description for Diana's temple that will match those provided for the other two. The painted images of Diana which he first describes show her in her most familiar role as goddess 'Of huntyng and of shamefast chastitee' (2055). But there is nothing soft and vulnerable about her virginal purity; prominently featured in the wall-paintings is Acteon, metamorphosed into a stag and torn to pieces by his own hounds 'For vengeaunce that he saugh Diane al naked' (2066). The story makes Diana's hunting the manifestation of an aggressive, Amazonian quality in her chastity, a vindictive rejection of masculinity. Yet Diana is not only the defender of chastity, but also, in her role as Lucina, the protectress of women in childbirth. At the foot of her statue there is represented a woman struggling in the throes of birth:

> A womman travaillynge was hire biforn;
> But for hir child so longe was unborn,
> Ful pitously Lucyna gan she calle
> And seyde, 'Help, for thou mayst best of alle!' (2083–6)

When Emily visits the temple, her prayer to Diana recalls these two contradictory images of womanhood. As an Amazon, Emily identifies passionately with the first and shrinks from the second:

> 'Chaste goddesse, wel wostow that I
> Desire to ben a mayden al my lyf,
> Ne nevere wol I be no love ne wyf.
> I am, thow woost, yet of thy compaignye,
> A mayde, and love huntynge and venerye,
> And for to walken in the wodes wilde,
> And noght to ben a wyf *and be with childe.*
> Noght wol I knowe compaignye of man.'
>
> (2304–11; my italics)

'[T]o ben a wyf and be with childe': Emily's resistance to marriage is also a resistance to childbirth, a clinging to the virginal separateness that stands aloof from suffering, reacting to male intrusion with the 'vengeaunce' and 'ire' that Diana turned on Acteon. Childbirth leads in the opposite direction – towards patience ('Lerneth to suffre') and away from ire.

Yet Emily already in her prayer shows an openness to pity for the 'bisy torment' of Palamon and Arcite (2320) that testifies to her capacity for wifehood, and she acknowledges that her destiny may 'be shapen so' that she must accept one of them as her husband (2323–4). And indeed the goddess declares that this is so, and that the fires on the altar will symbolically reveal to her her 'aventure of love' before she leaves the temple (2357). Emily's response echoes the patient submissions of the *Melibee*:

> 'I putte me in thy proteccioun,
> Dyane, and in thy disposicioun.' (2363–4)

surrender to the authority of another

Emily's submission to marriage and child-bearing is a submission to 'aventure'; it parallels and re-enacts the knight's readiness to 'take his aventure' (1186), making male and female experience a mirror for each other. Here as in the *Man of Law's Tale* and the *Clerk's Tale*, childbirth is the quintessence of patience, of the suffering-as-allowing that finds strength in responding rather than dictating. So the male hero is 'feminized' not just in respect of the culturally developed identification of certain qualities – flexibility, responsiveness, tenderness of feeling – as 'feminine', but also, and ultimately, in respect of the determining difference of childbirth, the fundamental 'necessitee' that persists through cultural variation. Minimal as Chaucer's references to childbirth are, their careful deliberateness suggests that it is the crucially female experience from which he develops and validates his conception of womanhood.

Of course, the image of childbirth as powerful suffering is as much a cultural construct imposed on biology as the stereotypes of feminine weakness and helplessness. Its significance is that it is a construct that aims to break down the ancient dichotomies between active/strong/male and passive/weak/female. Chaucer's writings dissolve these dichotomies not merely by the obvious route of showing the strength in women or the tender feelings in men, but more importantly, by identifying the strength in the apparently passive role of acceptance, and by insisting on this as the truly heroic role for men and women alike. The Boethian heroism exemplified in Constance and Griselda cannot be reduced to a convenient ideal for women and social inferiors; its first and most important model is in Boethius himself, who fits neither category. Chaucer's rooting of the ideal in 'womanhood' does not marginalize woman, but centralizes her, making her experience the exemplar for male heroism. Hers is the 'triumph of patience', the power that takes its origin in a calm acknowledgement of ultimate powerlessness. The male hero learns from her the renunciation of the self-directed activity that realizes itself as 'oppressioun', 'ire' and 'tirannye', moulding himself to her patience and her pity as the qualities that follow the onward movement of life itself.

The difficulty of finding terms to talk about the Chaucerian concept of 'active suffering' is a measure of how thoroughly this concept has been discarded, and how firmly fixed the division between 'active' and 'passive' has become. The result for feminism is something like an impasse, for women can identify neither with the 'passivity' that colludes with oppression, nor with the 'activity' that mimics male dominance. Feminist readings of Chaucer (such as Delany's interpretation of the *Man of Law's Tale* quoted in Chapter 4) customarily reject 'passivity' as a female role without noticing that this involves concurring in the male definition of 'activity' as inherently superior. Thus, in an often illuminating discussion of Criseyde's 'socialization as woman', David Aers attributes her refusal of Troilus's suggestion that they elope together to her internalisation of the (masculine) social values that 'subordinate human relations and Eros to power structures and militaristic glory' (1980, 128); her social training teaches her 'to *accommodate* to an antagonistic reality rather than rebel' (135), and the role of 'stoical "reason" and "patience"' is merely to 'confirm her resignation' to her fate (134). The corollary of this is Aers's approval of Troilus's 'active and independent' proposal of elopement, which is seen as a potential act of rebellion against 'the crippling social reality' that will eventually destroy their love (134). This interpretation is an ingenious way of deflecting criticism from Criseyde to society's expectations of women, but it ignores Chaucer's careful comparison between the proposed elopement and the 'ravysshyng of women' that brought about this 'male-instigated war' (133); it was just such an 'act of rebellion' against social conventions on Paris's part that led to the 'long and totally destructive' conflict of which Aers disapproves (134). And if it is objected that it was not Paris's abduction of Helen, but Menelaus's insistence on his marital rights that led to the Trojan war, then the logical conclusion of this is that the Trojans are fighting in *defence* of Eros (embodied in Paris's liaison with Helen) against Menelaus's definition of women as property.

More important than these excursions into the imagined hinterland of the text, however, is the fact that Aers's reading creates a series of contradictions and paradoxes which it fails to confront. On this reading, Criseyde becomes the mouthpiece of male values from which Troilus, though a man, is mysteriously exempt. And if it is male ideology that trains him in his 'active and independent role', then it is male ideology that trains him to rebel against male values. Masculine ideology is both rejected by Aers (the exaltation of militarism) and approved (active and independent resistance). Meanwhile the *real* innovation in this scene – that a woman insists on taking charge of her own destiny, and her male lover acquiesces in this – is lost to view, as is Chaucer's careful discrimination between the masculinity that expresses itself in easy action, and the masculinity that expresses itself in the far harder act of control (see above, pp. 130–1).

I cite this discussion not as an egregious example of misreading – Aers's fundamental emphasis on the very real 'social pressures, repressions and fears' (128) against which the mutual love of Troilus and Criseyde must be achieved is genuinely illuminating – but because it shows the confusions created by the modern stereotyping of activity and passivity, and by the automatic preference for the former. The commitment to activity is, indeed, implicit in criticism itself, the critic's duty being so often conceived as the pinpointing of where and why things go wrong, and identification of the way disaster could be avoided by the more prudent reader. So it is necessary to insist again that Criseyde's exchange does not make her betrayal inevitable; any of the possibilities she hypothesizes as likely to bring about her return to Troy could have realized itself (IV 1345–414). Her betrayal is due neither to masculine ideology nor to feminine weakness (though these may have a role to play in the contingencies that create the conditions for it), but to the human propensity to change with changing circumstances. 'Activity' cannot solve the problem, because it cannot eradicate change, it can only realize it in a different form. Elopement might have ensured Criseyde's fidelity, or it might simply have led to a different betrayal. At any rate, it cannot eradicate the possibility of betrayal – and it is the knowledge of this *possibility*, the knowledge that stability is not to be found in human affairs, that the experience of the poem brings home to us, and that lies at the heart of its tragedy.

That Criseyde's Boethian resignation creates the circumstances for her betrayal is not an indictment of it, but a bitter irony that gives emotional depth to the tragedy. Chaucer's commitment to Boethian philosophy, that is, embraces the recognition that no philosophy can outrun the reach of human tragedy. But the irony derives its power precisely from his commitment to the axioms with which Criseyde persuades Troilus to accept her departure and so lays the grounds for his own unhappiness.

> 'And forthi sle with resoun al this hete!
> Men seyn, "The suffrant overcomith," parde;
> Ek "Whoso wol han lief, he lief moot lete."
> Thus maketh vertu of necessite
> By pacience, and thynk that lord is he
> Of Fortune ay that naught wole of hire recche,
> And she ne daunteth no wight but a wrecche.' (IV 1583–9)

It is in the *Franklin's Tale* and the *Knight's Tale* that we see the positive face worn by these maxims – that we see patience conquering and Theseus making virtue out of necessity. The active power of passivity is there released, whereas in the tragic action of *Troilus* it is thwarted in Troilus and debased in the dishonest compromise of Criseyde. The *Knight's Tale* and the *Franklin's Tale* embrace the possibility of such tragedy as potential aspects of their own narratives, but they evade these potentialities by harnessing change to the rhythms of patience and pity, not denying it as 'activity' would, but channelling it into a creative role as the agent of a responsiveness that merges actant and patient into one.

A feminist reading of Chaucer needs, not to perpetuate the sterile antitheses between active and passive, to stigmatize female passivity only to find that the obverse of this is approval of male activity, but rather to recuperate Chaucer's careful integration of activity and passivity into a fully human ideal that erases male/female role-divisions. To do so is to enrich the range of twentieth-century gender models, limited as it is to shuffling the 'active' and 'passive' counters back and forth between the male and female ends of the board. And it is also to see that Chaucer's contribution is not least the contribution of an ideal for *men*. The question 'are women good or bad?' is relentlessly turned back on the sex that produces it, and transforms itself into the question 'what makes a good man?' And to that question women both give and *are* the answer.

Conclusion

Thise been the cokkes wordes, and nat myne;
I kan noon harm of no womman divyne.

(*Nun's Priest's Tale* 3265–6)

The preceding chapters have stressed Chaucer's originality in creating models of both female and male behaviour that erase traditional gender boundaries and dissolve the power-structures on which they rest. But the *Canterbury Tales* is not entirely lacking in examples of traditional gender roles. We see them above all in the fabliau-tales – in, for example, the miller of the *Reeve's Tale*, who goes armed to the teeth to impress his ladylike wife with his manly courage.

Ther dorste no wight clepen hire but 'dame';
Was noon so hardy that wente by the weye
That with hire dorste rage or ones pleye,
But if he wolde be slayn of Symkyn
With panade, or with knyf, or boidekyn.
For jalous folk ben perilous everemo –
Algate they wolde hire wyves wenden so. (3956–62)

We see these traditional roles likewise in January's pathetic belief that sexual desire is by definition masculine, even when he has to arouse it by laborious artificial means, and that it is the sexual act itself, rather than his own person, that will 'greetly offende' his innocent young wife (*Merchant's Tale* 1829). And again in the marital relationship of the *Shipman's Tale*, where the merchant buttresses his husbandly authority with the imposing mysteries of the business world, and his wife ripostes with the claims of the kitchen and the dinner-table, where female rule is undisputed (214–38). The comedy in examples such as these is generated precisely from the shrewd observation that identifies the conventionalized nature of these male-female roles – that recognizes role-*play* as a constant feature of human behaviour. So that to acknowledge the presence of traditional male-female relationships in these instances is at the same time to acknowledge that they are not represented as 'natural' but as a series of learned rituals through which male and female roles are constructed.

The wittiest and most original dramatisation of these traditional relationships is however acted out, not between human beings, but between a couple of chickens. Of all the married couples in the *Canterbury Tales*, it is Chauntecleer and Pertelote who give us a classic illustration of the distribution of roles in a conventional marriage. This is not simply because of the comic effect to be

gained from transposing the human into the animal, but because the gulf
between the animal actor and the human interpretation applied to the action
reveals the cultural construct imposed on raw experience. So the gaudy colouring of a farmyard cock is read as a testimony of aristocratic splendour
(2859–64). Natural instinct makes him an astrologer, unerringly marking the
'ascencioun/Of the equynoxial' (2855–6). And fantasies of male potency realize themselves in his relations with his seven hens, which blamelessly unite
polygamy with romantic love for 'faire damoysele Pertelote' without threat of
either jealousy or sexual restraint (2866–76). Animal copulation is sublimated
into love by the rituals of human courtship.

It is the episode of Chauntecleer's dream in particular that shows the construction of gender differences by representing them as pressures exerted by
each sex on the other. Terrified by his dream of the fox, the cock groans aloud
in his sleep, and when he explains his distress to his wife ('Yet of his look for
feere almoost I deye': 2906), she responds to him with horrified dismay:

> 'Avoy!' quod she, 'fy on yow, hertelees!
> Allas,' quod she, 'for, by that God above,
> Now han ye lost myn herte and al my love!
> I kan nat love a coward, by my feith!
> For certes, what so any womman seith,
> We alle desiren, if it myghte bee,
> To han housbondes hardy, wise and free,
> And secree – and no nygard, ne no fool,
> Ne hym that is agast of every tool,
> Ne noon avauntour, by that God above!
> How dorste ye seyn, for shame, unto youre love
> That any thyng myghte make yow aferd?
> Have ye no mannes herte, and han a berd?' (2908–20)

Culture masquerades as nature in the assumption of a link between a 'mannes
herte' and 'a berd'; it is the fact that this horrified question is addressed to a
naturally beardless cock that unmasks the connection as a construction rather
than a natural fact. Since his maleness does not entail a beard, why should it
entail physical bravery?

Chauntecleer has masculinity thrust upon him. And this is a fair exchange for
the imposition of delicate femininity on 'faire damoysele Pertelote'. The pressure on women to conform to an image of meek and gentle femininity
inevitably translates itself into a pressure on men to be brave and strong. Denied
direct expression, female aggression routes itself through men, as Harry Bailly
complains when contrasting his own wife with Melibee's Prudence:

> 'And if that any neighebor of myne
> Wol nat in chirche to my wyf enclyne,
> Or be so hardy to hire to trespace,

Whan she comth hoom she rampeth in my face,
And crieth, "False coward, wrek thy wyf!
By corpus bones, I wol have thy knyf,
And thou shalt have my distaf and go spynne!'
Fro day to nyght right thus she wol bigynne.
"Allas," she seith, "that evere I was shape
To wedden a milksop, or a coward ape,
That wol been overlad with every wight!
Thou darst nat stonden by thy wyves right!"
      This is my lif, but if that I wol fighte;
And out at dore anon I moot me dighte,
Or elles I am but lost, but if that I
Be lik a wilde leoun, fool-hardy.
I woot wel she wol do me slee som day
Som neighebor, and thanne go my way;
For I am perilous with knyf in honde,
Al be it that I dar nat hire withstonde,
For she is byg in armes, by my feith ...'

(*Monk's Prologue*, 1901–21)

Pertelote fuels the myth of masculine bravado in the same way, talking away her husband's cowardice by insisting that his bad dream is merely a product of indigestion, and must be dosed away with laxatives. The graceful serenity of the romantic heroine is sustained by the desperate underwater paddling of domestic nagging:

'Now sire,' quod she, 'whan we flee fro the bemes,
For Goddes love, as taak som laxatyf.
Up peril of my soule and of my lyf,
I conseille yow the beste – I wol nat lye –
That bothe of colere and of malencolye
Ye purge yow; and for ye shal nat tarie,
Though in this toun is noon apothecarie,
I shal myself to herbes techen yow
That shul been for youre hele and for youre prow.' (2942–50)

The cock is as eager to preserve his masculine dignity as is his wife, but he is equally eager to avoid taking any laxatives. He therefore resorts to a learned demonstration of the importance of dreams, as a way of achieving both ends at the same time. Female practicality is pounded into submission by the heavy guns of masculine rhetoric, relentlessly reiterating the same point, 'that dremes been to drede' (3063). It is only when this imposing rhetorical edifice is complete that the undignified nature of its foundation – the cock's hatred of 'venymes' laxatives – becomes clear (3153–6). Chauntecleer's last 'ensaumple', Hector's dismissal of his wife Andromache's premonitory dream of his death (3141–8), ironically reflects his own masculine resistance to female interference.[1]

The reassertion of male independence involves reinscribing female impotence: by flattering gallantry ('faire Pertelote so deere': 3105), Chauntecleer coaxes his wife back into the romantic role that effectively neutralizes her power to intervene in action, limiting her role to the decorative and the pleasurable:

> 'Now lat us speke of myrthe, and stynte al this.
> Madame Pertelote, so have I blis,
> Of o thyng God hath sent me large grace;
> For whan I se the beautee of youre face,
> Ye been so scarlet reed aboute youre yen,
> It maketh al my drede for to dyen;
> For al so siker as *In principio*,
> *Mulier est hominis confusio* –
> Madame, the sentence of this Latyn is,
> "Womman is mannes joye and al his blis."
> For whan I feele a-nyght your softe syde –
> Al be it that I may nat on yow ryde,
> For that oure perche is maad so narwe, allas –
> I am so ful of joye and of solas,
> That I diffye bothe sweven and dreem.' (3157–71)

The double perspective that unites the human and the gallinaceous to produce the compliment to Pertelote's 'scarlet reed' eyes, or the frisson of *amour lointain* that is all the narrow perch will allow, yields more than comedy. It also points to the sublimation of biology into ideational concept. The sexual conventions that disguise themselves as 'natural' in human behaviour are revealed as both arbitrary and superfluous when transferred to a cock and a hen. Beauty is merely whatever route the sexual appetite chooses to channel itself through, and the same can be said of all the other niceties of wooing.

It is this awareness of ideational convention that provides a context for understanding the comic mistranslation of *Mulier est hominis confusio*. Chaucer critics hitherto have assumed that this is a joke at the expense either of Pertelote's ignorance of Latin, or of Chauntecleer's, though they have been unable to agree as to which. The question does not need to be resolved, since the true import of the joke is much wider. The bland co-existence of the Latin tag and its contradictory English gloss is rather a comic reflection of the comfortable cohabitation of such polarized views of women in conventional male ideology. The true butt of the joke is neither the cock nor the hen, but the male stereotyping which fails

---

[1]   Chaucer may have been inspired here by *Renart le Contrefait*, where the hen Pinte uses the same example to show the value of women's counsel, ignoring the fact that it implicitly undermines her own counsel to dismiss dreams as unimportant. The irony is equivalent, although it works in the opposite direction (Pratt, 1972, 648–50).

to confront its own contradictory attitudes, preferring to keep them both in play for use as convenient. Their nonchalant juxtaposition here is an indication that they share the same function: that of establishing masculine dominance, whether by aggressive misogyny or by condescending gallantry. One way or the other, Chauntecleer needs to subdue the female in order to maintain his own masculine superiority. At this moment, he chooses the gentler option of gallantry; misogyny is kept in reserve for later on, when things go wrong.

> And with that word he fley doun fro the beem,
> For it was day, and eke his hennes alle,
> And with a chuk he gan hem for to calle,
> For he hadde founde a corn, lay in the yerd.
> Real he was, he was namoore aferd.
> He fethered Pertelote twenty tyme,
> And trad hire eke as ofte, er it was pryme.
> He looketh as it were a grym leoun,
> And on his toos he rometh up and doun;
> Hym deigned nat to sette his foot to grounde.
> He chukketh whan he hath a corn yfounde,
> And to hym rennen thanne his wyves alle.
> Thus roial, as a prince is in his halle,
> Leve I this Chauntecleer in his pasture. (3172–85)

In this passage we can see how necessary a role women play in constructing male importance. The female is necessary to define the male; Chauntecleer's 'royal' pride rides on a sustaining underswell of female deference. The double perspective that matches the proud posturings of royalty with the natural strutting of a cock again 'denaturalizes' both aristocratic and masculine pre-eminence. A real-life cock is inevitably innocent of interpreting its own behaviour in this way; it is the human being who needs to *represent* his behaviour to himself, constructing social and sexual hierarchies to support his sense of his own importance.

The care which Chaucer takes to prise loose the (animal) action of this tale from the (human) ideational constructions which are elaborated upon it, becomes especially apparent when the fox finally arrives. For, in the first place, the lengthy argument about dreams, and indeed the dream itself, are shown to have been completely superfluous, since the cock is *naturally* programmed to take alarm at the sight of his natural enemy.

> Nothyng ne liste hym thanne for to crowe,
> But cride anon, 'Cok! cok!' and up he sterte
> As man that was affrayed in his herte.
> For natureelly a beest desireth flee
> Fro his contrarie, if he may it see,
> Though he never erst hadde seyn it with his ye. (3276–81)

The story starts afresh, as it were, from this point; natural instinct performs the same function as the warning dream, with a lot less trouble. Intellectual debates about the possibility of knowing the future, predestination, free will and destiny, are rendered redundant by the simple operation of animal instinct. And so are the theories that blame women for the disasters that befall men, which have likewise been appliquéd on to this barnyard incident.

> My tale is of a cok, as ye may heere,
> That tok his conseil of his wyf, with sorwe,
> To walken in the yerd upon that morwe
> That he hadde met that dreem that I yow tolde.
> Wommennes conseils been ful ofte colde;
> Wommannes conseil broghte us first to wo
> And made Adam fro Paradys to go,
> Ther as he was ful myrie and wel at ese.
> But for I noot to whom it myght displese,
> If I conseil of wommen wolde blame,
> Passe over, for I seyde it in my game.
> Rede auctours, where they trete of swich mateere,
> And what they seyn of wommen ye may heere.
> Thise been the cokkes wordes, and nat myne;
> I kan noon harm of no womman divyne. (3252–66)

It is the impossibility of attaching this passage at any point to the narrative which it purports to interpret that frees the animal level of the action from the human ideation with which it is surrounded, and enables us to see the latter as a construct. As we have seen for ourselves, the cock did *not* take 'conseil of his wyf' on the significance or otherwise of his dream; on the contrary, he vigorously rejected her view in favour of his own. In order to create this blatant contradiction between story and moral Chaucer has reversed the situation in Branch II of the *Roman de Renart*, where it is the cock who dismisses his dream and the hen who insists on its significance (Bryan and Dempster, 1941, 652–3).[2] Chaucer's Chauntecleer fails to internalize his *own* arguments on dreams, for the very good reason that – as we have seen – they were generated only by his desire to avoid taking laxatives. The same interpretative facility with which the cock so successfully fended off the medicinal dose is here set to work by the teller of the tale to conjure up a male alibi out of the ready store of antifeminist clichés, with a sublime indifference to the facts of the

---

2   Chaucer may, as Pratt suggests (1972, 425–33) simply be following the little-known *Renart le Contrefait*, in which the hen likewise advises her husband to cast off his fears of the dream, boasting as she does so of the value of woman's counsel; it is significant, if so, that Chaucer not only chooses to follow this less obvious source, but also brings out the ironic divergence between the course of events and an antifeminist interpretation of them by placing the narrator's strictures on 'wommanes conseil' *after* Chauntecleer has decisively rejected it.

case. The purely strategic nature of this rhetoric is underlined by the fact that the accusation against women is no sooner made than it is withdrawn, retiring behind the conventional apology to the possibly offended audience, and the passing of responsibility, first, to other 'auctours', and then, the absurdity reaching its peak, to the *cock* ('Thise been the cokkes wordes'). The antifeminist writer's attempt tó evade responsibility for his own misogynistic comments is here brilliantly parodied and ridiculed (Mann, 1991); bereft of either the 'wommannes conseil' or the 'cokkes wordes' which would lend it plausibility, the accusation-cum-apology is revealed as a pure smokescreen. Like all the rhetorical paraphernalia superimposed on the action in this tale, it functions as a verbal strategy behind which men can disguise from themselves the realities of their own lives.

The moral Chauntecleer draws from his experience is a moral about blindness.

> 'For he that wynketh, whan he sholde see,
> Al wilfully, God lat him nevere thee!' (3431–2)

But as the *Merchant's Tale* has already shown us, men will voluntarily take refuge in mental blindness even when a miracle restores their physical sight; 'as good is blynd deceyved be/As to be deceyved whan a man may se' (2109–10). The *Nun's Priest's Tale* is a comic acknowledgement of the human inability to act without the protection of illusions – without the ideational constructions that will give grandeur and significance to human actions, whether by heroic history and legend, by theories of fate and free will, of hubris and nemesis, or of the baleful effects of women. It is part of Chaucer's clear-sightedness that he sees gender-stereotyping as part of these traditional patterns imposed on events. But it is equally part of his clear-sightedness that he recognizes the impossibility for human beings to divest themselves of this ideational clothing entirely. Prising off the layers of rhetoric reveals no fundamental human truth, but only a brute animality – a tale 'of a cok and hen'. To be human is by definition to be committed to the mental constructs which differentiate human from animal – to be committed to *representing* one's actions to oneself within given frameworks. It is only in the recognition that these frameworks are constructed, not naturally determined, that potential freedom lies, for it is a recognition that human beings can construct themselves anew, in the image they desire. Chaucer's work embodies his own attempt at reconstruction, shifting and reworking traditional patterns into radically new forms. In the preceding chapters I have tried to show how much there is still to be learned from his attempt, and how deep is its engagement with human experience, in ways still readily accessible today. But in the last resort, it is not any particular configuration of gender-relationships, but simply the demonstration that reconstruction is possible, that is the most valuable contribution he has to make.

Excursus: Wife-Swapping in Medieval Literature

The starting-point of this chapter is an article by Felicity Riddy called 'Engendering Pity in the *Franklin's Tale*' (Evans and Johnson, 1994, 54–71). The argument of this article is that the 'gentilesse' which is a key value in the tale 'has to do with relations between men' (56); like 'fredom', it is class-based and gender-based, and is not a quality that women are expected or indeed allowed to manifest. This claim partly depends on a general observation about the role of the 'gentil' lover in relation to the lady he loves: his 'gentilesse' 'is defined by his capacity to hold off, to refrain from consummation, while he endlessly beseeches pity' (58). The lover thus *needs* the lady to be hard-hearted, forever inaccessible, in order to demonstrate his own capacity for sexual restraint (cf. Fradenburg, 1986, 39) – and that capacity is demonstrated, not for the benefit of the lady, but to enhance his reputation with other men. '[H]is self-abasement is not feminizing, but is rather … a means of self-definition in relation to other men' (57). In the *Franklin's Tale*, of course, the hitherto inaccessible lady suddenly becomes available, as Dorigen finds herself bound by the literal form of the promise she has made, when Aurelius manages to fulfil its impossible condition by removing all the rocks from the coast of Brittany. Arveragus now demonstrates his 'gentilesse' by urging Dorigen to keep her promise, but Aurelius matches Arveragus's 'gentilesse' with his own by sending her back to her husband untouched ('here is a young gentleman who … is not going to betray his class', 61).[1] In doing so he *also* preserves her necessary inaccessibility. Dorigen's role in all this is, according to Riddy, simply to 'provide the occasion for the show of "pitee" on the part of Aurelius that will save her and at the same time define him as a gentleman'. 'The *raison d'être* of Dorigen's humiliation turns out to be to permit a display of "gentilesse" on the part of the men' (61). Dorigen herself 'collude[s] in the tale's underlying view of her sexuality as property which the men propose to pass backwards and forwards between them in order to establish their status' (62).[2]

I find this an interesting and challenging reading of the *Franklin's Tale*, but one that leaves out important sections of the tale – for example, the description

---

[1] Cf. Weisl, 1995, 115: 'It is not Dorigen's sorrow that moves Aurelius to *gentilesse*; rather it is Arveragus' great *gentilesse* that causes him to give up his claim. Dorigen remains a commodity of male exchange. Just as Arveragus has sent her to Aurelius, he now sends her back again.' Crane (1994, 49) also discusses the homosocial aspects of the 'erotic rivalry' between Arveragus and Aurelius.

[2] In support of this view: Riddy quotes lines 1003–5, where Dorigen expresses surprise that any man would want to make love to a married woman, whose husband 'hath hir body whan so that hym liketh'. This question merits larger discussion than I have room for here, but it may be noted that Dorigen is simply referring to what was a legal reality until the latter part of the twentieth century, and not indicating her own opinion.

of the relationship between Dorigen and Arveragus at the beginning of the tale, and also the concluding section which shows the 'gentilesse' of the clerk who lets Aurelius off the promised payment, and thus carries this virtue outside the sphere of court culture. I shall return to these sections of the tale later on.[3] Rather than proceeding directly to a competing analysis of the *Franklin's Tale*, what I want to do is to approach it via an elaborate detour through other literary texts, taking my cue from the remark just quoted about Dorigen's sexuality being 'property which the men propose to pass backwards and forwards between them in order to establish their status'. Although Riddy gives no supporting citations for this comment, an implicit context may be locatable in (first), Eve Kosofsky Sedgwick's work on the socially-instituted bonds between men that she calls 'homosociality' ([1985] 1992), and (second), the work on the exchange of women as a means of creating and consolidating social bonds which originated with Claude Lévi-Strauss's *The Elementary Structures of Kinship* ([1949] 1969). Lévi-Strauss claimed that the incest taboo, supported by elaborate kinship systems defining who one may or may not marry, functions to create social bonds by enforcing marriage outside the immediate family or social group. This conception was both extended and criticized in an influential essay by Luce Irigaray called 'Women on the Market' and an equally influential essay by Gayle Rubin called 'The Traffic in Women',[4] who argued that the exchange of women installs sexual oppression as an essential element in the social system. There are obvious problems in collapsing non-Western societies with modern Europe,[5] and in addition, the equation

---

3   There is also some equivocation as to whether the tale is a critique or an endorsement of the class-based/gender-based values that Riddy finds in it. She herself attributes these values to 'the narrator' – that is, the Franklin, whose own concern with 'gentilesse' is evident in the link that connects his tale with the Squire's, and also in the concluding question as to which of the three men – Arveragus, Aurelius, and the clerk – was 'the mooste fre', a question addressed, significantly, to the male pilgrims ('Lordinges'). But Riddy also suggests that this concluding question is left open as an invitation 'to dissident readers to provide their own answers or indeed to engage in a dialogue with the tale' (65), which would allow for the possibility that Chaucer is exposing rather than endorsing the sexual-political ideologies that Riddy finds embodied in it. Since I take a different view of these ideologies, I do not pursue this question further, but those who share Riddy's view would need to determine an answer to it before passing judgement on Chaucer.
4   Irigaray, 1985, 170–9; see also the following essay, ibid., 192–7; Rubin (1975) 1997, 27–62. Eve Kosofsky Sedgwick declares that René Girard, Freud, and Lévi-Strauss, 'especially as he is interpreted by Gayle Rubin', provide 'the basic paradigm of "male traffic in women"' that underlies her book (16; see also 25–7).
5   Irigaray leaps straight from Lévi-Strauss's analysis of tribal societies in Asia and Africa to twentieth-century Europe, as if the same social practices obtained in both, while Rubin has a tendency to treat these 'primitive' societies according to a developmental model, as if they represented some earlier stage of our own history somehow surviving to the present day. She tries to circumvent this problem, not very happily, by using Lacan and suggesting that sexual oppression has become lodged in the human psyche. The 'striking fit' which Rubin sees between Freud and Lévi-Strauss (51) is not so striking when one considers the place of Freud in the intellectual context to which Lévi-Strauss belonged. Eve Kosofsky Sedgwick

of gift exchange with commodity exchange which is implicit in this model has been subjected to a powerful and thoughtful critique in Marilyn Strathern's *The Gender of the Gift* (1988; see especially 311–39). I would therefore like to bypass the larger social and anthropological issues here in order to look at the exchange of women in a much more precise and limited *literary* context: that is, the context of the many medieval stories which represent the exchange of women – wife-swapping, as I have called it in my title – in various different forms. I hope that these stories will provide fruitful comparisons and contrasts with the *Franklin's Tale* which can form the basis for a re-evaluation of its supposed 'homosociality'.

In a number of these tales, wife-swapping is presented as a supreme demonstration of male friendship. One of the oldest stories of this type is the tale of Lantfrid and Cobbo, a Latin poem preserved in the manuscript collection of secular lyrics known as the 'Cambridge Songs'.[6] The manuscript, now Cambridge, University Library, Gg.5.35, was written at St Augustine's, Canterbury, in the mid-eleventh century, though the nature of its contents suggests that the collection of lyrics it contains was originally compiled in the Rhineland. Like other poems in this collection, 'Lantfrid and Cobbo' is evidently older than the Cambridge manuscript; fragments of it are found in a Turin manuscript of the late tenth century, and part of the first stanza appears as a pen-trial in a St Gall manuscript of the tenth or eleventh century. There is also a later version of the poem in rhythmic verse.[7] The tale is brief enough to quote in its entirety.

1a. Omnis sonus cantilene   trifariam fit:
nam aut fidium concentu sonus constat
pulsu plectro manuque,
ut sunt discrepantia vocum variis
chordarum generibus;
1b. Aut tibiarum canorus   redditur flatus,
fistularum ut sunt discrimina queque

cautions against treating the formulations of her book 'as cross-cultural or (far more) universal' (1992, 19); it is not clear how this insistence on the cultural (in this instance, European) specificity of her arguments fits her earlier declaration of reliance on Lévi-Strauss and Rubin (see preceding note).

6   I quote Ziolkowsi's text, with the substitution of v for u where it has consonantal value, a few minor changes in punctuation, and one more substantial change in punctuation at 5.12–13 (where Ziolkowski puts a full stop at the end of line 12, and translates '... let me return to you. Look, as life is your companion,/ may you leave as brother to brother/ one memento'). I have also adopted the reading 'memorum' from the Turin manuscript at 4.7, as did Bulst. The translation I give here is my own. In stanza 7, the musical instrument is unspecified; I have used the term 'lyre' as a word that most readily conjures up for modern readers the type of instrument indicated, with strings and a hollow soundbox (*timpanum*). Christopher Page (personal communication) suggests that it was most likely a lyre of the type found at Sutton Hoo, which was known in various forms all over Northern and central Europe.

7   Printed in Strecker's edition of the *Cambridge Songs*, 1966, 18–20.

folle ventris orisque
tumidi flatu perstrepentia pulchre
mente mulcisonant;
2a. Aut multimodis gutture canoro idem sonus redditur
plurimarum faucium hominum volucrum animantiumque
sicque inpulsu <flatu> guttureque agitur.
2b. His modis canamus carorum sotiorumque actus
quorum honore pretitulatur prohemium hocce pulchrum,
Lantfridi Cobbonisque pernobili stemmate.

1a. All musical sounds take one of three forms:
for either the sound comes from the harmony of strings,
struck with plectrum or hand,
as are the different notes from various types of strings,
1b. or a melodious breath is produced, as are the notes of pipes or flutes,
which, resonating from the bellows of stomach and mouth,
with swelling sound echo sweetly in the soul,
2a. or in various forms the sound is produced by a tuneful throat,
from the mouths of men, birds, and animals.
So the sound is brought forth by striking, by blowing, or by singing.
2b. In these modes let us sing the deeds of the dear friends and comrades
in whose honour this fair prologue is placed as a heading,
Lantfrid and Cobbo, of noble race.

3. Although one reads of	3. Quamvis amicitiarum
many sorts of friendship,	genera plura legantur,
they are not so famous	non sunt adeo preclara
as the one between those comrades	ut istorum sodalium,
who shared everything	qui communes extiterunt
to such an extent that neither	in tantum, ut neuter horum
of them possessed anything for	suapte quid possideret
himself – money, servants,	<nec> gazarum nec servorum
or clothing.	nec alicuius suppellectilis;
Whatever one of them wanted,	alter <h>orum quicquid vellet,
the wish was seconded by the other.	ab altero ratum foret.
[They were] peers in character,	more ambo coequales,
never at odds over anything,	in nullo umquam dissides,
as if the two were one person,	quasi duo unus essent,
alike in everything.	in omnibus similes.
4. Then Cobbo up and said	4. Porro prior orsus Cobbo
to his friend and brother:	dixit fratri sotio:
'This service of the king	'diu mihi hic regale
has long burdened me,	incumbit servitium,
so that I might not go to see	quod fratres affinesque

my family and friends,
and am forgetful of those
who are mindful of me.
So I shall return across the sea,
whence I came hither,
and satisfy their yearning
by going to see them.'

5. 'I cannot bear' said Lantfrid
'the dreadful life it would be
to live here without you.
So, bringing my wife,
I shall go with you, an exile,
as you have long been one with me,
paying recompense to your love.'
So they proceed and approach
the shore together.
Then Cobbo said to his comrade
'I beg you, brother, return;
I shall come back and see you
if I live.
One token of remembrance
give, as brother to brother:

6. Your wife, whom alone you have
kept to yourself,
give me, so that freely
I may enjoy her embrace.'
Without hesitation, he
cheerfully gave her hand to his.
'Enjoy her as you please, brother,
lest it be said that I seemed
to possess anything to myself.'
Then, the ship being ready,
he took her with him on the sea.

7. Lantfrid, standing on the shore,
to the strains of his lyre sings
'Cobbo, brother, keep faith
as you have done hitherto.
For it is shameful to follow one's desire,
and lose the honour of one's vow.
Let not brother become brother's disgrace.'
Thus, having sung a long time,

visendo non adeam,
immemor memorum.
ideo ultra mare revertar
unde huc adveni;
illorum affectui
veniendo ad illos
ibi satisfaciam.'

5. 'Tedet me' Lantfridus inquit,
'vite proprie tam dire,
ut absque te cis hic degam.
Nam arripiens coniugem
tecum pergam, exul tecum
ut tu diu factus mecum,
vicem rependens amori.'
sicque pergentes, litora maris
applicarunt pariter.
Tum infit Cobbo sodali:
'hortor, frater, redeas;
redeam visendo <te>,
en, vita comite;
unum memoriale
frater fratri facias:

6. Uxorem, quam solam tibi
vendicasti propriam,
mihi dedas, ut licenter
fruar eius amplexu.'
nihil hesitando, manum
manui eius tribuens, hilare
'fruere ut libet, frater, ea,
ne dicatur quod semotim
visus sim quid possidere.'
Classe tunc apparata
ducit secum in equor.

7. Stans Lantfridus super litus
cantibus chordarum ait
'Cobbo, frater, fidem tene,
hactenus ut feceras,
nam indecens est affectum
sequendo voti honorem perdere;
dedecus frater fratri ne fiat.'
sicque diu canendo

while gazing after him,	post illum intuitus,
on seeing him no more,	longius eum non cernens
he broke his lyre on a rock.	fregit rupe timpanum.

8. But Cobbo, who cannot bear to see	8. At Cobbo collisum
his brother injured,	fratrem non ferens
quickly returns and soothes him.	mox vertendo mulcet:
'Here you have, sweet friend,	'En habes, perdulcis amor,
what you gave, untouched	quod dedisti, intactum
by the experience of love.	ante amoris experimentum.
Now there is nothing further	iam non est quod experiatur ultra;
to be tested, and I shall	ceptum iter relinquam.'
abandon the journey begun.'	

The story proper is preceded by a preface on the three different kinds of music: that produced by stringed instruments, that produced by wind instruments, and that produced from human or animal throats. The connection between this preface and the tale itself is created by a pun on the word 'fides', which is used in the very first line to mean 'stringed instrument' (or 'string'), and in line 7.3 in its more usual sense of 'faith, loyalty'.[8] So the 'concentus fidium' ('the harmony of strings') in the proem becomes the model for the 'concentus fidium' ('harmony of loyalties') illustrated in the behaviour of the two friends. The pun is reinforced by the picture of Lantfrid playing his lyre on the shore as he begs his friend to keep faith, and smashing it on the rock when he thinks all is lost.

The song, and its termination by the breaking of the musical instrument, give 'Lantfrid and Cobbo' its pathos, but it is a pathos that belongs solely to the husband's position. Lantfrid's wife is not named, and her reaction to this situation does not enter the story. Her importance lies only in the potential threat that she poses to the bond of male friendship, as the one possession that might not be shared between them. Jan Ziolkowski points out that both Lantfrid and Cobbo use neuter pronouns to refer to her ('quid possidere', 6.9; 'quod dedisti', 8.5), as if she belonged to the category of objects, like the other things they share (3.6–11). This is true, but if the language used by the two men *pretends* that she is like these objects, Lantfrid's anguish reveals that she is *un*like them in that she may be exchanged but not used. That is, it is essential to the bond between the two men that Cobbo renounces sexual possession of her – not because of her feelings in the matter, but for the sake of his friend's honour. The surface asymmetry demonstrates a deeper symmetry, in that each of

---

8   In the notes to his edition of the poem, Jan Ziolkowski (1988, 180–81) calls the shift from the preface to the tale 'deliberately disjunctive', though he afterwards says that 'the two are held together through the common theme of accord, first in music and then in social relationships'. He sees a kind of implicit pun on 'chords' and 'accords', but he overlooks the overt pun on 'fides'.

the two brothers acts as if the other's interests were his own: Lantfrid's gesture says, in effect, 'since we are one, my wife is yours', while Cobbo's gesture replies 'since we are one, your honour is mine'. The relationship between the two men absorbs into itself the relationship between husband and wife.

'Lantfrid and Cobbo' may be seen as an early harbinger of the twelfth-century vogue for friendship as an ideal, promoted by treatises such as Ailred of Rievaulx's *De Spirituali Amicitia* and Peter of Blois's *De amicitia christiana*, which refashioned Cicero's *De amicitia* into Christian forms.[9] Another early harbinger of this ideal is the story of Amis and Amiloun, which exists in many different versions in many languages, including medieval Latin, Old French, Anglo-Norman, and Middle English. Its oldest surviving form likewise belongs to the eleventh century, when a monk of Fleury named Rodulfus Tortarius made it the main subject of a verse epistle on the subject of friendship.[10] Rodulfus begins by citing classical examples – Euryalus and Nisus from the *Aeneid*, Damon and Pythias, Tideus and Polynices. However, all these ancient heroes were outdone by Amicus and Amelius, as he calls his heroes, who proved their devotion to each other by supreme acts of self-sacrifice. First, Amicus risked his life by taking his friend's place in a judicial combat; then, when Amicus was stricken by leprosy, Amelius killed his two children in order to cure his friend by bathing him in their blood. The friendship is further demonstrated in the way that the two men treat each other's women, an aspect of the story which is most fully developed in its later versions.[11] Here, as in 'Lantfrid and Cobbo', it appears that the perfect unity between these two friends (who are so alike no one can tell them apart) may be disturbed by relations with the female sex. In the Middle English version, Amiloun's parents die and he goes home and marries a wife. Meanwhile, Belisaunt, the daughter of the duke at whose court the two friends were brought up, falls in love with Amis, and uses emotional blackmail (she threatens to cry rape if he refuses) to bully him into becoming her lover (565–672). In the Old French version, she

9   See Leclercq, 1945; Raby, 1965, esp. 601–2; see also, on the poem that Raby is discussing, Dronke, 1997, 275–92; McGuire, 1988; Haseldine, 1999, especially the first essay by James McEvoy (3–44) on the theory of friendship in the Latin Middle Ages from 350 to 1500.

10   Ed. Ogle and Schullian, Epistula II (256–67). Unfortunately, McGuire (see previous note) does not discuss Rodulfus Tortarius's collection.

11   I refer primarily to the Middle English *Amis and Amiloun*, preserved in four manuscripts, the oldest of which is the celebrated Auchinleck manuscript (*c*. 1330), and to the Old French version *Ami et Amile*, preserved in one thirteenth-century manuscript. (References given in the text are to the lines of the Middle English and to the stanzas of the Old French version.) The Middle English romance is closer to an Anglo-Norman version, *Amis e Amilun*. In both the Anglo-Norman and Middle English versions the names of the heroes are reversed (that is, the leprous friend is Amiloun, whereas in Rodulfus and the Old French version it is Amicus/Ami). For a survey of all the different versions of the story, see Leach's edition, pp. ix–xiv; his division of these variants into a 'romantic' group and a 'hagiographic' group is, however, untenable. The works listed in note 9 above do not deal with the chivalric type of friendship exemplified by the 'blood-brotherhood' between knights; see on this Keen, 1962.

creeps into his bed and deceives him into thinking that she is only a serving-maid (stanzas 39–40). The duke's steward, who likewise represents a threat to the friendship since he had tried to replace Amiloun in Amis's affections, betrays the love-affair to the duke; Amis offers to swear his innocence and prove it in a trial by combat. Since his oath will be false, however, he is worried about the outcome of the battle, and he therefore gets Amiloun to undertake both oath and combat in his stead. This means that when Amiloun wins, and the duke betroths his daughter to him as a reward, Amiloun has won the right to his friend's wife. (In the Old French version, this interpretation is reinforced by the fact that the victor is not just betrothed but actually married to the daughter, and his subsequent leprosy is said to be a punishment for this bigamous marriage; he shows the taint of sexual connection in his body, as it were, although he has never enjoyed his friend's woman.) Meanwhile, in order to prevent suspicions about Amiloun's true identity, Amis has been sent to take his place in the marital bed. As a sign of his fidelity to his friend, he places a sword in the bed between himself and Amiloun's wife, telling her that he has a sickness that means he must not touch her (1165–76). Each knight, therefore, is in the position of being able to take possession of the other's woman, and each demonstrates that his fidelity to his friend is the primary consideration.

The women themselves are estimated according to their willingness to endorse the primacy of male friendship. Amiloun's wife shows herself to be a bad woman by her furious anger when her husband reveals that Amis has taken his place in her bed for two weeks while he was away fighting on his behalf (1477–1500); she refuses, that is, to accept the claims of male friendship. It is no surprise, therefore, that she turns Amiloun out of the house when he becomes leprous, for which she is severely punished at the end of the story. In the Old French version, the subordination of the wife (Lubias) to the claims of male friendship is crudely reinforced by the husband's instructions to his friend: she will, he tells him, make sexual advances to him, which he is to refuse, and if she becomes fractious, he is to strike her (stanza 60).[12] Lubias also defines herself as evil by attempting to disrupt male bonding; she falsely tells her supposed husband that his friend has made sexual advances to her (stanza 66), little imagining that she is saying this to the friend himself. In the Middle English version, Amiloun shows even greater trust: he does not give Amis any instructions about abstaining from sex with his wife, and is pleasantly surprised when he learns from her about the sword in the bed (1465–73). Belisaunt at first seems to represent a similar threat to male loyalties when she persuades Amis to betray his fidelity to her father by becoming her lover, but she later redeems herself. First of all, she becomes surety for Amis's promise to return for the trial by combat, and secondly, she endorses Amis's decision to kill their two children in order to cure his friend. 'God may send us more

---

[12] He does indeed strike her, but for other reasons, when they first meet. She accuses him, her supposed husband, of having an affair with Belissant, and curses her, at which Amile, who is of course Belissant's lover, strikes her 'as his companion had told him' (stanza 62).

children', she tells Amis, 'and to save your friend I would die myself' (2389–400). Belisaunt, that is, is identified as a good wife because she completely accepts the over-riding claims of male friendship. So, at the end of the tale, there is no imbalance between the two friends because Amis has a wife and Amiloun does not, since the marital relationship is, as in 'Lantfrid and Cobbo', absorbed into the relationship between the two men.

In this tale, therefore, the role of women is to support male homosociality, and male friendship is demonstrated in a concern for the chastity of the friend's woman as part of his honour. But as in 'Lantfrid and Cobbo', the exchange remains at a symbolic level; friendship is sustained by its not being actualized. A later variation on this theme appears in *Sir Gawain and the Green Knight*: although the lord of the castle and Gawain are not friends, and Gawain is unaware that it is the lord himself who has instructed his wife to offer herself to him, a 'homosocial' sense of what is due to his host obliges him to refuse her sexual advances.[13] These examples might make it seem that wife-swapping in medieval literature is a rather tame affair, a titillating possibility which is never acted upon. In fact, the exchange *does* lead to sexual consummation elsewhere, notably in *Athis and Prophilias*, an early thirteenth-century romance which exists in two versions, the longer of them comprising over 20,000 lines.[14] The first half of this gargantuan romance derives from a short exemplum in the *Disciplina Clericalis* (Exemplum II) of Petrus Alfonsi,[15] which has been reworked into a long narrative about two devoted friends. Prophilias is a young Roman who has been sent to Athens for his education, and who there becomes the devoted friend of Athis. Eventually, Athis's family arrange his betrothal to a beautiful girl called Cardïones. Again, heterosexual attachments appear as a threat to the male bond; Athis tells Prophilias that he is afraid that his marriage will diminish their friendship, but Prophilias assures

---

13   Gawain's reluctance to betray his host is referred to at lines 1773–5. In this romance, the homosocial is firmly distinguished from the homoerotic, as Carolyn Dinshaw's perceptive analysis (1994) has shown.

14   For date, authorship, and other details, see *Grundriss der romanischen Literaturen des Mittelalters* IV, vol. 1, 278–80, and vol. 2, 74–5.

15   On the wide diffusion of this work, see Tolan, 1993. The exemplum in question is the Story of the Perfect Friend: a merchant from Baldach is welcomed as a guest by an Egyptian merchant with whom he had previously had only long-distance communications; he falls sick with love, and when he is shown all the women in the house in order to determine which of them is the cause, it turns out that the Egyptian merchant's betrothed is responsible. The Egyptian merchant relinquishes her and her dowry to his friend. Later, he loses his wealth, goes to Baldach to ask his friend for help, but is prevented from doing so by shame. He confesses falsely to a murder in order that he might die, but his friend saves him by confessing to the murder himself. Eventually the real murderer is shamed into confessing. The true story comes out and all three are pardoned; the merchant of Baldach gives his friend half his wealth and he then returns to Egpyt.

On the *Disciplina Clericalis* as the source for *Athis et Prophilias*, see Staël von Holstein, 1909, 44–8. Among the literary progeny of this exemplum is Lydgate's *Fabula Duorum Mercatorum* (*Minor Poems*, ed. MacCracken, 2: 486–516); cf. Schirmer, 1961, 238.

him it will not. On the day of his betrothal, Athis invites Prophilias to come and see his bride; Prophilias immediately falls madly in love with her. His love is so great it makes him ill, and his anguish is increased by the thought that it is treachery to feel this way about his friend's (almost) wife. There is a long account of Prophilias's tormented state, and the debates between Love and Wisdom (Savoirs) that enact themselves in his mind. The wedding takes place as planned, but immediately afterwards, Athis interrogates Prophilias as to the cause of his malady and discovers the truth. He invents an ingenious plan to save his friend, preferring his own shame to Prophilias's death. Using Prophilias's sickness as a pretext, he says he will have a bed made up for him in his own room; then, when they have all gone to bed, he will get up and allow Prophilias to take his place in bed beside Cardïones. This plan is duly executed. It is a scene of high emotional drama. Athis puts out the light, and is then assailed by doubts. How can he betray the faith he has just pledged to his wife? On the other hand, how can he allow his friend to die for so trivial a cause? He ought not to consent to anything that would dishonour himself or his wife – but then again, there are lots of beautiful women around, and he can't let his friend die for love of this one (983–94). He kisses his wife seven times, then turns away from her. Cardïones falls asleep.

Prophilias on his side is equally racked by doubt. He longs for Cardïones, but asks himself what man alive would give his wife to another (1005–18). Athis just said what he did to cheer him up (1019–22). Meanwhile, Athis, impelled by pity for Prophilias and the thought that no one will know what he is about to do, gets out of bed – only to be overwhelmed with a sense of his own folly. How can he bring about his own shame in this way? (1045–55) Is it his fault if Prophilias is sick? – No! (1057–61) There is no man alive who would not rather see him die than give him his wife (1064–6). He gets back into bed. But soon he is once more tormented by his feelings for Prophilias. Their love and friendship have been so great; they match each other in might, spirit, appearance, character and will – and now their companionship is ruptured for the sake of a woman! He tells himself that Prophilias would have given him *his* wife, if their situations had been reversed. He puts his feet out of bed – then pulls them in again. After much tossing and turning, he jumps out of bed, and starts to go over to Prophilias, but three times he turns back (1143–6). Finally he makes it all the way to Prophilias and tells him to take his place beside Cardïones. Prophilias goes over to the bed but is then assailed by self-reproach. How can he do such treachery to his friend (1161–70)? He turns back to his own bed, but Love stops him halfway. He sits down in the middle of the bedroom. Love and Wisdom hold another debate (1185–98), which Love wins, so that finally he gets into Athis's bed and makes love to Cardïones. The author admits it was 'vilenie', but excuses him on the grounds that any man will try to save his own life, and he did this at his friend's bidding (1237–54). The two friends then swap beds again.

I have recounted this scene at some length for two reasons. The first is to show that its long interior monologues, filled with conflicts between contradictory emotions, resemble the similar monologues that we find in the context of hetero-sexual love in other romances (for example, the works of Chrétien de Troyes). The emotional fervour and bittersweet tensions of this relationship bring the homosocial close to the homoerotic.[16] The second reason is to show that in all these exquisitely protracted doubts and deliberations, Cardïones's thoughts/feelings/wishes are never considered. Neither friend worries that he might be committing treachery or 'vilenie' against *her* by involving her in sex-ual relations with Prophilias without her consent or even knowledge. What holds back both Athis and Prophilias is the shame brought to the husband by having another man enjoy his wife. Cardïones is a mere cipher, who is con-veniently and sublimely oblivious to all the to-ings and fro-ings in her bed-room, and who contentedly dozes (on her wedding night!) until such time as the man she thinks is her husband requires her sexual compliance, without even speaking a word to her (Athis has told Prophilias not to say anything at all, lest she recognize him; 927–8).

The nightly substitution continues for some time, with Cardïones still sus-pecting nothing. Eventually however a message arrives to say that Prophilias's father is dying, and he must return to Rome. Once again Prophilias is plunged into anguish at the thought that he must leave Cardïones behind. Again, Athis takes pity on him and rescues him. He reveals that loyalty to his friend has kept him from having sexual relations with his wife. He will make this public, so that his marriage can be dissolved, and Prophilias can marry Cardïones and take her home to Rome. Prophilias gratefully accepts this offer. This means, of course, that the truth must now be revealed to Cardïones. Athis asks her if she likes the man who has made love to her (1525–8). She replies that certainly, she loves her 'seignor', on whom she has fixed her heart. Athis asks if he who loves her more than himself had to depart, what would she do? She says she would go with him.[17] Once Cardïones has made her declaration, we are told, Athis sadly realizes she has made her choice, and he tells her the truth. He then takes her by the hand to Prophilias and tells Cardïones that this is her new hus-band. Cardïones is understandably bewildered. How can this be? she asks Athis; *you* married me. True, he says, and now I have given you to another. 'I never heard of such a thing,' she protests, 'taking wives and giving them away. Did you take me only for whoredom?' She concludes that she has been vilely shamed by two men, and weeps bitterly; Prophilias comforts her. And that is the last we hear of Cardïones's feelings. Athis carries out his plan; Cardïones's relatives and his own are angry, but they see that the only thing is to make the best of it and acquiesce in the transfer of Cardïones from Athis to

16   Cf. the poems in Stehling, 1984.
17   This exchange does not seem to be so much an attempt at psychological preparation as a rather clumsy imitation of the scene in Chrétien's *Yvain* where Lunete gets Laudine to promise to reconcile 'the knight with the lion' with his lady – who is, of course, Laudine herself. Verbal formulae (what Chrétien calls the 'jeu de vérité') become the autonomous determinants of action.

Prophilias. Cardïones is taken off to Rome and disappears from the story for a good while; when she reappears she is Prophilias's loving wife (she eventually dies of grief when she thinks he has been killed in battle).

Meanwhile, Athis is reviled by his kin and deprived of his inheritance. He follows Prophilias to Rome, looking for his help, but is so worn down by poverty that Prophilias and Cardïones fail to recognize him in the street. Despairing, Athis confesses to a murder which he has not committed, in order that he may be put to death. At the eleventh hour, however, he is recognized by Prophilias, who promptly claims that *he* committed the murder, so that he may save his friend's life. Eventually both men are exonerated, and Prophilias takes Athis home and provides for his support. It might seem that the scores are now even, but not so. The gift of one woman has to be matched with the gift of another. Athis now falls desperately in love with Prophilias's sister Gaïte (who, unbeknown to him, feels the same way about him). Love-sickness overwhelms Athis just as it had earlier overwhelmed Prophilias, and is accompanied by similar internal debates, since Athis's poverty prevents him from revealing his feelings. Gaïte meanwhile is going through her own anguished debates, worrying about whether Athis cares for her at all, about whether he'll treat her the same way he treated Cardïones, and finally, about the fact that she is already promised as a bride to King Bilas. Eventually Prophilias divines that his friend's sickness is due to love – but for whom? Is it Gaïte, or has Athis belatedly fallen in love with his one-time wife, Cardïones? Gloomily, he decides that if this is so, he will be obliged to relinquish her to his friend, as his friend once relinquished her to him. He is thus very happy to find out that Athis is indeed in love with his sister. He immediately sets to work on his friend's behalf, working out a plan that his father Evas should keep his word to Bilas by handing Gaïte over to him, but that then Prophilias and his followers will attack Bilas's men and win her back by force.

We are still only half-way through this enormously long romance, but the rest of the story need not detain us. It is sufficiently evident that male homosociality is sealed by the exchange of women: Athis gives Prophilias his wife, Prophilias gives Athis his sister. (The wrongs done to Bilas are finally righted by giving him Athis's sister.) In neither of these transactions is there even a whiff of the ecclesiastical doctrine that the validity of a marriage depended on the consent of both partners, a view which, according to Georges Duby, was given increasing emphasis from the twelfth century onwards.[18] Cardïones can hardly be said to consent to sexual consummation with Prophilias since she is ignorant of his identity. Gaïte is madly in love with Athis, but neither her father nor her brother thinks of advancing that as a reason to Bilas for failure to give her to him as his wife. Her passion for Athis is convenient for the plot, since it ensures her co-operation in her own kidnapping from Bilas. But it is of no public concern in determining male rights to her.

[18]   See Duby, 1978, esp. 21, 43, 63, 69.

The narrative which makes up the first part of *Athis and Prophilias* is retold by Boccaccio in the *Decameron* as the story of Titus and Gisippus, the Eighth Story of the Tenth Day.[19] Like Athis, Gisippus relinquishes his wife Sophronia to his friend Titus, and Titus in return attempts to save Gisippus's life by falsely confessing to the murder of which Titus is held guilty. Titus then marries off Gisippus to his sister Fulvia, without any of the complications that attend on this event in *Athis and Prophilias*. For Boccaccio too the story illustrates the power of friendship, which can elicit such extraordinary acts of self-sacrifice. He makes a perfunctory nod in the direction of the consensual basis for marriage by having Titus ask Sophronia, just before he makes love to her, whether she wishes to be his wife. Thinking that it is Gisippus playing some kind of game, she naturally answers in the affirmative, whereupon Titus replies 'And I want to be your husband', and places a ring on her finger. The sexual consummation completes a *de facto*, if clandestine, marriage. When the truth comes out, Sophronia is violently upset and goes back to her father's house. But after letting things simmer down for a little, Titus decides to take a firm line with her family and that of Gisippus – they are, after all, only Greeks, who always make a lot of fuss unless sternly dealt with. He summons them to a temple, where he first points out that what has happened must have been destined by the gods, simply by virtue of the fact that it has happened. Since, however, he acknowledges that many people are incapable of following such an intellectual train of thought, he will convince them that Gisippus has not in fact injured them but done them a favor. They wanted to give Sophronia to a young man and a philosopher, and Gisippus gave her to a young man and a philosopher. They gave her to a noble youth, Gisippus to a nobler; they gave her to a rich young man, Gisippus to a richer. They gave her to a young man who did not love her, Gisippus to one who loved her better than life itself. To cap it all, he, Titus, is a Roman, and his city is far greater than Athens, so he can be of great assistance to his kinsfolk. As for Sophronia, she may complain of the deception, but she agreed to be his wife; if she failed to ask who he was, that was her fault. This stirring speech has the desired effect: Sophronia's kinsmen decide that it is better to have Titus as a friend than as an enemy. As for Sophronia herself, 'being a sensible girl', as Boccaccio puts it, she makes a virtue of necessity, and transfers her affections to Titus.

So far, we have looked at two types of story, in both of which the exchange of women is motivated by the claims of friendship. In the first type ('Lantfrid and Cobbo' and *Amis and Amiloun*), sexual consummation is refused, while in the second (*Athis and Prophilias* and the story of Titus and Gisippus), it takes place, but in both cases the result is a strengthening of male bonds as against male-female bonds. These stories, that is, do indeed endorse male homosociality. However, it should also be noted that they are entirely conscious of the extreme and indeed preposterous nature of the events they describe. These are

19   On *Athis and Prophilias* as a direct source for Boccaccio's story, see Staël von Holstein, 1909, 116–20.

not everyday instances of the social exchange of women (such as occur, for example, in Chaucer's *Knight's Tale*, when the dying Arcite recommends his 'wife' Emily to his friend Palamon, or when Theseus seals an alliance with Thebes by promoting their marriage).[20] On the contrary, in both types there is a notably transgressive quality to the exchange of women: it threatens or actually destroys male honour, whether that of the husband or of other male kin, and only the over-riding claims of male friendship can reinscribe this social disgrace as a positive value. Athis sacrifices the honour of himself and his family to help his friend, embracing poverty and shame. Prophilias causes his father to break his word to Bilas, in effect if not literally, and creates enmity between Rome and Bilas's people in order to secure his sister for his friend. Like heterosexual love in the Tristram stories, male friendship is here conceived as an individual bond which over-rides larger social claims. The exchange of women does not demonstrate qualities that prove one's membership of a class; on the contrary, it shows that the power of male friendship is strong enough to sanction betrayal of class values. It is an ideal that transcends normal social relations.

In a third type of story, the two men involved are not friends at all; they are connected only by the fact that, as in the *Franklin's Tale*, one is the husband and one the would-be lover of the same woman. The husband unwittingly precipitates

---

[20]   Crane (1994, 52–4) and Ingham (1998, 23–35) discuss homosociality in the *Knight's Tale*. I do not have space to consider it in full here, but hope to return to it at a later date.

Perhaps this is the place to mention the Provençal romance *Daurel e Beton*, which represents something of a hybrid type between realism and romance. Here Duke Bevis has sworn comradeship to his vassal Guy, and promised that Guy shall marry his wife and inherit his property after his death in the event that he dies childless. Charlemagne then marries his sister Esmengart to Bevis; Guy immediately falls in love with her, and says to Bevis, apparently in joke: 'I'll tell you what I want – how lovely my lady is, so beautifully made! Will you give me my share, as we agreed?' Bevis innocently jokes back, 'Comrade, ask the Almighty Father to kill me off quickly, and then, as you like her, she shall be yours!' Guy does indeed kill Bevis with a spear while they are out boar-hunting. As he dies, Bevis tells Guy to place the boar's tusks in his side instead of the spear, so that everyone will think he was killed by the boar. He says he knows why Guy killed him: 'it's because you wanted my wife so much. God help me and forgive me my sins, if only you had told me, I would have given her to you, her and all her great inheritance! I would have gone overseas. For God's sake, don't hurt her! Ask good King Charles to give her to you; he'll do that, you're a man of good reputation, well respected.' He asks Guy to protect his baby son Beton, but Guy contemptuously refuses. The rest of the narrative tells how Beton is saved by the minstrel Daurel (at the cost of his own son's life), and eventually takes revenge on Guy. In this story, Bevis's fidelity as a friend is demonstrated by his willingness to surrender his wife, even when Guy has murdered him; Guy's treachery, on the other hand, is shown in his covetousness of his friend's wife. Although the offer of the wife remains at a theoretical level, the ideal of friendship and male loyalty appears in Bevis's behaviour and in its inversion in Guy. As in *Amis and Amiloun*, women are subordinated to male plans; Bevis does not consider Esmengart's feelings about marriage to Guy; knowing that he is Bevis's murderer, she is nevertheless obliged to marry him by her brother Charlemagne, who ignores her protests because he has been won over by a gift of treasure from Guy. Quotations are from the translation by Shirley, 1997, 20, 29.

his wife's acceptance of the lover's advances, but when the lover discovers this, he voluntarily renounces the offered sexual consummation. The story of Rollo in Walter Map's *De Nugis Curialium* (Dist. iii, c. 5) is an example of this type. Rollo, a man of great name and achievement in chivalry, but no victim of jealousy, has a fair wife who is courted unsuccessfully by a young man called Resus. Eventually he decides that it is not surprising if the wife prefers Rollo, who has accomplished so much more than he has, and he therefore sets out to emulate Rollo by embarking on a military career which wins him a great reputation, but still leaves the lady obdurate. One day, however, when Resus by chance rides by Rollo and his wife, Rollo praises him to his wife as 'the noble wonder of our time, a man distinguished for birth, beauty, character, wealth, renown, and every earthly gift' (ed. James, 1994, 273). Fired by this description, since she knows her husband's sincerity and truthfulness, the wife immediately summons Resus and admits him to her bedroom. In case he is wondering why she has finally capitulated, she tells him that Rollo was the cause. Starting back from the bed, Resus proclaims that Rollo shall never be requited with wrong for his goodness; 'it were discourteous of me to stain that couch, which the whole world denied and he gave to me' (ed. James, 1994, 275).

This story too can be classed as 'homosocial' in that the narrative events *create* a bonding between the two men which ultimately excludes the wife who had seemed central to their relationship. Modelling himself on Rollo, Resus comes to match his nobility and generosity, prizing them above mere sexual gratification. Meanwhile, the wife is progressively devalued, as is shown by the fact that she is unable to appreciate the qualities either of her husband or her lover on her own account. The lover's qualities have to be mediated to her by her husband; her husband's qualities are mediated to her by her lover. She becomes merely the occasion for them to demonstrate these qualities (as Riddy suggests Dorigen is in the *Franklin's Tale*).

A similar story is told by Giraldus Cambrensis in his *Gemma Ecclesiastica* (II.xii), which in turn seems to have inspired a tale in a late fourteenth-century story collection called *Il Pecorone* (I.1), written by an imitator of Boccaccio called Giovanni Fiorentino.[21] A young Sienese nobleman called Galgano is in love with a lady called Minoccia, wife of a knight named Stricca, but she refuses his advances. One day Stricca meets Galgano out hawking, and invites him to his house, but Galgano refuses. His sparrowhawk, however, chases a magpie over Stricca's garden wall. Minoccia asks her husband if he knows whose hawk it is, and he replies that it is Galgano's; moreover it matches its master in quality, for there is no nobler youth in Siena. Again the husband's praise transforms the wife's attitude to her lover, and she sends for Galgano to come to her the next time her husband is away. They are already lying naked

---

21   On Giraldus as a source for *Il Pecorone*, see Hinton, 1917–18. Hinton also proposes that Giraldus is the source, direct or indirect, of another example of this type, the story of Bertramo d'Aquino in Masuccio Salernitano, *Il Novellino*, Novella XXI. The *Novellino* was first published in 1476.

in bed together when Galgano asks Minoccia the reason for her sudden change of heart. When she tells him about the sparrowhawk episode, he immediately jumps out of bed, protesting that he will never do 'villania' to a man who has shown him such courtesy. Here too the narrative forges a bond of mutual admiration between the men that bypasses the wife and leaves her looking cheap. This impression is increased by the sexual frisson which is implied in the sparrowhawk's seizure of the magpie, which suggests her sudden awakening of interest is physical in nature; Galgano's refusal of sexual gratification thus contrasts with her capitulation to sexual desire.

It should by now be clear that in all these tales, whatever their individual differences, women are erased, marginalized or degraded in the interests of male friendship or moral solidarity. In the last two examples, unlike the earlier ones, the wife is given a role in the action in that she initiates her own transfer from husband to lover, but this role serves ultimately to demonstrate her moral inferiority to the men and to reveal their greater nobility. In the earlier examples, the wife's reaction to being passed from one friend to another is simply ignored ('Lantfrid and Cobbo'), treated as recalcitrance (*Amis and Amiloun*), or discounted as female emotionalism (*Athis and Prophilias*). Against this background, the *Franklin's Tale* forms, in my view, a striking contrast. Two major differences are that, first, the wife's passage from husband to lover is motivated not by her husband's witting or unwitting action, but by her own freely-given promise; [22] second, her own reactions to the situation are not only vividly imagined and described, but are made central to the moral evaluation of what is envisaged at this point.

The ground was partly prepared for Chaucer by his source, the story of Tarolfo told by Boccaccio in Book IV of the *Filocolo* (ed. Marti, 474–93). A slightly different version appears in the *Decameron* as the Fifth Story of the Tenth Day. In Boccaccio, as in the *Franklin's Tale*, the lady binds herself to her would-be lover by promising to be his if he accomplishes a task which she judges to be impossible (in this case, creating a spring garden in the depths of

---

[22] This is also the case in the oriental analogues assembled by Clouston, 1888, 289–340. Since these tales belong to social and cultural contexts very different from those of western Europe, and since they are available to me only in Clouston's English summary, I have excluded them from my discussion. It may be noted, however, that they differ from the *Franklin's Tale* in that (a) whether casual or seriously meant, the wife's promise is made before her marriage, and (b) the marriage is not eulogized as it is in Chaucer's tale, and the husband and wife are not shown as agonized by the situation in the same way as Arveragus and Dorigen.

The wife's promise is also crucial in a story told in the life of the twelfth-century troubadour Guillem of Saint-Leidier (now Saint-Didier). Having been rejected by the wife of the viscount Heraclius of Polignac, who told him she would grant him her love only if her husband commanded it, Guillem composed a song in which the speaker urged a lady to give her love to an anonymous lover (whose identity the lady would know), and got her husband to sing it to her, Remembering her earlier promise, the viscountess felt herself obliged to accept Guillem's suit (Boutière and Schutz, *Biographies des troubadours*, 1964, 280–83).

winter). And here too she is grief-stricken when this impossible task is carried out, so that she does not incur the suspicion of fickleness or sensuality. But it remains the case that Tarolfo's final renunciation of her seems to arise not so much out of pity for her as out of admiration for the 'great generosity' shown by her husband: 'he began to say to himself that anyone who considered doing a base act to a man who was so generous would be deserving of a grave reproach' (trans. Cheney and Bergin, 261). In the *Decameron*, this impression is strengthened: the lover Ansaldo is 'deeply moved' by the 'liberality' of Gilberto, the husband, and says to the lady 'God forbid that I should ever impair the reputation of one who shows compassion for my love' (trans. McWilliam, 760). The lover's admiration for the husband is sealed by the fact that 'from that day forth, Gilberto and Messer Ansaldo became the closest of loyal friends' (trans. McWilliam, 761).

What sets Chaucer's version off from Boccaccio's, and transforms the structure of its meaning is, in the first place, the long prefatory passage in which he describes the courtship and marriage of Arveragus and Dorigen (in the *Filocolo* as in the *Decameron*, the marriage is simply 'given'). The marriage is *primary*, in both senses of the word; it is this heterosexual relationship, and not male friendship, that provides a model for the values that are enacted in the tale. 'Gentilesse' is only one of these values; far more important is patience, which is the subject of a long eulogy from the narrator, in which marriage takes on the lineaments of friendship. (Note the use of the word 'freendes' in line 762.)

> For o thyng, sires, saufly dar I seye,
> That freendes everych oother moot obeye,
> If they wol longe holden compaignye. (761–3)

The 'compaignie' that bonds male knights in (say) the romances of Chrétien de Troyes here appears in the form of a heterosexual relationship. The sacrifices it calls for do not take the extreme and dramatic forms that they do in 'Lantfrid and Cobbo', *Amis and Amiloun*, or *Athis and Prophilias*, but instead consist in patience, which is here conceived as a series of day-to-day and minute-by-minute adjustments to the other's needs and desires, changes of mood and physical imbalances, adjustments that make space for the other person and so satisfy the mutual desire for freedom.

> Love is a thyng as any spirit free.
> Wommen, of kynde, desiren libertee,
> And nat to been constreyned as a thral;
> And so doon men, if I sooth seyen shal.
> Looke who that is moost pacient in love,
> He is at his avantage al above.
> Pacience is an heigh vertu, certeyn,
> For it venquysseth, as thise clerkes seyn,

Thynges that rigour sholde nevere atteyne.
For every word men may nat chide or pleyne.
Lerneth to suffre, or elles, so moot I goon,
Ye shul it lerne, wher so ye wole or noon;
For in this world, certein, ther no wight is
That he ne dooth or seith somtyme amys.
Ire, siknesse, or constellacioun,
Wyn, wo, or chaungyng of complexioun
Causeth ful ofte to doon amys or speken.
On every wrong a man may nat be wreken.
After the tyme moste be temperaunce
To every wight that kan on governaunce.
And therfore hath this wise, worthy knyght,
To lyve in ese, suffrance hire bihight,
And she to hym ful wisly gan to swere
That never sholde ther be defaute in here. (767–90)

What is important about this passage is that it shows 'trouthe' realizing itself through patience. The unanimity of heart and thought between a man and a woman is created out of a ceaseless process of adjustment and adaptation. Stability is founded on change.

Of course the moment does eventually come when a more dramatic and extraordinary kind of 'suffrance' is called for. Dorigen binds herself by her playful promise to give Aurelius her love if he removes all the rocks from the coast of Brittany, and he manages to do this with the help of a magician, so that, against all expectations, she is called upon to keep her word, and Arveragus is called upon to urge her to do so. As in the 'homosocial' tales, an extreme and improbable situation is used to illustrate and exalt an ideal. But this time the ideal is the relation between husband and wife rather than male friendship. It is crucial that what is required of Arveragus at this point in the tale is an act of submission to *Dorigen's promise*. He relinquishes his wife to another man, not because of the promptings of male friendship or class solidarity, but because of his respect for her 'trouthe'. This is emphasized a number of times – first, in his words to Dorigen:

'Ye, wyf,' quod he, 'lat slepen that is stille.
It may be wel, paraventure, yet to day.
Ye shul youre trouthe holden, by my fay!
For God so wisly have mercy upon me,
I hadde wel levere ystiked for to be
For verray love which that I to yow have,
But if ye sholde youre trouthe kepe and save.
Trouthe is the hyeste thyng that man may kepe' –
But with that word he brast anon to wepe. (1472–80)

In 'Lantfrid and Cobbo', 'fides' is a masculine virtue; in the *Franklin's Tale*, a woman's 'trouthe' is taken as seriously as a man's. Note, again, that Arveragus's words are spoken 'in freendly wyse', recalling the earlier identification of friendship with the marital relationship.[23] The sacrifice that elsewhere one male friend cheerfully makes for another here becomes the sacrifice that Arveragus makes for love of his wife. (That is, the sacrifice *of* the wife here becomes a sacrifice *to* the wife.)

It is often said that Arveragus is, at this moment of crisis, forced to reassume the 'maistrye' he has relinquished and to order Dorigen to keep her promise. But, as I have argued in Chapter 3 (90, 92), the combination of command and submission in his response exactly illustrates the fusion of 'lordshipe' and 'servage' described in the opening eulogy of patience. The *easy* (and obvious) order for him to give would be to tell Dorigen to forget about her promise, and to deal with Aurelius himself, using the threat of masculine force. Instead, he regards himself as bound by what she has promised just as she regards herself.[24] Dorigen too is in no doubt that this is the source of her husband's command, as she shows when she answers Aurelius's enquiry as to where she is going, 'half as she were mad',

> 'Unto the gardyn, as myn housbonde bad,
> *My trouthe for to holde* – allas, allas!' (1512–13)

---

23   Stephen Knight (1983, 49–50) has commented on the 'cognitive dissonance caused by the reading "frendly"', which is evident in scribal substitution of more conventional variants, such as 'spedely', 'sondry', 'good', 'humble', at this point. The scribes, that is, seem to have found the use of the word unexpected here, and thus unwittingly testify to its importance.

Arveragus's response is in striking contrast to that of the husband in the *Decameron*, whose reaction on hearing of his wife's promise is to become 'extremely angry'; calming down, he nevertheless reproves her and tells her she did wrong to play with words in this way. However, knowing the purity of her intentions, he tells her to keep her promise, unless she can persuade Ansaldo to let her off, not least because he is rather afraid of what the magician might do if they refused. One may suspect a punitive element in his command: since he knows that the lady has no desire for the extramarital liaison, it will teach her to be more circumspect in future if she is forced to go through with it. The wife's peevish comment to Ansaldo certainly suggests a dissatisfaction with her husband that never appears in Dorigen:

'Sir, I am led here, not because I love you or because I pledged you my word, but because I was ordered to come by my husband, who, having more regard to the labours of your unruly love than to his own or his wife's reputation, has constrained me to call upon you' (trans. McWilliam, 760).

24   Cf. Martin, 1990, 128: 'the resonant words "truth" and "honour" ... traditionally have a much narrower field of reference for women than for men. They are usually synonymous with chastity, sometimes held to be the *only* female virtue. According to this usage, Arveragus's masculine honour, in complement to his wife's, might be saved by fighting a duel with Aurelius. This would be his equivalent of her hypothetical suicide. Instead, the husband acknowledges that his wife's "truth" is as important as his own and should operate in the public world of contracts and social life, not only in the private sanctum of the marital relationship.'

Aurelius likewise perceives that this is Arveragus's paramount concern, as appears in his words to Dorigen:

> 'Madame, seyth to youre lorde Arveragus
> That sith I se his grete gentillesse
> To yow, and eek I se wel youre distresse,
> That him were levere han shame (and that were routhe)
> *Than ye to me sholde breke thus youre trouthe...*' (1526–30)

And again, when he is recounting what has happened to the magician:

> He seide, 'Arveragus, of gentillesse,
> Hadde levere dye in sorwe and in distresse
> *Than that his wyf were of hir trouthe fals.*' (1595–7)

In contrast to (say) *Amis and Amiloun*, where the wife's 'trouthe' is identified as synonymous with that of her husband, here the husband's 'trouthe' is identified with his wife's.

Dorigen's promise thus acts as an external constraint on both husband and wife. Neither can identify it as a willed action; it represents neither Arveragus's wish to transfer his wife to another man nor Dorigen's wish to transfer herself. If Arveragus authorizes her to keep her promise, this is because only he can release her from the earlier promise of fidelity which she had made to him. And it is by yielding to the claims of her promise to Aurelius that Arveragus preserves her 'trouthe' to himself. For if promises can be broken, what would become of the 'trouthe' that binds Dorigen to Arveragus? Paradoxically, therefore, the act that threatens to dissolve their marriage is also the one that reaffirms the value on which it is founded.

The *Franklin's Tale* is thus the only one of the stories we have looked at that gives a woman's 'trouthe' the same status as a man's. It is also the only one to confront the experience of non-consensual sex from the woman's point of view. In a long desperate soliloquy, Dorigen contemplates the need to keep her promise to Aurelius, and compares herself to a long list of women who killed themselves in order to avoid rape or expunge its memory. Felicity Riddy thinks that this shows the falseness of the courtly lover's position: once the lady is made accessible by male endeavour, he finds himself cast in the role of a rapist (1994, 60). But that is surely the point that the story makes: no true lover would wish to have his lady on any other basis than her own unforced choice of him (a point that the author of *Athis and Prophilias* seems incapable of grasping). The anguished words which reveal to Aurelius that Dorigen's promise is forcing her to a totally unwilled sexual act – and is not the sign of a lingering wish to be able to accept his love – provoke his pity and dissolve his desire. What Aurelius glimpses in Dorigen's reply is 'the love bitwix yow two', a love that he has it in his power to pollute forever. If he speaks admiringly of Arveragus's 'gentillesse', his final praise is for Dorigen, as 'the treweste

and the beste wyf/ That evere yet I knew in al my lyf' (1539–40). His renunciation of her is an acknowledgement that her marriage is not simply an incon-
venient obstacle to his desires, but a living part of her personhood; as Priscilla
Martin puts it (1990, 128–9), he recognizes that she is 'a person independent
of her relationship with him and his fantasies about her'. And the tale does not
end with the establishment of a bond between Arveragus and Aurelius, but with
the re-affirmation of the bond between Arveragus and Dorigen:

> Arveragus and Dorigen his wyf
> In sovereyn blisse leden forth hir lyf.
> Nevere eft ne was ther angre hem bitwene.
> He cherisseth hire as though she were a queene,
> And she was to hym trewe for everemoore. (1551–5)

The marriage is confirmed in the primary position it held at the beginning of
the tale. Meanwhile, instead of becoming best friends with Arveragus (like
Gilberto and Ansaldo in the *Decameron*), Aurelius is left to forge a new bond
with the clerk-magician, a man not of his class, but equally capable of a 'gentil dede' (1611). The function of this narrative coda is to extend the notion that
the stability and harmony represented by 'trouthe' are the result of a ceaseless
process of adjustment and adaptation, as they are in the marital relationship of
Arveragus and Dorigen. But in emotional terms, this homosocial relationship
is distinctly second-best (rather like that between Humphrey Bogart and the
police captain at the end of *Casablanca*)[25] in comparison with the rapturous
happiness of Arveragus and Dorigen.

   To sum up: in the other tales we have looked at, the renunciation of the wife,
whether by husband or by lover, testifies to a regard for the other man. In the
Franklin's Tale, it testifies to Arveragus's regard for his wife, and to Aurelius's
regard for Arveragus's regard for his wife. Within the context of the generally
homosocially-oriented literature we have looked at, the *Franklin's Tale* stands
out as unusual, and its unusualness deserves to be acknowledged. Its story is
wildly improbable, and hardly meant as a model for human behaviour in any
straightforward sense. But what it celebrates is the power of a commitment to
'trouthe' – the power of the kind of blind surrender that Chaucer calls patience –
to awaken a response in the human heart, a response that matches the initial

---

25   *Casablanca* has obvious affinities with the narratives considered in this paper, but
offers an interesting twist on the pattern: in this case, it is the lover (Rick Blaine), not the
husband (Victor Laszlo), who is at first the party 'betrayed' by the apparent infidelity of Ilse
Lund, which turns out to be her adherence to an earlier marital relationship. Rick is eventually linked to the husband in a homosocial relationship, forged by their sense of larger
duties created by the war, but since Ilse too participates in this greater commitment to political rather than emotional claims (and indeed for most of the film bears the major responsibility for making this choice), she is not degraded by Rick's eventual renunciation of her.
All three main characters are thus bonded by their commitment to a cause external to their
individual desires.

self-surrender and transforms what had seemed a deadlocked situation into harmony and happiness. It is in this conception of the miraculous power of 'trouthe' to remake the world in the image of the self-sacrificing hero/heroine that the *Franklin's Tale* most nearly resembles 'Lantfrid and Cobbo' (as also the latter part of *Amis and Amiloun*, not to mention *Sir Gawain and the Green Knight*). But here again, what marks out Chaucer's tale is that the liberating commitment to 'trouthe' is not made by a male hero, but by a husband and wife, united in their values, their dilemmas, and their trust in each other.[26]

---

[26] This chapter was delivered as the Chambers Memorial Lecture at University College, London, in March 2000, and as the Bastian Lecture at Centre College, Danville, Kentucky, in March 2001. An earlier draft was presented to the medieval graduate seminar at Harvard University. I am grateful for the comments and suggestions which I received on all these occasions. Chris Cannon read a draft and made helpful comments; Katherine O'Brien O'Keeffe gave welcome advice. I would also like to acknowledge a much older debt to a lecture given by Peter Dronke, in which he compared 'Lantfrid and Cobbo' with the story of Rollo, *Il Pecorone*, and the *Franklin's Tale*.

Bibliography

The bibliography includes all works cited in the text or notes of this book, together with others that are of special importance to its argument; it is not a list of all works consulted in its preparation, still less of all those falling within its general field. Quotations of Chaucer are from *The Riverside Chaucer*, ed. L. D. Benson (Boston, Mass.: Houghton Mifflin, 1987). The Riverside version of *The Canterbury Tales* has also been issued separately in a revised edition by Larry Benson (Boston, Mass.: Houghton Mifflin, 2000). I have also used the edition of *Troilus and Criseyde* by B. A. Windeatt (London: Longman, 1984). Translations in the text are my own unless there are specific indications otherwise.

References to primary works in languages other than English are keyed to the sectionalisation (book, chapter, line, etc.) used in the original texts, except where (as in the case of the Abelard–Heloise correspondence) such sectionalisation is absent; in that case I have cited the pagination of the translation as being most widely accessible to readers. Those interested in the Latin original can readily find the corresponding passages in the editions of the *Letters* listed below. Line-numbering for the *Romance of the Rose* follows Lecoy's edition, which is the basis of Horgan's translation; Dahlberg's translation follows the older edition by Langlois, but may be matched with Lecoy by means of Dahlberg's table of correspondences between the two texts.

Primary Works

Abelard, Peter, *Historia Calamitatum*, ed. J. Monfrin (Paris: J. Vrin, 1967) [trans. Radice in *Letters*, below].

Abelard, Peter, *Theologia Christiana*, *Opera Theologica* vol. II, ed. E. M. Buytaert, Corpus Christianorum Continuatio Medievalis XII (Turnhout: Brepols, 1969).

Abelard–Heloise Correspondence:

Muckle, J. T., ed., 'The Personal Letters Between Abelard and Heloise', *Mediaeval Studies* 15 (1953) 47–94 [Letters I–IV].

Muckle, J. T., 'The Letter of Heloise on Religious Life and Abelard's First Reply', *Mediaeval Studies* 17 (1955) 240–81 [Letters V–VI].

McLaughlin, T. P., ed., 'Abelard's Rule for Religious Women', *Mediaeval Studies* 18 (1956) 241–92 [Letter VII].

Radice, B., trans., *The Letters of Abelard and Heloise* (Harmondsworth: Penguin Books, 1974).

Amis and Amiloun:

Amis and Amiloun [Middle English], ed. M. Leach, EETS o.s. 203 (London: Oxford University Press, 1937).

Ami et Amile [Old French], ed. P. F. Dembowski, CFMA (Paris: Honoré Champion, 1969).

Ami and Amile, trans. S. N. Rosenberg and S. Danon (Ann Arbor, Mich.: University of Michigan Press, 1996).

Amis e Amilun [Anglo-Norman], pp. 111–87 in *Amis und Amiloun: Zugleich mit der altfranzösischen Quelle*, ed. E. Kölbing (Heilbronn: Henninger, 1884). Trans. Judith Weiss in *The Birth of Romance: An Anthology* (London: Dent, 1992).

Andreas Capellanus, *On Love*, ed. and trans. P. G. Walsh (London: Duckworth, 1982).

Athis et Prophilias:
Li Romanz d'Athis et Prophilias, ed. A. Hilka, 2 vols, Gesellschaft für romanische Literatur 29, 40 (Dresden: Niemeyer, 1912–1916).

Avianus, *Fabulae*, in *Minor Latin Poets*, ed. and trans. J. W. Duff and A. M. Duff, vol. I (London: Heinemann, 1982).

Barthes, R., *A Lover's Discourse: Fragments* [1977], trans. R. Howard (London: Jonathan Cape, 1979).

Benoît de Sainte-Maure, *Le Roman de Troie*, ed. L. Constans, 6 vols, SATF (Paris, Firmin-Didot, 1904–12).

Blamires, A., ed., *Woman Defamed and Woman Defended: An Anthology of Medieval Texts* (Oxford: Clarendon Press, 1992).

Boccaccio, Giovanni, *Tutte le Opere*, ed. V. Branca, 12 vols (Milan: Mondadori, 1964–), *Filocolo* in vol. I (1967), *Filostrato* and *Teseida* in vol. II (1964); *Decameron* in vol. IV (1976); *De Mulieribus Claris* in vol. X (1967).
The Decameron, trans. G. H. McWilliam (Harmondsworth: Penguin, 1972).
Filocolo, trans. D. Cheney and T. G. Bergin (New York and London: Garland, 1985).
Concerning Famous Women, trans. G. A. Guarino (London: George Allen and Unwin, 1964).

Cambridge Songs:
Carmina Cantabrigiensia ed. W. Bulst (Heidelberg: Carl Winter, 1950).
Carmina Cantabrigiensia, ed. K. Strecker (Berlin: Weidmann, 1926; repr. 1966).
The Cambridge Songs, ed. and trans. Jan Ziolkowski [originally published 1994], (Tempe, Ariz.: Medieval and Renaissance Texts and Studies, 1998).

Chaucer's Boccaccio: Sources of Troilus and the Knight's and Franklin's Tales, ed. and trans. N. R. Havely (Cambridge: D. S. Brewer; Totowa, N.J.: Rowman and Littlefield, 1980).

Chrétien de Troyes, *Le Chevalier de le Charrete*, ed. M. Roques, CFMA (Paris: Honoré Champion, 1968).

Chrétien de Troyes, *Yvain*, ed. T. B. W. Reid (Manchester: Manchester University Press, 1942).

Chrétien de Troyes, *Arthurian Romances*, trans. W. W. Kibler (Harmondsworth: Penguin, 1991).

Christine de Pisan, Jean Gerson, Jean de Montreuil, Gontier et Pierre Col, *Le Débat sur le Roman de la Rose*, ed. E. Hicks (Paris: Honoré Champion, 1977).

[Christine de Pisan et al.] *La Querelle de la Rose: Letters and Documents*, trans. Joseph L. Baird and John R. Kane, North Carolina Studies in the Romance Languages and Literature (Chapel Hill: University of North Carolina, 1978).

Christine de Pisan, *The Book of the City of Ladies*, trans. E. J. Richards (London: Pan Books, 1983).

Claudian, *De Raptu Proserpinae*, ed. J. B. Hall (Cambridge: Cambridge University Press, 1969).

Claudian, *De Raptu Proserpinae*, trans. M. Platnauer, in *Claudian*, vol. II, Loeb Classical Library (London: Heinemann; Cambridge, Mass.: Harvard University Press, 1922).

Dante Alighieri, *The Divine Comedy*, [text with translation], trans. C. S. Singleton, 3 vols in 6 (Princeton: Princeton University Press, 1970–5).

Dante Alighieri, *Il Convivio*, ed. M. Simonelli (Bologna: Riccardo Pàtron, 1966).

Dante Alighieri, *The Banquet*, trans. C. Ryan (Saratoga, Calif.: Anma Libri, 1989).

Daurel e Beton:
  A Critical Edition of the Old Provençal Epic 'Daurel e Beton', ed. A. S. Kimmel (Chapel Hill: University of North Carolina Press, 1971).
  Daurel and Beton, trans. Janet Shirley (Felinfach: Llanerch Publishers, 1997).

Davies, R. T., ed., *Medieval English Lyrics: A Critical Anthology* (London: Faber and Faber, 1963).

De Coniuge non Ducenda: *Gawain on Marriage: The Textual Tradition of the* De Coniuge Non Ducenda *with Critical Edition and Translation* by A. G. Rigg (Toronto: Pontifical Institute of Mediaeval Studies, 1986).

Defoe, Daniel, *Roxana: The Fortunate Mistress*, ed. J. Jack (London: Oxford University Press, 1969).

Deguileville, Guillaume de, *Le Pèlerinage de l'âme*, ed. J. J. Stürzinger, Roxburghe Club (London: Nichols and Sons, 1895).

Deschamps, Eustache, *Miroir de Mariage*, in *Oeuvres Complètes*, vol. IX, ed. G. Raynaud, SATF (Paris: Firmin-Didot, 1894).

Epistola Valerii: see Map, Walter.

Giovanni Fiorentino, *Il Pecorone*, ed. Enzo Esposito, Classici Italiani Minori (Ravenna: Longo, n.d.). Trans. T. Roscoe, in *The Italian Novelists*, vol. I (London: Septimus Prowett, 1825), 283–90.

Giraldus Cambrensis, *Gemma Ecclesiastica*: *Giraldi Cambrensis Opera*, vol. II, ed. J. S. Brewer, Rolls series (London: Longman: 1862).
  The Jewel of the Church, trans. J. J. Hagen (Leiden: Brill, 1979).

Gower, John, *Confessio Amantis*, ed. G. C. Macaulay, 2 vols, EETS e.s. 81–2 (London: Oxford University Press, 1900–1901, repr. 1969).

Guillaume de Lorris: see *Romance of the Rose, The.*

Hawes, Stephen, *The Pastime of Pleasure*, ed. W. E. Mead, EETS o.s. 173 (London: Oxford University Press, 1928).

Hervieux, L., ed., *Les Fabulistes latins*, 2nd edn, 5 vols (Paris: Firmin-Didot, 1893–9; repr. New York: Burt Franklin, n.d.).

Higden, Ranulph, *Polychronicon*, ed. C. Babington and J. R. Lumby, 9 vols, Rolls series (London: H.M.S.O., 1865–86; repr. 1964–75).

Hoccleve, Thomas: *Selections from Hoccleve*, ed. M. C. Seymour (Oxford: Clarendon Press, 1981).

Innocent III, Pope: Lotario dei Segni (Pope Innocent III), *De Miseria Condicionis Humanae*, ed. [with English trans.] R. E. Lewis (Athens, Ga.: University of Georgia Press, 1978).

Jean de Meun: see *Romance of the Rose, The.*

Jehan le Fèvre: *Les Lamentations de Matheolus et le Livre de Leesce de Jehan le Fèvre, de Ressons*, ed. A. G. Van Hamel, 2 vols, Bibliothèque de l'Ecole des Hautes Etudes 95–6 (Paris: Emile Bouillon, 1893–1905).

Jerome, *Adversus Jovinianum*, PL 23, cols 211–338.

Jerome, *Adversus Jovinianum* trans. W. H. Fremantle in *St Jerome: Letters and Select Works*, ed. H. Wace and P. Schaff, A Select Library of Nicene and Post-Nicene Fathers of the Christian Church, vol. 6 (Oxford: Parker; New York: Christian Literature Co., 1893).

John of Salisbury, *Policraticus*, ed. C. C. I. Webb, 2 vols (Oxford: Clarendon Press, 1909; repr. Frankfurt a.M.: Minerva, 1965).

John of Salisbury, *Frivolities of Courtiers and Footprints of Philosophers, Being a Translation of the First, Second and Third Books, and Selections from the Seventh and Eighth Books of the Policraticus of John of Salisbury*, trans. J. B. Pike (Minneapolis: University of Minnesota Press; London: Oxford University Press, 1938).

Julian of Norwich: *A Book of Showings to the Anchoress Julian of Norwich*, ed. E. Colledge and J. Walsh, 2 vols (Toronto: Pontifical Institute of Mediaeval Studies, 1978).

Lydgate, John, *Minor Poems*, ed. H. Noble MacCracken, 2 vols, EETS e.s. 107, o.s. 192 (London: Oxford University Press, 1911–34).

Macrobius, *Saturnalia*, ed. J. Willis (Leipzig: Teubner, 1963).

Map, Walter, *De Nugis Curialium/Courtiers' Trifles*, ed. and trans. M. R. James, rev. C. N. L. Brooke and R. A. B. Mynors (Oxford: Clarendon Press, 1983, repr. with bibliographical note, 1994) [*Epistola Valerii* at Dist. IV, cap. iii–v].

Masuccio Salernitano, *Il Novellino*, ed. S. S. Nigro (Rome and Bari: Laterza, 1975). *The Novellino of Masuccio*, trans. W. G. Waters (London: no publisher, n.d.).

Marbod of Rennes, *Liber Decem Capitulorum*, PL 171, cols 1693–1716 [Capitulum III: De Meretrice; Capitulum IV: De Matrona].

Marie de France, *Fables*, trans. Mary Lou Martin (Birmingham, Ala.: Summa Publications, 1984) [with parallel French text].

Matheolus: see Jehan le Fèvre.

Miller, Robert P., ed., *Chaucer: Sources and Backgrounds* (New York; London: Oxford University Press, 1977) [includes translations of relevant portions of Jerome, *Adv. Jov.*, Walter Map's *Epistola Valerii*, Heloise's *dissuasio*, and *The Romance of the Rose*].

Oliphant, Margaret: *Autobiography and Letters of Mrs Margaret Oliphant*, ed. Mrs H. Coghill ([originally published 1899] Leicester: Leicester University Press, 1974).

Osbert of Clare, *Letters*, ed. E. W. Williamson (London: Oxford University Press, 1929).

Ovid, *Ars Amatoria* and *Remedia Amoris*, in *The Art of Love, and Other Poems*, ed. and trans. J. H. Mozley, Loeb Classical Library (London: Heinemann; Cambridge, Mass.: Harvard University Press, 1962).

Ovid, *Heroides and Amores*, ed. and trans. G. Showerman, Loeb Classical Library (London: Heinemann; Cambridge, Mass.: Harvard University Press, 1963).

Ovide moralisé, ed. C. de Boer, 5 vols, Verhandelingen der koninklijke Akademie van Wetenschappen, Afdeeling Letterkunde, n.s. 15.21, 30^3, 37, 43 (Amsterdam: Johannes Müller, 1915–68).

Pamphilus, ed. S. Pittaluga, in *Commedie latine del XII e XIII secolo*, vol. III (Genoa: Istituto de Filologia Classica e Medievale, Università di Genova, 1980).

Pamphilus: 'Pamphilus, De Amore: An Introduction and Translation', T. J. Garbaty, *ChuuR* 2 (1967) 108–34.

Peter of Blois, *Epistola LXXIX*, PL 207, cols 243–7.

Peter of Blois, 'Grates ago Veneri' [*Carmina Burana* 72; *Arundel Lyrics* 10], trans. F. Adcock, *The Virgin and the Nightingale* (Newcastle upon Tyne: Bloodaxe Books, 1983), no. XII.

Petrarch, Francis, *Rerum familiarum libri: Le familiari*, ed. V. Rossi (Florence: Sansoni, 1933–42).

Petrarch, Francis, *Letters on Familiar Matters*, trans. A. S. Bernardo, vol. I (I–VIII) (Albany, N.Y.: State University of New York Press, 1975); vols II–III (IX–XVI and XVII–XXIV) (Baltimore: Johns Hopkins University Press, 1982–5).

Petrarch, Francis, *Epistolae Seniles*, in *Francisci Petrarchae Opera*, 3 vols (Basle, 1554).

Petrarch, Francis, *Letters of Old Age*, trans. A. S. Bernardo, S. Levin, and R. A. Bernardo, 2 vols (Baltimore and London: Johns Hopkins University Press, 1992).

Petrarch, Francis, *Trionfi*, ed. Vinicio Pacca and Laura Paolino (Milan: Mondadori, 1996).

Petrus Alfonsi, *Disciplina Clericalis*, ed. A. Hilka and W. Söderhjelm, Acta Societatis Scientiarum Fennicae 38.4 (Helsingfors: Drukerei der Finnischen Litteraturgesellschaft, 1911).

> *The Scholar's Guide*, trans. J. R. Jones and J. E. Keller (Toronto: Pontifical Institute of Mediaeval Studies, 1969).

Quintilian, *Institutio Oratoria*, ed. and trans. H. E. Butler, 4 vols. (London: Heinemann, 1966–9).

Rabelais, François, *Le Tiers Livre*, in *Oeuvres Complètes*, vol. I, ed. P. Jourda (Paris: Garnier, 1962).

Rabelais, François, *Le Tiers Livre*, trans. J. M. Cohen, in *The Histories of Gargantua and Pantagruel* (Harmondsworth: Penguin, 1955).

Rodulfus Tortarius, *Carmina*, ed. M. B. Ogle and D. M. Schullian (Rome: American Academy in Rome, 1933).

Romance of the Rose, The.

> Guillaume de Lorris and Jean de Meun, *Le Roman de la Rose*, ed. F. Lecoy, 3 vols (Paris: Honoré Champion, 1966–70).

> Guillaume de Lorris and Jean de Meun, *The Romance of the Rose*, trans. Frances Horgan (Oxford: Oxford University Press, 1994).

> Guillaume de Lorris and Jean de Meun, *The Romance of the Rose*, trans. Charles Dahlberg (Hanover, New England; London: University Press of New England, 1971).

Serlo of Bayeux, 'Ad Muriel Sanctimonialem', ed. T. Wright, pp. 233–41 in *The Anglo-Latin Satirical Poets and Epigrammatists of the Twelfth Century*, vol. 2, Rolls Series (London: Longman, 1872).

Sir Gawain and the Green Knight, ed. J. R. R. Tolkien and E. V. Gordon, rev. Norman Davis, (Oxford: Clarendon Press, 1968).

Stehling, T., trans., *Medieval Latin Poems of Male Love and Friendship* (New York and London: Garland, 1984).

Vergil: *P. Vergili Maronis Opera*, ed. R. A. B. Mynors (Oxford: Clarendon Press, 1969).

Secondary Works

Adams, J. N., *The Latin Sexual Vocabulary* (London: Duckworth, 1982).

Aers, D., *Chaucer, Langland and the Creative Imagination* (London, Boston, Henley: Routledge and Kegan Paul, 1980).

Ames, R. M., 'The Feminist Connections of Chaucer's *Legend of Good Women*', pp. 57–74 in *Chaucer in the Eighties*, ed. J. N. Wasserman and R. J. Blanch (Syracuse, N.Y.: Syracuse University Press, 1986).

Beidler, P. G., ed., *Masculinities in Chaucer: Approaches to Maleness in the 'Canterbury Tales' and 'Troilus and Criseyde'* (Cambridge: D. S. Brewer, 1998).

Benson, D. E., 'The Marriage "Encomium" in the *Merchant's Tale*: A Chaucerian Crux', *ChauR* 14 (1979–80) 48–60.

Blamires, A., 'Chaucer's Revaluation of Chivalric Honor', *Mediaevalia* 5 (1979) 245–69.

Bloch, R. H., 'Medieval Misogyny', *Representations* 20 (1987) 1–24.

Bloch, R. H., 'Chaucer's Maiden's Head: "The Physician's Tale" and the Poetics of Virginity', *Representations* 28 (Fall 1989) 113–34.

Bloomfield, M. W., 'The Man of Law's Tale: A Tragedy of Victimization and a Christian Comedy', *PMLA* 87 (1972) 384–90.

Blum, M., 'Negotiating Masculinities: Erotic Triangles in the *Miller's Tale*', pp. 37–52 in *Masculinities in Chaucer*, ed. P. Beidler (Cambridge: D. S. Brewer, 1998).

Bolgar, R. R., *The Classical Heritage and its Beneficiaries from the Carolingian Age to the End of the Renaissance* (London: Cambridge University Press, 1954).

Boutière, J., and A.-H. Schutz, *Biographies des troubadours*, 2nd edn (Paris: Nizet, 1964).

Bronson, B. H., 'Afterthoughts on the Merchant's Tale', *Studies in Philology* 58 (1961) 583–96.

Brown, E., Jr, 'Biblical Women in the Merchant's Tale: Feminism, Antifeminism, and Beyond', *Viator* 5 (1974) 387–412.

Brown, E., Jr, 'Chaucer, the Merchant, and their Tale: Getting Beyond Old Controversies', *ChauR* 13 (1978–9) 141–56, 247–62.

Bryan, W. F., and G. Dempster, *Sources and Analogues of Chaucer's Canterbury Tales* (Chicago: University of Chicago Press, 1941; repr. New York: Humanities Press, 1958).

Bugge, J., *Virginitas: An Essay in the History of a Medieval Ideal* (The Hague: Martinus Nijhoff, 1975).

Burnley, J. D., *Chaucer's Language and the Philosophers' Tradition* (Cambridge: D. S. Brewer; Totowa, N.J.: Rowman and Littlefield, 1979).

Burrow, C., *Epic Romance: Homer to Milton* (Oxford: Clarendon Press, 1993).

Burrow, J. A., 'Irony in the *Merchant's Tale*', *Anglia* 75 (1957) 199–208.

Butler, J., *Bodies That Matter: On the Discursive Limits of 'Sex'* (New York and London: Routledge, 1993).

Bynum, C. W., *Jesus as Mother: Studies in the Spirituality of the High Middle Ages* (Berkeley: University of California Press, 1982).

Cabassut, A., 'Une dévotion médiévale peu connue: la dévotion à "Jésus notre mère"', *Revue d'ascétique et de mystique* 25 (1949) 234–45.

Caie, G. D., 'The Significance of the Early Chaucer Manuscript Glosses (with special reference to the *Wife of Bath's Prologue*)', *ChauR* 10 (1975–6) 350–60.

Cannon, C., '*Raptus* in the Chaumpaigne Release and a Newly Discovered Document Concerning the Life of Geoffrey Chaucer', *Speculum* 68 (1993) 74–94.

Cannon, C., 'Chaucer and Rape: Uncertainty's Certainties', *SAC* 22 (2000) 67–92.

Carruthers, M., 'The Wife of Bath and the Painting of Lions', *PMLA* 94 (1979) 209–22; repr. with an Afterword, pp. 22–53 in *Feminist Readings in Middle English Literature: The Wife of Bath and All Her Sect*, ed. R. Evans and L. Johnson (London and New York: Routledge, 1994).

Chesterton, G. K., *Chaucer* (London: Faber and Faber, 1932; repr. 1962).

Clasby, E., 'Chaucer's Constance: Womanly Virtue and the Heroic Life', *ChauR* 13 (1978–9) 221–33.

Clemen, W. H., *Chaucer's Early Poetry* (London: Methuen, 1963).

Clouston, W. A., 'The Damsel's Rash Promise: Indian Original and Some Asiatic and European Variants of Chaucer's Franklin's Tale', pp. 289–340 in *Originals and Analogues of Some of Chaucer's Canterbury Tales*, ed. F. J. Furnivall, E. Brock, and W. A. Clouston, Chaucer Society (London: Trübner & Co., 1888).

Condren, Edward I., 'The Clerk's Tale of Man Tempting God', *Criticism* 26 (1984) 99–114.

Cox, C. S., *Gender and Language in Chaucer* (Gainesville, Fla.: University Press of Florida, 1997).

Crampton, G. R., *The Condition of Creatures: Suffering and Action in Chaucer and Spenser* (New Haven: Yale University Press, 1974).

Crane, S., 'Alison's Incapacity and Poetic Instability in the Wife of Bath's Tale', *PMLA* 102 (1987) 20–8.

Crane, S., *Gender and Romance in Chaucer's Canterbury Tales* (Princeton, N. J.: Princeton University Press, 1994).

d'Alverny, M.-T., 'Comment les théologiens et les philosophes voient la femme', *Cahiers de civilisation médiévale* 20 (1977) 105–29.

Dean, R. J., 'Unnoticed Commentaries on the *Dissuasio Valerii* of Walter Map', *Mediaeval and Renaissance Studies* 2 (1950) 128–50.

Delany, S., *Chaucer's House of Fame: The Poetics of Skeptical Fideism* (Chicago: University of Chicago Press, 1972).

Delany, S., *Writing Woman: Women Writers and Women in Literature, Medieval to Modern* (New York: Schocken Books, 1983): 'Womanliness in the *Man of Law's Tale*', pp. 36–46 [originally published 1974–5]; 'Slaying Python: Marriage and Misogyny in a Chaucerian Text', pp. 47–75; 'Sexual Economics, Chaucer's Wife of Bath, and *The Book of Margery Kempe*', pp. 76–92 [originally published 1975].

Delany, S., *Medieval Literary Politics: Shapes of Ideology* (Manchester and New York: Manchester University Press, 1990): 'Rewriting Woman Good: Gender and the Anxiety of Influence in Two Late-Medieval Texts', pp. 74–87 [originally published 1986]; 'Strategies of Silence in the Wife of Bath's Recital', pp. 112–29; 'The Haunted Work: Politics and the Paralysis of Poetic Imagination in *The Physician's Tale*', pp. 130–40 [originally published 1981]; ' "*Mulier est hominis confusio*": The Anti-Popular *Nun's Priest's Tale*', pp. 141–50 [originally published 1984]; 'Women, Nature and Language: Chaucer's *Legend of Good Women*', pp. 151–65.

Delany, S., *The Naked Text: Chaucer's Legend of Good Women* (Berkeley, Los Angeles, and London: University of California Press, 1994).

Delhaye, P., 'Le Dossier antimatrimonial de l'*Adversus Jovinianum* et son influence sur quelques écrits latins du XIIᵉ siècle', *Mediaeval Studies* 13 (1951) 65–86.

Diamond, A., 'Chaucer's Women and Women's Chaucer', pp. 60–83, 282–4 in *The Authority of Experience: Essays in Feminist Criticism*, ed. A. Diamond and L. R. Edwards (Amherst: University of Massachusetts Press, 1977).

Dietrich, S., ' "Slydyng" Masculinity in the Four Portraits of Troilus', pp. 205–220 in *Masculinities in Chaucer*, ed. P. Beidler (Cambridge: D. S. Brewer, 1998).

Dinshaw, Carolyn, *Chaucer's Sexual Poetics* (Madison and London: University of Wisconsin Press, 1989).

Dinshaw, C., 'A Kiss is Just a Kiss: Heterosexuality and its Consolations in *Sir Gawain and the Green Knight*', *diacritics* 24 (1994) 205–26.

Donaldson, E. T., 'Idiom of Popular Poetry in the Miller's Tale', [originally published 1951], pp. 13–29 in his *Speaking of Chaucer* (London: Athlone Press, 1970).

Donaldson, E. T., 'The Effect of the Merchant's Tale', pp. 30–45, in his *Speaking of Chaucer* (London: Athlone Press, 1970).

Donaldson, E. T., 'Designing a Camel; Or, Generalizing the Middle Ages', *Tennessee Studies in Literature* 22 (1977) 1–16.

Donovan, M. J., 'The Image of Pluto and Proserpina in the *Merchant's Tale*', *Philological Quarterly* 36 (1957) 49–60.

Dronke, P., 'Peter Abelard: *Planctus* and Satire', pp. 115–49 in *Poetic Individuality in the Middle Ages: New Departures in Poetry 1000–1150* (Oxford: Clarendon Press, 1970; 2nd edn, Westfield College, University of London, 1986).

Dronke, P., 'Francesca and Heloise', [originally published 1975], pp. 359–85 in his *The Medieval Poèt and his World* (Rome: Edizioni di Storia e Letteratura, 1984).

Dronke, P., *Intellectuals and Poets in Medieval Europe* (Rome: Edizioni di Storia e Letteratura, 1992): 'Abelard and Heloise in Medieval Testimonies', pp. 247–94 [originally published 1976]; 'Dido's Lament: From Medieval Latin Lyric to Chaucer', pp. 431–56 [originally published 1986].

Dronke, P., *Sources of Inspiration: Studies in Literary Transformation, 400–1500* (Rome, 1997).

Duby, G., *Medieval Marriage: Two Models from Twelfth-Century France*, trans. E. Foster (Baltimore and London: Johns Hopkins University Press, 1978).

Eade, J. C., ' "We ben to lewed or to slowe": Chaucer's Astronomy and Audience Participation', *SAC* 4 (1982) 53–85.

Elliott, J. R., Jr, 'The Two Tellers of *The Merchant's Tale*', *Tennessee Studies in Literature* 9 (1964) 11–17.

Engle, L., 'Chaucer, Bakhtin, and Griselda', *Exemplaria* 1 (1989) 429–59.

Evans, R., and L. Johnson, eds., *Feminist Readings in Middle English Literature: The Wife of Bath and All Her Sect* (London and New York: Routledge, 1994).

'La Femme dans les civilisations des Xe–XIIIe siècles: Colloque', *Cahiers de civilisation médiévale* 20 (1977) 93–263.

Ferrante, J. M., *Woman as Image in Medieval Literature from the Twelfth Century to Dante* (New York and London: Columbia University Press, 1975).

Fradenburg, L. O., 'The Wife of Bath's Passing Fancy', *SAC* 8 (1986) 31–58.

Frank, R. W., Jr, *Chaucer and* The Legend of Good Women (Cambridge, Mass.: Harvard University Press, 1972).

Friedman, J. B., *Orpheus in the Middle Ages* (Cambridge, Mass.: Harvard University Press, 1970).

Friend, A. C., 'Chaucer's Version of the *Aeneid*', *Speculum* 28 (1953) 317–23.

Fries, M., ' "Slydynge of Corage": Chaucer's Criseyde as Feminist and Victim', pp. 45–59, 279–82 in *The Authority of Experience: Essays in Feminist Criticism*, ed. A. Diamond and L. R. Edwards (Amherst: University of Massachusetts Press, 1977).

Fyler, J. M., *Chaucer and Ovid* (New Haven: Yale University Press, 1979).

Gottfried, B., 'Conflict and Relationship, Sovereignty and Survival: Parables of Power in the *Wife of Bath's Prologue*', *ChauR* 19 (1984–5) 202–24.

Gravdal, K., *Ravishing Maidens: Writing Rape in Medieval French Literature and Law* (Philadelphia: University of Pennsylvania Press, 1991).

Gray, D., 'Chaucer and "Pite" ', pp. 173–203 in *J. R. R. Tolkien, Scholar and Storyteller: Essays in Memoriam*, ed. M. Salu and R. T. Farrell (Ithaca, N.Y.: Cornell University Press, 1979).

Green, R. F., 'Women in Chaucer's Audience', *ChauR* 18 (1983–4) 146–54.

Green, R. F., 'Chaucer's Victimized Women', *SAC* 10 (1988) 3–21.

Green, R. F., *A Crisis of Truth. Literature and Law in Ricardian England* (Philadelphia: University of Pennsylvania Press, 1999).

Grundriss der romanischen Literaturen des Mittelalters IV, Le roman jusqu'à la fin du XIIIᵉ siècle (Heidelberg: Carl Winter, 1978–84), vol. 1, ed. J. Frappier and R. R. Grimm, and vol. 2, ed. R. R. Grimm.

Hall, L. B., 'Chaucer and the Dido-and-Aeneas Story', Mediaeval Studies 25 (1963) 14 8–59.

Hanna, R., III, 'Some Commonplaces of Late Medieval Patience Discussions: An Introduction', pp. 65–87 in The Triumph of Patience: Medieval and Renaissance Studies, ed. G. J. Schiffhorst (Orlando: University Presses of Florida, 1978).

Hanna, R., III, and T. Lawler, Jankyn's Book of Wikked Wyves (Athens, Ga., and London: University of Georgia Press, 1997).

Hanning, R. W., 'From Eva and Ave to Eglentyne and Alisoun: Chaucer's Insight into the Roles Women Play', Signs 22 (1977) 580–99.

Hanning, R. W., 'Roasting a Friar, Mis-taking a Wife, and Other Acts of Textual Harassment in Chaucer's Canterbury Tales', SAC 7 (1985) 3–21.

Hansen, E. T., Chaucer and the Fictions of Gender (Berkeley, Los Angeles, and Oxford: University of California Press, 1992).

Haseldine, J., ed., Friendship in Medieval Europe (Stroud, Glos.: Sutton Publishing, 1999).

Heimmel, J. P., 'God Is Our Mother': Julian of Norwich and the Medieval Image of Christian Feminine Divinity (Salzburg: Institut für Anglistik and Amerikanistik, University of Salzburg, 1982).

Hexter, R. J., Ovid and Medieval Schooling: Studies in Medieval School Commentaries on Ovid's Ars Amatoria, Epistulae ex Ponto and Epistulae Heroidum (Munich: Arbeo, 1986).

Hinton, J., 'Walter Map and Ser Giovanni', Modern Philology 15 (1917–18) 203–9.

Hoffman, R. L., 'Jephthah's Daughter and Chaucer's Virginia', ChauR 2 (1967–8) 20–31.

Howard, D. R., 'Experience, Language and Consciousness: "Troilus and Criseyde," II, 596–931', [originally published 1970], pp. 159–80 in Chaucer's Troilus: Essays in Criticism, ed. Stephen A. Barney (London: Scolar Press, 1980).

Ingham, P. C., 'Homosociality and Creative Masculinity in the Knight's Tale', pp. 23–35 in Masculinities in Chaucer, ed. P. Beidler (Cambridge: D. S. Brewer, 1998).

Irigaray, L., This Sex Which Is Not One [French original published 1977], trans. C. Porter with C. Burke (Ithaca, N.Y.: Cornell University Press, 1985): 'Women on the Market', pp. 170–91; 'Commodities Among Themselves', pp. 192–7.

Jacobs, K., 'The Marriage Contract of the Franklin's Tale: The Remaking of Society', ChauR 20 (1985) 132–43.

Jacobus, M. 'The Difference of View', pp. 10–21 in Women Writing and Writing About Women, ed. M. Jacobus (London: Croom Helm; New York: Barnes and Noble, 1979).

Johnson, L., 'Reincarnations of Griselda: Contexts for the Clerk's Tale?', pp. 195–220 in Feminist Readings in Middle English Literature: The Wife of Bath and All Her Sect, ed. R. Evans and L. Johnson (London and New York: Routledge, 1994).

Keen, M., 'Brotherhood in Arms', History 47 (1962) 1–17.

Keiser, G. R., 'The Middle English Planctus Mariae and the Rhetoric of Pathos', pp. 167–93 in The Popular Literature of Medieval England, ed. T. J. Heffernan (Knoxville: University of Tennessee Press, 1985).

Kelly, H. A., Love and Marriage in the Age of Chaucer (Ithaca, N.Y.: Cornell University Press, 1975).

Kelly, H. A., 'Meaning and Uses of *Raptus* in Chaucer's Time', *SAC* 20 (1998) 101–65.

Kirk, E. D., ' "Who Suffreth More Than God?": Narrative Redefinition of Patience in *Patience* and *Piers Plowman*', pp. 88–104 in *The Triumph of Patience: Medieval and Renaissance Studies*, ed. G. J. Schiffhorst (Orlando: University Presses of Florida, 1978).

Kirkpatrick, R., 'The Griselda Story in Boccaccio, Petrarch and Chaucer', pp. 231–48 in *Chaucer and the Italian Trecento*, ed. P. Boitani (Cambridge: Cambridge University Press, 1983).

Kiser, L. J., *Telling Classical Tales: Chaucer and the* Legend of Good Women (Ithaca, N.Y.: Cornell University Press, 1983).

Kittredge, G. L., 'Chaucer's Discussion of Marriage' [originally published 1911–12], pp. 188–215 in *Chaucer: Modern Essays in Criticism*, ed. E. Wagenknecht (New York: Oxford University Press, 1959).

Knapp, P. A., 'Alisoun Weaves a Text', *Philological Quarterly* 65 (1986) 387–401.

Knight, S., 'Textual Variants: Textual Variance', *Southern Review* 16 (1983) 44–54.

Laskaya, A., *Chaucer's Approach to Gender in the Canterbury Tales* (Cambridge: D. S. Brewer, 1995).

Leclercq, J., 'L'amitié dans les lettres', *Revue du moyen âge latin* 1 (1945) 400–10.

Leicester, H. M., Jr, 'Of a Fire in the Dark: Public and Private Feminism in the *Wife of Bath's Tale*', *Women's Studies* 11 (1984) 157–78.

Leicester, H. M., Jr, 'The Wife of Bath as Chaucerian Subject', pp. 201–10 in *SAC, Proceedings No. 1 1984* (Knoxville, Tenn.: The New Chaucer Society, 1985).

Leube, E., *Fortuna in Karthago: Die Aeneas-Dido-Mythe Vergils in den romanischen Literaturen vom 14. bis zum 16. Jahrhundert* (Heidelberg: Carl Winter, 1969).

Lévi-Strauss, C., *The Elementary Structures of Kinship* [rev. edn of French original published 1967], trans. J. H. Bell, J. R. von Sturmer, and R. Needham (Boston: Beacon Press, 1969).

Levy, B. S., 'The Meanings of *The Clerk's Tale*', pp. 385–409 in *Chaucer and the Craft of Fiction*, ed. L. A. Arrathoon (Rochester, Mich.: Solaris Press, 1986).

Leyerle, J., ed., *Marriage in the Middle Ages* [five papers included in *Viator* 4 (1973) 413–501].

Lipking, L., *Abandoned Women and Poetic Tradition* (Chicago and London: University of Chicago Press, 1988).

Lowes, J. L., 'Chaucer and the *Miroir de Mariage*', *Modern Philology* 8 (1910–11) 165–86, 305–34.

Lowes, J. L., 'Is Chaucer's *Legend of Good Women* a Travesty?', *Journal of English and Germanic Philology* 8 (1909) 513–69.

Lumiansky, R. M., 'Chaucer and the Idea of Unfaithful Men', *Modern Language Notes* 62 (1947) 560–2.

Mann, J., *Chaucer and Medieval Estates Satire* (Cambridge: Cambridge University Press, 1973).

Mann, J., 'Chaucer and the Medieval Latin Poets: Part B', pp. 172–83 in *Writers and their Background: Geoffrey Chaucer*, ed. D. Brewer (London: Bell and Sons, 1974; repr. Cambridge: D. S. Brewer, 1990).

Mann, J., 'Troilus' Swoon', *ChauR* 14 (1980) 319–35.

Mann, J., 'Chaucerian Themes and Style in the *Franklin's Tale*', pp. 133–53 in *The New Pelican Guide to English Literature*, ed. B. Ford, vol. I, Part One (Harmondsworth: Penguin Books, 1982).

Mann, J., 'Parents and Children in the *Canterbury Tales*', pp. 165–83 in *Literature in Fourteenth-Century England*, ed. P. Boitani and A. Torti (Tübingen: Gunter Narr; Cambridge: D. S. Brewer, 1983) [1983a].

Mann, J., 'Satisfaction and Payment in Middle English Literature', *SAC* 5 (1983) 17–48 [1983b].

Mann, J., 'Chance and Destiny in *Troilus and Criseyde* and the *Knight's Tale*', pp. 75–92 in *The Cambridge Chaucer Companion*, ed. P. Boitani and J. Mann (Cambridge: Cambridge University Press, 1986).

Mann, J., 'Shakespeare and Chaucer: "What is Criseyde Worth?" ', pp. 219–42 in *The European Tragedy of Troilus*, ed. P. Boitani (Oxford: Clarendon Press, 1989).

Mann, J., *Apologies to Women* (Cambridge: Cambridge University Press, 1991) [1991a].

Mann, J., 'The Authority of the Audience in Chaucer', pp. 1–12 in *Poetics: Theory and Practice in Medieval English Literature*, ed. P. Boitani and A. Torti (Cambridge: D. S. Brewer, 1991) [1991b].

Mann, J., 'Anger and "Glosynge" in the *Canterbury Tales*', *Proceedings of the British Academy* 76 (1991) 203–23 [1991c].

Mann, J., 'Sir Gawain and the Romance Hero', pp. 105–17 in *Heroes and Heroines in Medieval English Literature. A Festschrift Presented to André Crépin on the Occasion of his Sixty-Fifth Birthday*, ed. Leo Carruthers (Cambridge: D. S. Brewer, 1994).

Mann, J., 'Chaucer and Atheism', *SAC* 17 (1995) 5–19.

Manning, S., 'Chaucer's Constance, Pale and Passive', pp. 13–23 in *Chaucerian Problems and Perspectives: Essays Presented to Paul E. Beichner C.S.C.*, ed. E. Vasta and Z. P. Thundy (Notre Dame, Ind.: University of Notre Dame Press, 1979).

Martin, P., *Chaucer's Women: Nuns, Wives and Amazons* (London: Macmillan, 1990).

Matthews, W., 'The Wife of Bath and All Her Sect', *Viator* 5 (1974) 413–43.

McAlpine, M. E., *The Genre of Troilus and Criseyde* (Ithaca, N.Y. and London: Cornell University Press, 1978).

McGuire, B. P., *Friendship and Community: The Monastic Experience 350–1250* (Kalamazoo, Mich: Cistercian Publications, 1988).

McInerney, M. B., ' "Is This a Mannes Herte?": Unmanning Troilus through Ovidian Allusion', pp. 221–35 in *Masculinities in Chaucer*, ed. P. Beidler (Cambridge: D. S. Brewer, 1998).

McLaughlin, M. M., 'Peter Abelard and the Dignity of Women: Twelfth Century "Feminism" in Theory and Practice', pp. 287–333 in *Pierre Abélard, Pierre le Vénérable*, Colloques Internationaux du CNRS 546 (Paris: Editions du CNRS, 1975).

Middleton, A., 'The Clerk and his Tale: Some Literary Contexts', *SAC* 2 (1980) 121–50.

Mieszkowski, G., 'The Reputation of Criseyde 1155–1500', *Transactions of the Connecticut Academy of Arts and Sciences* 43 (1971) 71–153 (New Haven: Archon Books, 1971).

Moi, T., 'Desire in Language: Andreas Capellanus and the Controversy of Courtly Love', pp. 11–33 in *Medieval Literature: Criticism, Ideology and History*, ed. D. Aers (Brighton: Harvester, 1986).

Moore, A. K., 'Chaucer and Matheolus', *Notes and Queries* 190 (1946) 245–8.

Morris, L. K., *Chaucer Source and Analogue Criticism: A Cross-Referenced Guide* (New York: Garland, 1985).

Morse, C. C., 'The Exemplary Griselda', *SAC* 7 (1985) 51–86.

Murtaugh, D. M., 'Women and Geoffrey Chaucer', *ELH* 38 (1971) 473–92.

Muscatine, C., *Chaucer and the French Tradition* (Berkeley and Los Angeles: University of California Press, 1957).

Muscatine, C., 'The Wife of Bath and Gautier's La veuve', pp. 109–14 in *Romance Studies in Memory of Edward Billings Ham*, ed. U. T. Holmes (Hayward, California: Valencia Press, 1967).

Norton-Smith, J., *Geoffrey Chaucer* (London: Routledge and Kegan Paul, 1974).

Otten, C. F., 'Proserpine: *Liberatrix Suae Gentis*', *ChauR* 5 (1970–1) 277–87.

Overbeck, P. T., 'Chaucer's Good Woman', *ChauR* 2 (1967–8) 75–94.

Panofsky, E., '"Imago Pietatis": Ein Beitrag zur Typengeschichte des "Schmerzenmanns" and der "Maria Mediatrix"', pp. 261–308 in *Festschrift für Max J. Friedländer zum 60. Geburtstage* (Leipzig: E. A. Seemann, 1927).

Patterson, L., '"For the Wyves love of Bathe": Feminine Rhetoric and Poetic Resolution in the *Roman de la Rose* and the *Canterbury Tales*', *Speculum* 58 (1983) 656–95.

Patterson, L., 'Chaucer's Pardoner on the Couch: Psyche and Clio in Medieval Literary Studies', *Speculum* 76 (2001) 638–60.

Percival, F., *Chaucer's Legendary Good Women* (Cambridge: Cambridge University Press, 1998).

Perella, N. J., *The Kiss Sacred and Profane* (Berkeley and Los Angeles: University of California Press, 1969).

Pinder, W., 'Die dichterische Würzel der Pietà', *Repertorium für Kunstwissenschaft* 42 (1920) 145–63.

Pratt, R. A., 'Jankyn's Book of Wikked Wyves: Medieval Antimatrimonial Propaganda in the Universities', *Annuale Mediaevale* 3 (1962) 5–27.

Pratt, R. A., 'Three Old French Sources of the Nonnes Preestes Tale', *Speculum* 47 (1972) 422–44, 646–68.

Raby, F. J. E., '*Amor* and *Amicitia*: A Medieval Poem', *Speculum* 40 (1965) 599–610.

Reid, T. B. W., 'The She-Wolf's Mate', *Medium Aevum* 24 (1955) 16–19.

Richmond, V. B., '"Pacience in Adversitee": Chaucer's Presentation of Marriage', *Viator* 10 (1979) 323–54.

Ricks, C., *T. S. Eliot and Prejudice* (London: Faber and Faber, 1988).

Riddy, F., 'Engendering Pity in the *Franklin's Tale*', pp. 54–71 in *Feminist Readings in Middle English Literature: The Wife of Bath and All Her Sect*, ed. R. Evans and L. Johnson (London and New York: Routledge, 1994).

Rowe, D. W., *Through Nature to Eternity: Chaucer's Legend of Good Women* (Lincoln and London: University of Nebraska Press, 1988).

Rubin, G., 'The Traffic In Women: Notes on the "Political Economy" of Sex' [originally published 1975], pp. 27–62 in *The Second Wave: A Reader in Feminist Theory*, ed. Linda Nicholson (New York and London: Routledge, 1997).

Saintonge, C., 'In Defense of Criseyde', *Modern Language Quarterly* 15 (1954) 312–20.

Salter, E., *The Knight's Tale and The Clerk's Tale* (London: Edward Arnold, 1962).

Saunders, C., *Rape and Ravishment in the Literature of Medieval England* (Cambridge: D. S. Brewer, 2001).

Schibanoff, S., 'Taking the Gold Out of Egypt: The Art of Reading as a Woman', pp. 83–106 in *Gender and Reading: Essays on Readers, Texts and Contexts*, ed. E. A. Flynn and P. P. Schweickart (Baltimore and London: Johns Hopkins

University Press, 1986); repr. pp. 221–45 in *Feminist Readings in Middle English Literature: The Wife of Bath and All Her Sect*, ed. R. Evans and L. Johnson (London and New York: Routledge, 1994).

Schibanoff, S., 'The New Reader and Female Textuality in Two Early Commentaries on Chaucer', *SAC* 10 (1988) 71–108.

Schirmer, W. F., *John Lydgate: A Study in the Culture of the XVth Century*, trans. Ann E. Keep (London: Methuen, 1961).

Schleusener, J., 'The Conduct of the *Merchant's Tale*', *ChauR* 14 (1979–80) 237–50.

Schmitz, G., *Die Frauenklage: Studien zur elegischen Verserzählung in der englischen Literatur des Spätmittelalters und der Renaissance* (Tübingen: Max Niemeyer, 1984).

Sedgewick, G. G., 'The Structure of the *Merchant's Tale*', *University of Toronto Quarterly* 17 (1947–8) 337–45.

Sedgwick, E. K., *Between Men: English Literature and Male Homosocial Desire*, 2nd edn (New York: Columbia University Press, 1992).

Shores, D. L., '*The Merchant's Tale*: Some Lay Observations', *Neuphilologische Mitteilungen* 71 (1970) 119–33.

Showalter, E., 'Towards a Feminist Poetics', pp. 22–41 in *Women Writing and Writing About Women*, ed. M. Jacobus (London: Croom Helm; New York: Barnes and Noble, 1979).

Smalley, B., *English Friars and Antiquity in the Early Fourteenth Century* (Oxford: Basil Blackwell, 1960).

Staël von Holstein, L. F. W., *Le roman d'Athis et Prophilias: étude littéraire sur ses deux versions* (Uppsala: Almqvist & Wiksell, 1909).

Stiller, N., *Eve's Orphans: Mothers and Daughters in Medieval English Literature* (Westport, Conn.: Greenwood Press, 1980).

Strathern, M., *The Gender of the Gift* (Berkeley and Los Angeles: University of California Press, 1988).

Sturges, R. S., *Chaucer's Pardoner and Gender Theory: Bodies of Discourse* (Basingstoke and London: MacMillan, 2000).

Tatlock, J. S. P., 'Chaucer's *Merchant's Tale*', *Modern Philology* 33 (1935–6) 367–81.

Taylor, B., 'The Medieval Cleopatra: the Classical and Medieval Tradition of Chaucer's *Legend of Cleopatra*', *Journal of Medieval and Renaissance Studies* 7 (1977) 249–69.

Thundy, Z. P., 'Matheolus, Chaucer and the Wife of Bath', pp. 24–58 in *Chaucerian Problems and Perspectives: Essays Presented to Paul E. Beichner C.S.C.*, ed. E. Vasta and Z. P. Thundy (Notre Dame, Ind.: University of Notre Dame Press, 1979).

Tolan, J., *Petrus Alfonsi and his Medieval Readers* (Gainesville, Fla.: University Press of Florida, 1993).

Turner, W. A., 'Biblical Women in *The Merchant's Tale* and *The Tale of Melibee*', *English Language Notes* (1965) 92–5.

Utley, F. L., *The Crooked Rib: An Analytical Index to the Argument about Women in English and Scots Literature to the End of the Year 1568* (Columbus: Ohio State University Press, 1944).

Walther, H., *Proverbia Sententiaeque Latinitatis Medii Aevi*, 5 vols and index (Göttingen: Vandenhoeck and Ruprecht, 1963–9).

Webster, R., *Why Freud Was Wrong: Sin, Science and Psychoanalysis*, rev. edn (London: HarperCollins, 1996).

Weisl, A. J., *Conquering the Reign of Femeny: Gender and Genre in Chaucer's Romance* (Cambridge: D. S. Brewer, 1995).

Weissman, H. P., 'Late Gothic Pathos in *The Man of Law's Tale*', *Journal of Medieval and Renaissance Studies* 9 (1979) 133–53.

Wentersdorf, K. P., 'Theme and Structure in the Merchant's Tale: The Function of the Pluto Episode', *PMLA* 80 (1965) 522–7.

Wiesen, D. S., *St Jerome as a Satirist: A Study in Christian Latin Thought and Letters* (Ithaca, N.Y.: Cornell University Press, 1964).

Wilson, K. M., and E. M. Makowski, *Wykked Wyves and the Woes of Marriage: Misogamous Literature from Juvenal to Chaucer* (Albany, N.Y.: State University of New York Press, 1990).

Wimsatt, J. I., *The Marguerite Poetry of Guillaume de Machaut* (Chapel Hill: University of North Carolina Press, 1970).

Young, K., 'Chaucer's Appeal to the Platonic Deity', *Speculum* 19 (1944) 1–13.

Index

References to pages may also include further citations in the footnotes on the page(s) in question. Where an index topic appears *only* in a footnote, this is indicated by the addition of 'n' to the page number (to avoid confusion where the page number is in Roman type, a space intervenes between it and the 'n'). Entries for fictional characters in Chaucer's works are cross-referenced in the entries for the work in question *only* in cases where they contain references not included in the latter entries.

CHAUCER STUDIES